What people are saying about A Busy Cook's Guide to Spices:

"Second only to Joy of Cooking. I've cooked for many years, professionally for a while, and didn't fully understand the hows and whys of spices. Linda has put together a cook's resource that should be in every kitchen."

Edward J. Bisiar, author of the children's book
A Visitor in the Dark

"Your approach in explaining the mystery of spice usage is to be commended. Not only is your well-written book an excellent resource for the novice in the kitchen, it is a quick reference for the food professional. Everyone should have a copy."

Joe Ames, New Ringgold, PA
www.theingredientstore.com

"This book is wonderful for a person like me who doesn't have a lot of back ground in combining spices/flavorings and foods...when I bought some lamb recently, all I had to do was check out the page relating to lamb to receive wonderful info on how to cook it, which seasonings go best with lamb and I even found some preparation ideas."

Janet Walsh
Denver, Colorado

"The leisurely cook, browser and food historian will find much to enjoy in this conveniently arranged reference. Bursting with valuable information, the folklore/history sidebar provides interesting background, with flavor blends and substitutions expanding its usefulness. This is a book every kitchen should contain."

Iva Freeman, Director of Library Services
Kendall College, Evanston, Illinois

"When customers come into our store to purchase spices they are attracted to this great resource. It helps them expand their use of spices to cook more creatively."

Jim & Kathleen Curtis, Owners
Village Roaster Coffee & Tea
Lakewood, Colorado

"I have been having a great time with Guide to Spices. Especially enjoy the history, folklore and origins. I never knew it made a difference when herbs were added. I guess I just dump everything in at the beginning."

Marilyn Nelson
Vadnais Heights, MN

A Busy Cook's Guide to Spices

How to Introduce New Flavors to Everyday Meals

by

Linda Murdock

BELLWETHER BOOKS
Denver, Colorado

2011, 8th Printing

Other books by Linda K. Murdock:

A Busy Cook's Guide to Flavor-Packed Cookies & Bars

Publisher/Order Information (also see last page):
Bellwether Books
P O Box 9757
Denver, CO 80209
www.bellwetherbooks.com
303-765-1220
Send comments to: *sales@bellwetherbooks.com*

ISBN-13: 978-0-9704285-0-9   (ISBN 10: 0-9704285-0-2)   Spiral bound

LCCN: 00-093582

Murdock, Linda.
A busy cook's guide to spices : how to introduce new flavors to everyday meals / Linda Murdock
Denver, Colo. : Bellwether Books, c2001
234 p. ; 22 cm.
Includes index.
ISBN-13: 978-0-9704285-0-9 Spiral bound
ISBN-10: 0-9704285-0-2
1. Spices. 2. Cookery (Spices)
641.6383 M941bu   00-093582

10 9 8
Printed in United States of America

Dedication

To my mother, Jean Ellen Leiby (1924-1980),
one of 400,000 women who served during WWII.
She once told me she wanted to write a book.

A traditional toast for weddings and housewarmings:

Bread! That this house may never know hunger.

Salt! That life may always have flavor.

And wine! That joy and prosperity may reign forever.

Disclaimer

This book is designed to provide information on spices and how to cook using them. The publisher and author are not engaged in rendering any medical recommendations or services, especially as noted under Historical Remedies or anywhere else in this book. These "remedies" are included for informational and entertainment purposes only and refer to both modern and historical uses no longer in practice. If medical assistance is necessary for any of the ailments or situations listed, the services of a competent professional is advised.

This book is not all-encompassing, nor is it a definitive text on flavorings. It is a complement to other cookbooks and resources on the subject of spices, herbs and flavorings. You are encouraged to read more about flavorings and to tailor that knowledge to your individual needs.

Every effort has been made to edit thoroughly and to make this book as accurate as possible. However, there may be errors both typographical and in content. Thus, use this book only as a guide. This book contains information on spices, herbs and flavorings only up to the date it was printed.

This guide was written to entertain and to educate. The author and Bellwether Books shall not be liable or responsible to any person or entity due to any loss or harm caused, or claimed to be caused, directly or indirectly by the contents in this book.

If you do not wish to be bound by the above disclaimer, you may return this book to the publisher for a full refund.

Special Thanks ⁓ Acknowledgements

The Denver Public Library and the Tattered Cover Bookstore, my research sources, made it easy to peruse a wide variety of books on spices and cooking.

My husband Scott, a willing guinea pig, encouraged me throughout the writing process. He converted my color photography to the computer and made the cover look professional. His allergies to MSG and other "natural flavorings" made me look for alternatives in seasoning foods and, as a result, led to less preservatives and more spice in our lives.

The overall look and design of this book would not have been possible without the help of my friend and graphic designer David Gonzales. He was very patient and generous with his time and encouragement. He came up with numerous suggestions throughout the writing process. He helped with tips on how to do indoor photography and lent me some of his camera equipment. His wife Bev even loaned me some of her cookbooks.

Thanks must also include Kass Johns for her excited enthusiasm for the project and for giving me recipes, books and the video tape on cheese, a passion we both share. Whenever I floundered, she reassured me that the concept was worth the effort. She went above and beyond the call with her editing. Foolish of me to think she wouldn't find much. She tried to keep me honest, consistent and grammatically correct. Any errors that remain uncorrected, are mine alone.

Jan, a good friend, clipped articles of interest and persuaded me to attend various wine and beer tastings as research for those sections. (It was difficult work, but someone had to do it.) Her editorial suggestions throughout the book have made it more valuable and useable.

Eric Forte recommended years ago that I buy spices by weight instead of in a jar from the grocery store. Perhaps it is he, who is ultimately responsible for getting me hooked on spices and flavorings.

For the countless other friends and people who encouraged me with their favorable opinions of the overall concept, I will be contacting you to buy a copy! After three years of gestation, long for us humans, I bet you never thought I'd finish it.

About the Author

Linda Murdock, like most of us mere mortals, spends her time juggling between family and work, while trying to come up with new dinner ideas 365 times a year! Prior to owning a print shop, she worked in the tax department of a gold mining firm, in the accounting department of a small railroad company and as a stock broker. She has a major in mathematics and history in preparation for teaching. Just the background you need for writing a book on spices! Her other published project to date was a genealogical calendar of her family that was donated to both the Wisconsin and the South Carolina Historical Societies.

A Busy Cook's Guide to Spices was typeset in the Minion family of fonts.

Table of Contents

Special Charts and Lists

Introduction

We all eat basic foods—meats, vegetables, starches, fruits, breads, salads and, of course, desserts. Flavor in foods usually comes from fat, which tastes good, but is not necessarily good for us. So, why not avoid the fat and add flavorings instead. After all, if we all eat the same things, then it must be just a matter of arranging them in the right quantities with the right flavorings that makes for so many cookbooks!

Most books on spices and flavorings are arranged alphabetically by spice. But I rarely go home and say I am going to cook with "coriander" tonight and have something come to mind. Likewise, if I want to cook chicken, I may not find a recipe with my favorite spices. Worse, I may find a recipe, but it requires going to the store for half the ingredients or the recipe will say, which is the kiss of death for me, "prepare the night before" or "simmer 2 hours." Who has that kind of time? This book attempts to solve these problems.

I realize many of us are in a rut and buy the same groceries week after week. This book allows you to prepare the same dishes and yet create new taste sensations through the better knowledge and use of flavorings and spices. It also includes Preparation Ideas meant to stir your imagination, expand your menus and get you out of the kitchen quickly. This is not to say there aren't a few time consuming and/or challenging concoctions included. After all there are those cold winter days, when I just want to spend time in the kitchen.

Ultimately I wrote **A Busy Cook's Guide to Spices** for me. I get bored with the same food week after week. I also prefer to cook by taste rather than by recipe, especially for the evening meals. In the course of researching this book, however, I discovered how little I really know about cooking. This led to more research and sections on *How to Cook* and the *Buying Guide*. I also inserted lots of little tips and charts on cooking that are important to understand if you are going to experiment with flavors or make healthy alterations. Equivalency charts and flavor substitutions are also included in the back of the book to keep you from having to run to the store.

When I told one of my friends, who knew me before I was married, that I was writing a cookbook, he was surprised and amused. He knew my "I can't cook" reputation. If I can "come out," there just may be a hidden cook in all of us. So, this book is for all of you, who eat the same thing week after week, who eat on a budget, who get tired of eating out, who have little time and don't want to spend it cooking, and who above all "can't cook." Take a chance. Try spicing up your life a little. You just may discover new taste sensations without having to learn all new recipes.

*H*ow to *G*et *S*tarted ... Q.&A.

What is a Spice vs. an Herb? Although definitions vary, there are distinctions between herbs and spices. Herbs are green leaves, and sometimes stems, of fresh or dried plants, shrubs or trees, grown in temperate climates. Spices are usually black, brown or red in color, are grown in the tropics and have a more pungent flavor than herbs. Spices come from everything but the leaves of the plant, that is the buds, fruits, berries, roots and/or bark. Some plants are both a spice and an herb, as in, dill seed and dill weed or cilantro and coriander.

Do I Use Fresh, Dried or Extracts? Fresh spices and herbs are the best as far as flavor is concerned. They are the least concentrated and should be used 4 parts fresh to 1 part dried. Finely cutting fresh herbs and spices releases more of their flavor. Dried flavorings are easier to store, more readily available when cooking and more concentrated than fresh. They are less expensive if purchased by weight at specialty shops. *Generally use ¼ teaspoon dried or ground flavoring for every 2 servings (or 1 pound) until you become familiar with its taste.* Dried flavorings can be added sooner than fresh when cooking. *Save fresh herbs until the end or you will cook out all the flavor.* Extracts are the most concentrated form of a seasoning and should be used by the drop—3 to 6 drops for every 2 servings.

Will I Like the Flavor? In learning about unfamiliar flavorings, trust your sense of smell to tell you a lot about the taste. If something smells good to you, it is likely that you will enjoy the taste of it, too. To be safe buy in small quantities until you become more aware of the flavor. Seasonings are not just for taste. Sometimes it is just the color, aroma or texture of a flavoring that you want. Consult *The Four Tastes and How to Use Them* on further hints to repair any spicing errors.

How Long Do I Keep Spices? To prolong the life of spices and herbs keep them in a cool dark place in an airtight container. Keep them away from heat, that is, not close to the stove or a sunny window. Most dried flavorings begin loosing their pungency after 3 months and should be replaced within a year. You can test the flavor retention of seasonings by grinding them. If they give off an odor the flavor should still be intact. Better yet, date them when they are purchased and buy smaller quantities, so they will always be fresh. Seed spices may be toasted in a dry skillet for 3-5 minutes to prolong their flavor.

*H*ow to *G*et *S*tarted . . . Q. & A. continued

Why Did You Include . . .? In addition to the most common herbs and spices, I have included other items that are used to enhance the flavor of food. Examples of non-spices are beer, lemon juice and nuts. Cheese and tomato are so important that they are included as both a flavoring and a food.

Why Didn't You Include . . .? Excluded from the page-by-page list are most herb blends, such as poultry seasoning, which you can mix for yourself or buy mixed in jars. These blends are defined under *Other Blends and Flavorings Defined* in the back of Section 1. Also defined are the difficult to obtain, uncommonly used seasonings or ones that taste similar to flavorings already detailed. I have included some difficult to mix blends, such as curry powder, five-spice powder and liquid flavor enhancers, such as Liquid Smoke and Tabasco.

Me? Make My Own Blends? Although you can buy spice blends, generally it is less expensive to buy dried seasonings by weight at a health food or spice store and mix them yourself. That way you can create your own blends. Use the *Flavor Blends* chart in the middle of the book for Italian, French or other cuisines. It will get you started, if you do not know which spices are used for a particular kind of food. Blend the spices in the ratio indicated and put them in their own labeled jar in your spice cabinet. Later, vary the ratios to enhance the flavors you like.

How Does Cooking Effect Flavor? Timing is everything in preparing a meal. Some spices lose potency the longer they are cooked, while others, like cayenne, get stronger with cooking. Heat can both enhance and destroy flavors, because the heat allows essential oils to escape. Slow cooking is usually best. Microwaving may not allow for flavor release in some herbs, so do a taste test and add more if necessary.

How Does Not Cooking Effect Flavor? Cold foods, such as potato salad, and uncooked foods, such as cucumbers, can absorb flavor, so be more generous with the seasonings and add them early on. Likewise, freezing foods can destroy flavors, so it is best to add them after they are reheated for serving. Another trick that works well in uncooked foods, such as salads, is to blend your dried seasonings with an equal amount of fresh parsley, which takes on their flavor, makes them taste fresher and expands the quantity.

*H*ow to *G*et *S*tarted . . . Q. & A. continued

What If I Put in Too Much? If you overdo a flavoring and want to lessen the potency, peel a potato and add it raw to the dish before serving. Stir it around to help absorb the overdone flavor. If the dish is too acidic, as is common with tomato recipes, add a little sugar to the dish. It is fun to experiment by picking flavors from two of the taste groups of sweet, salty, sour (acidic) and bitter. The best known combination is with sweet and sour flavorings. If using sweet spices, also try adding some cayenne or other hot spice. If your Italian-flavored spaghetti tastes a little bland, add a tablespoon of vinegar to help kick in the spices.

What Are My Recommendations? Here are my top 30 flavorings:

Allspice	Fennel	Nuts
Bay Leaf	Five-Spice Powder	Onions
Caraway Seed	Garlic	Oregano
Cardamom	Ginger	Pepper, Black
Cayenne	Honey (flavored)	Rosemary
Cheese	Lemon Juice	Savory
Chili Powder	Liquid Smoke	Shallot
Cinnamon	Maple Extract	Soy Sauce (Tamari)
Cumin	Mint	Thyme
Curry Powder	Mustard	Vanilla

Won't Changing the Recipe Ruin It? Substitutions are acceptable and necessary at times. Remember as we get older the taste buds diminish, so you need to add more spice to your life, literally. Substituting or adding your favorite spices in place of what is recommended in a recipe is better than running to the store. See *Flavor Substitutions* in the back of the book. Adding seasonings, unlike changing the amount of flour or eggs in a baking recipe, will not change the chemistry or the overall results.

So What's Stopping You? Keep plenty of recipe cards around to jot down your own creations and add them to the *Preparation Ideas* under the appropriate food in Section 2. And there you have it—a meal suited to your own particular taste, done in a time frame that gets you out of the kitchen quickly, using the same basic foods you have always used, but with a subtle difference that makes it newly appealing to everyone in the family.

A Brief History of Spices

Spices and herbs first came into use probably by accident. Humans ate plants to survive. If plants were poisonous, that knowledge was passed to survivors. With the domestication of plants and animals around 8000 BC, we reduced food varieties from what was available in a nomadic lifestyle to what was planted in a set area. We came to eat what our parents ate for thousands of years.

The earliest knowledge of spices in Europe was about 3000 BC, via caravan routes in the Middle East. The Egyptians used herbs for embalming circa 2000 BC. Their need for exotic herbs helped stimulate world trade. In fact, the word spice comes from the same root as *species,* meaning "kinds of goods." By 1000 BC China and India had a medical system based upon herbs. Thus, early uses were connected with magic, medicine, religion, tradition, preservation and hygiene (or more likely, smells resulting from the lack of hygiene).

Herbs were first used in their native habitats and became known elsewhere through conquest and travel. The Greeks were influenced by India, especially after Alexander the Great (356-323 BC) conquered Persia. Theophrastus (371-287 BC) categorized 450 plants and the Greeks spread that information to the Roman Empire. The most important discovery prior to the European spice trade were the monsoon winds (40 AD). Sailing from Eastern spice growers to Western European consumers gradually replaced the land-locked spice routes once dominated by the Middle East.

After the Dark Ages (500-1000) and Marco Polo's Far East visit (mid-1200s) there was renewed interest in the spice trade. The key spices were pepper, cloves, nutmeg, mace and later, cinnamon and ginger. When the Ottomans closed land routes, a search for spices and their profits (as high as 32,000%) created a *gold rush* for a sea route to the East by first, the Portuguese and Spanish, and then the Dutch and English. A secondary impetus was the desire to find the real Garden of Eden, still believed to be in existence somewhere in the East.

Like the Middle Eastern merchants, European spice traders did everything to keep others from removing seedlings. The Dutch cut down every nutmeg tree on an island claimed by the English. To ensure a monopoly they traded this island and gave up New Amsterdam (Manhattan) in return. With the New World came new spices, including allspice, peppers, vanilla and chocolate. Although new settlers brought herbs to the North American continent, before 1750 it was thought that you could not grow plants or trees outside their native habitat, which was true with tropical plants. This belief kept the spice trade, with America as a late comer, profitable well into the 19th century.

This book covers only a fraction of the flavorings available worldwide. Travel, a desire for variety, and immigrants from around the globe, continue to expand America's knowledge of these once unfamiliar flavorings and makes international cuisine both more accessible and acceptable.

Section 1: Flavorings and How They Are Used

This alphabetical list of flavorings, including a few spice blends, covers the first half of the book. Some seasonings require special attention and more in-depth information as you will see. If a seasoning or blend of seasonings, such as fines herbes, is not listed, you may find it defined on the last few pages of this front section. Each seasoning contains the following information:

Flavor/Taste: Although somewhat subjective, a description of the flavor and/or taste is included as a guideline for each seasoning.

Use: "Use" means whether to use the flavoring SPARINGLY or GENEROUSLY, and whether to put it in at the BEGINNING or END of the cooking cycle. Some flavorings lose potency (basil) or become bitter (garlic) if cooked for long periods. Others increase in potency during cooking (cayenne) and can withstand prolonged heat (bay leaf). Foods or drinks, with which the flavoring is commonly used, are also listed here.

Mix with: Other flavorings that go well with the one listed are included under "Mix with." For example, nutmeg goes well with and is listed under the main heading of cinnamon. Refer also to the *Flavor Blends* Chart at the end of this section for more mixing guidelines.

Color & Form: For identification and recognition when purchasing, I have included the color of the flavoring and the form(s) in which it is most often found. This can be whole, ground or an extract. If some forms are not listed, it is most likely omitted to keep you from using the seasoning in that form. For example, some ground items, such as black pepper or coffee, lose flavor once ground and should be purchased whole.

At the bottom of each flavoring page are its **Historical Remedies,** its **Origin** and a little **Folklore/History.** This information is for your entertainment, so that you may dazzle your friends with your new knowledge.

....

Consult a physician before trying any of the medicinal remedies, since some of the cures are from ancient uses and may not be acceptable or even valid today.

Allspice

Flavor/Taste:
Like a mixture of cinnamon, nutmeg and cloves

Use:
Use ¼ tsp ground for 2 servings.
Add at the BEGINNING of cooking.
Use as a cinnamon substitute, as a marinade, in sauces and desserts and with sweet vegetables.

Mix with:
- Cinnamon
- Cloves
- Five-Spice Powder
- Nutmeg

Color & Form:
Brown berries, whole or ground

. . . .

❧ Historical Remedies ❧

Internally:
Antiseptic and anesthetic
Appetite stimulant
Lowers blood sugar

Externally:
Good on sore joints and muscles
Varicose veins

❧ Origin ❧
Allspice comes from the berries of an evergreen tree of the myrtle family. It is native to Jamaica and Central America.

❧ Folklore/History ❧

In the late 1600's, pirates learned to survive long sea voyages by preserving their foods. They found that combining allspice with smoking acted as a preservative. Thus, the French word *boucan* for barbequing gave these pirates a new name, buccaneers.

Allspice is also known as **Jamaica pepper**, since most of the world's supply comes from Jamaica.

Angelica

Flavor/Taste:
Like a juniper berry or a sweeter tasting celery; strong

Use:
Add at the END of cooking, although it is good for baking.
It minimizes the need for sugar and reduces acidity.
Use with candy, pastries, ham, pork, seafood and salads.

Mix with:
꙾Bay Leaf   ꙮGinger   ꙮOnion/Scallion

Color & Form:
Green leaf and thin, celery-like stem; oil from seeds are used
in gin and vermouth

ꙮ Historical Remedies ꙮ

Internally:
Dulls alcohol craving
Bronchitis-roots are used in a tea
Urinary problems

Externally:
Roots used to improve eyesight
Perfume

ꙮ Origin ꙮ
Angelica is a large perennial herb of the
parsley family. It is native to Northern Europe
and Russia.

ꙮFolklore/History ꙮ

The name Angelica comes from a legend
about a monk in 1665, who had a dream. In
it an angel told him about a plant that
would cure the plague.

Angelica supposedly blooms on May 8th,
the feast of St. Michael the Archangel, thus
its Latin name Angelica *archangelica*.

Laplanders used it for sever colic.

Angostura Bitters™

Flavor/Taste:
A bitter, citrusy, allspice flavor

Use:
Use SPARINGLY.
You may find Bitters in liquor stores.
Use in fruit salads, ice cream, sauces, soups, and cocktails.

Mix with:
- Cinnamon
- Cloves
- Lemon Juice
- Nutmeg
- Orange

Color & Form:
Brown liquid in bottles; high alcohol content

❧ Historical Remedies ❧

Internally:
Appetite stimulant
Digestive
Hiccup cure (place on a lemon wedge with sugar)

❧ Origin ❧
Bitters are extracted from the bark of a tree and mixed with rum, quinine and spices. The tree is native to Trinidad in the West Indies.

❧ Folklore/History ❧

The name comes from the old town of Bolívar in Venezuela and means narrowness, since it was near the narrows of the Orinoco River.

Angostura is a trade name for a particular brand of bitters and is the most common brand used for spicing up foods in the US.

Anise

Flavor/Taste:
Licorice flavor

Use:
Use ¼ tsp ground for 2 servings.
Use at the BEGINNING of cooking.
Use in breads, cheese, desserts, fruit, stews, carrots and slaw.

Mix with:

- Allspice
- Bay Leaf
- Cinnamon
- Curry Powder
- Fennel
- Garlic
- Nutmeg
- Nuts
- Oils & Fats-olive
- Parsley

Color & Form:
Whole gray seeds, ground powder or extract; in liquors (ouzo)

❧ Historical Remedies ❧

Internally:
Asthma, Congestion and Coughs
Breath freshener
Cramps or Gas
Laxative
Ulcers
Contains the vitamin: coline

❧ Origin ❧
Anise is the seed of a fruit in the parsley family. Unrelated to star anise, it is native to the Eastern Mediterranean and Egypt.

❧ Folklore/History ❧

The Romans mixed **aniseeds** (anise) and other spices to make a cake served after heavy meals, including wedding feasts. Some think the wedding cake tradition came from this custom. They also hung an anise plant near pillows to ward off bad dreams and seizures, and to restore youth.

A tax was once placed on anise to help repair the London Bridge. In Virginia an early law required each male settler to plant several aniseeds.

Arrowroot

Flavor/Taste:
Tasteless

Use:
Use 1 Tbsp arrowroot with 2 Tbsp water for 2 cups of liquid.
Use SPARINGLY, since it thickens about twice that of flour.
Mix with a cool liquid before adding to hot foods.
Use with children and elderly, who have difficulty with digestion.
Use as a thickener in puddings, pies, soups, sauces and gravies.

Do not stir too vigorously when using arrowroot for sauces or gravies, since it may actually thin it.

Mix with:
❧Most flavorings

Color & Form:
White roots finely ground in powder form

❧ Historical Remedies ❧

Internally:
Resistant to viruses
Helps with night blindness

❧ Origin ❧
Arrowroot comes from the roots of a tree. It is native to the West Indies and Central and South America.

❧ Folklore/History ❧

Arrowroot flour was used in the past in making cookies.

Arrowroot is a starch that has no taste and turns clear when it is cooked.

Mayans in Central America used arrowroot as a poultice for smallpox sores. The Arawak Indians used it as an antidote for poison arrows.

Asafoetida

Flavor/Taste:
Garlicky; smells like sulfur

Use:
Use SPARINGLY. A pinch is enough.
Use with vegetables, mushrooms, fish and as a salt substitute
in Indian dishes.

Mix with:

- Ginger
- Parsley
- Rosemary
- Thyme
- Tomato

Color & Form:
Solid, wax-like pieces; mostly seen as a white powder

❧ Historical Remedies ❧

Internally:
Antispasmodic
Bronchitis
Coughs
Gas preventative
Nerve and brain stimulant

❧ Origin ❧
Asafoetida is the dried sap in the stem of a
large perennial fennel plant. It is native to
Afghanistan and Iran.

❧ Folklore/History ❧

This spice is well known in India.

It comes from a Persian word *aza,* meaning
resin and the Latin word *fetida,* meaning
stinking.

It is the resin or sap that is sold in clumps or
ground into a powder.

Basil

Flavor/Taste:
Sweet, minty, mildly peppery taste; very aromatic;
Also in lemon, licorice and cinnamon flavor varieties

Use:
Use SPARINGLY, ⅛ tsp dried for 2 servings. Tear fresh leaves.
Add at the END, just before serving in hot dishes.
Use in eggs, meats, pastas, salads, vegetables (especially tomatoes),
peaches, berries, soups and in Italian and Mediterranean cooking.

Mix with:
Cilantro	Garlic	Oregano	Rosemary	Sage
Fennel	Mint	Parsley	Saffron	Thyme

Color & Form:
Fresh green leaves more flavorful than dried

Historical Remedies

Internally:
Headaches
Joint aches
Nausea

Externally:
Apply leaves to poisonous bites
Insecticide for cabbage and tomato plants

Origin
Basil is an intrusive annual plant belonging
to the mint family. It is native to India and is
a fairly recent discovery to the West.

Folklore/History

In Greek mythology, basilisk, from which
the word basil is derived, was a fire breathing
dragon that could walk on water. There are
American lizards in the genus Basiliscus,
which can also walk on water.

Basil repels mosquitoes and flies.

It was known as the Herb of Kings in ancient
Greece and the tomato herb in more recent
times. It is one of the Italian herbs including
rosemary, oregano, sage and thyme.

Dried stems may be used in a smoker.

Bay Leaf

Flavor/Taste:
Slightly bitter, usually not eaten; dominant flavor

Use:
Use SPARINGLY, 2-3 leaves for 4 servings or 1 leaf per quart.
Remove before serving.
Add at the BEGINNING, heat and moisture increases flavor,
as does cutting it. Overuse can cause bitterness.
Use with gumbo, stews, white sauces, soups and marinades.

Mix with:
- Allspice
- Fennel
- Garlic
- Lemon Juice
- Mustard
- Orange
- Parsley
- Thyme

Color & Form:
Whole light green dried leaves or more flavorful fresh leaves

❧ Historical Remedies ❧

Internally:
Coughs
Cramps
High blood pressure
Sedative

Externally:
In a tea for dandruff

❧ Origin ❧
Bay leaf is from a small laurel tree. It is
native to Asia Minor and the Mediterranean.
Most leaves now come from California.

❧ Folklore/History ❧

Bay leaf is also known as **sweet laurel**.

When Cupid hit Apollo with an arrow,
making him fall for Daphne, she begged the
gods to change her into something else—a
laurel tree. In honor of Daphne, Apollo
decreed that laurel leaves be a sign of courage
or accomplishment, thus "to win one's laurels"
refers to public recognition.

A wreath of laurels, known for its medicinal
values, was given to doctors at graduation.
Thus from *bacca lauris* comes "baccalaureate
degree" and the term "bachelor's degree," a
person too busy with his studies to marry.

Beer

Flavor/Taste:
Can be sweet (malty), watery, bitter, smokey or fruity

Use:
Use as a tenderizer for meats before cooking.
Use in batters to make crisp coatings when frying.
Use in chilis, fondues, stews, sauces and marinades.

The liquor content of beer, wine and other alcohol evaporates when cooked or heated.

Mix with:
Salty foods, such as pizza, nuts, pretzels and chips
Stout beers with hot spicy foods and blue-veined cheeses
Wheat beers with aromatic cream sauces
Light beers with Asian foods, salads, chilis, mustards and curries
Hoppy beers with basil, cilantro and rosemary

Color & Form:
Liquid ranging in color from light yellow, gold, red or dark brown

---

❧ Historical Remedies ❧

Internally:
"A drink a day keeps the doctor at bay and the heart in good stay."

Externally:
A saucer of beer kills garden slugs, that are attracted to the fermentation.

❧ Origin ❧

Beer comes from barley and other fermented grains, yeast, hops and water. Its alcohol content is usually 5% or less.

❧ Folklore/History ❧

In Babylonia 2000 BC a bride's father would supply mead to the new son-in-law for a month after the wedding. Because their calendar was lunar and the mead was made of honey, this month became known as a *honeymoon*.

English pub patrons ordered beer in pints and quarts. If they were unruly, the bartender would have them *mind their P's (pints) and Q's (quarts)*. English pub fans also had a whistle baked into their ceramic mugs. When they wanted a refill they would whistle. From this came the phrase *wetting your whistle*.

Matching Foods and Flavorings with Beer

Generally the spicier a meal is, the heartier the beer you should drink with it.

Ales (full, malty)	Wild game
Ales (India pale)	Hot, spicy, BBQ, rich fried foods, creamy sauces
Ales (pale or red fruity)	Asian spices, curry, ginger
Bock beers	Smoked meats, sausages
Bocks (double)	Desserts, chocolate
Fruity ales	Rich red meat
Fruity beers	Desserts, chocolate
High alcohol	Hot, spicy, BBQ
Lagers (dark, malty)	Smoked meats, sausages
Lagers (hoppy)	Fresh herbs, dill, tarragon, basil, rosemary
Lagers (strong)	Rich red meat, flavorful chicken, rich seafood
Pilsners	Shellfish, white meat, rich fried foods, creamy sauces, fresh herbs
Porters	Shellfish, desserts, chocolate
Stouts	Shellfish
Stouts (creamy)	Desserts, chocolate
Weiss (full flavored)	Shellfish

⟡ More Folklore/History ⟡

Vikings, who would drink a bucket of ale before battle, would fight without armor or even shirts. Thus, the term *berserk* meaning bare shirt from the wild Viking battles.

An admiral, known for his wool grogram coats and for watering down rum, was called Old Grog. Too much of this watered-down drink and you became *groggy*.

Before thermometers, brewers would dip a thumb into the mix to find the right temperature for adding yeast. Too cold and the yeast wouldn't grow; too hot and the yeast would die. This thumb in the beer is where we get *rule of thumb*.

Bouillon Cubes

Flavor/Taste:
Salty chicken, beef or vegetable flavors

Use:
Dissolve 1 cube in 1 cup of boiling water.
Dissolve in just a little water to have a substitute for soy sauce.
Add at the BEGINNING.
Use as a gravy, sauce or soup starter (stock or base).

Mix with:
↝Most unsalty flavorings

Color & Form:
Cubes wrapped in foil found in clear jars

↝ **Historical Remedies** ↝

Internally:
Colds

↝ **Folklore/History** ↝

Carl Knorr of Germany was credited with the development of the bouillon cube in the 1880's, while experimenting with the concept of convenience foods. His early mixes were made of seasonings, dried vegetables and flour.

↝ **Origin** ↝
Bouillon Cubes are boiled down and dehydrated juices from chicken, beef or vegetable stock.

Burnet

Flavor/Taste:
Like a tangy cucumber

Use:
Use toward the END of cooking.
Use in cream cheese dips, green salads, sauces, soups and teas.

Mix with:

- Basil
- Dill
- Garlic
- Marjoram
- Oregano
- Rosemary
- Tarragon
- Thyme

Color & Form:
Fresh, young green leaves

✦ Historical Remedies ✦

Internally:
High in vitamin C

Externally:
Used as a blood coagulant

✦ Origin ✦
Burnet comes from a small bushy perennial plant. It is native to Europe.

✦ Folklore/History ✦

The dried leaves, which have little flavor, were used in the Orient to help stop bleeding.

Translated it means "drink up blood" and does indeed have astringent qualities. In fact, soldiers would drink it in a tea before battle to avoid severe wounds.

Thomas Jefferson used burnet as fodder for his livestock.

Burnet is also known as **salad burnet**.

Butter/Margarine

Flavor/Taste:
Creamy, sweet, solidified oil that absorbs other flavors

Use:
It is essential in baking breads, cookies and pastries.
Use for sautéing seasonings and cooking meats.
Use with pastas, mushrooms, potatoes, rice and vegetables.

Mix with:
- Cinnamon
- Garlic
- Leeks
- Mustard
- Nuts
- Onion/Scallions
- Shallot
- Tarragon
- Turmeric

Color & Form:
Light yellow, hard in sticks, soft in tubs, extract; also salted or unsalted (does not store as long); whipped (air beaten into it); reduced calorie butter (40% fat, water, skim milk and gelatin)

1 tsp butter = 33 calories

Use *unsalted* butter to grease pans to keep food from sticking.

Soften butter sticks by microwaving on low for 15 seconds.

For recipes in this book margarine and butter are used interchangeably.

❖ Origin ❖

Both butter and margarine are 80% milk fat. Margarine was developed around 1900 as a butter substitute. It is 100% vegetable oil and is cheaper, but not as flavorful as butter. **Hydrogenation** is the process of changing a liquid oil into a solid saturated fat. The added hydrogen prevents oil from breaking down or smelling at high temperatures.

Saturated fats are "bad" and **unsaturated** fats are "good" as far as cholesterol is concerned. Low cholesterol margarines are made from canola, safflower or corn oil.

❖ Baking with Butter/Margarine ❖

1 cup butter = ½ lb butter = 2 sticks
1 cup of salted butter contains ½ tsp salt

Avoid low calorie or whipped butter for baking.

If using margarine instead of butter, it should have at least 60% milk fat. Some recipes, though, must have butter to bake correctly.

Clarified Butter-the clear liquid from melted butter after you skim off foam and remove the yellow solids on the bottom. It may be cooked at a higher temperature than butter. **Ghee** is clarified butter cookable at 375° F.

Flavored Butters/Margarines

Here is an easy way to make flavored butters or margarines. Just mix them, store in plastic containers and refrigerate a few days. They last about a month and get more flavorful over time. Unsalted butter won't keep as long. Use them on breads, vegetables, seafood or for sautéing. Also try spicing up ½ cup mayonnaise, instead of butter, for a more flavorful sandwich spread.

Breakfast Butter
1 Tbsp Mint
1 Tbsp Dill
½ cup softened Butter

Italian Butter
1 Tbsp Basil
1 Tbsp Oregano
1 Tbsp Thyme
½ cup softened Butter

Garlic Butter
1 Tbsp Garlic
1 Tbsp Marjoram
½ cup softened Butter

Corn or Potato Butter
½ tsp Rosemary
½ tsp Marjoram
½ cup softened Butter

Honey Butter
2⅔ Tbsp Honey
½ cup softened unsalted Butter

Lemon Butter
1 tsp grated Lemon zest
½ cup softened unsalted Butter

Cheese & Onion Butter
⅓ cup grated Parmesan Cheese
1⅓ Tbsp Chives
½ cup softened Butter

Crunchy Butter
1 Tbsp Chives
2 cloves Garlic
1 Tbsp Sesame Seeds
½ cup softened Butter

Mustard Butter
3 Tbsp Parsley
3 tsp prepared Mustard
⅔ tsp Oregano
½ cup softened Butter

French Butter
½ tsp Parsley
½ tsp Chives
½ tsp Tarragon
½ tsp minced Shallot
½ cup softened Butter

Hot & Spicy Butter
4 Tbsp Horseradish
½ cup softened unsalted Butter

Capers

Flavor/Taste:
Sour and salty

Use:
Use SPARINGLY, 1 tsp for 4 servings, at the BEGINNING of cooking. Rinse capers before using to remove excess salt.
Use with eggs, eggplant, salads, seafood, especially salmon, Italian sauces, olives, tomatoes and with boiled meats.

Mix with:
⊷Garlic　　　　　⊷Lemon Juice　　　⊷Soy Sauce

Color & Form:
Greenish to black buds pickled in a salty vinegar

- -

⊷ Historical Remedies ⊷

Internally:
Intestinal infections
Diarrhea

⊷ Folklore/History ⊷

Europeans used capers as a condiment over 2,000 years ago.

Capers are considered weeds where they thrive around the Mediterranean in open stony terrains.

⊷ Origin ⊷
Capers come from unopened buds of a perennial shrub. The shrub is native to the Mediterranean.

Caraway Seed

Flavor/Taste:
A mix of tangy dill and light licorice; nutty

Use:
Use SPARINGLY, 1 tsp for 4 servings. Crush seeds for more flavor.
Use at the END, during the last 15 minutes of cooking, or it may
turn bitter.
Use with breads, cookies, fruit, especially apples, meats and
many vegetables including sauerkraut, in soups and stews.

Mix with:
❧Cheese

Color & Form:
Brownish gray sickle-shaped seeds

❧ Historical Remedies ❧

Internally:
Asthma
Breath freshener
Cramps
Diarrhea
Nausea
Prevents gas

❧ Origin ❧
Caraway Seeds come from a hardy white-
flowered biennial of the parsley family. The
plant is native to India and Eastern Europe.

❧ Folklore/History ❧

One of 74 herbs grown in Charlemagne's
gardens. It has been in use in cooking and
medicine for over 5,000 years.

The name is from the ancient Arabs,
karawya.

Because the seeds disintegrate when they
ripen, seeds are picked when dew covered,
either early morning or late evening.

Popular in Austrian, Hungarian and
German cooking.

Cardamom

Flavor/Taste:
Light ginger with pine taste; aromatic

Use:
Use SPARINGLY, ¼ tsp (2 pods) for 4 servings. Dry roast seeds for more flavor. Use at the BEGINNING of cooking.
Use with breads, cookies, meats, Indian dishes, fruit pies, salads, rice and stews.

Cardamom neutralizes the odor of garlic.

Mix with:
- Anise
- Cinnamon
- Coriander
- Cumin
- Curry Powder
- Honey
- Wine-spiced

Color & Form:
Pods with black seeds inside; ground seeds

❧ Historical Remedies ❧

Internally:
Breath freshener
Heartburn
Reduces gas caused by garlic
Headaches (stimulant)
Makes acid in grains more digestible

❧ Origin ❧
Cardamom comes from a tall perennial bush of the ginger family. It is native to India and Southeast Asia.

❧ Folklore/History ❧

The third most expensive spice in the world after saffron and vanilla. The pods are cut with scissors off the plant by hand.

Greeks traded cardamom as early as the 4th century BC. It was also very popular in Roman times.

Cardamom is also spelled *cardamon*.

Cayenne

Flavor/Taste:
Burning hot taste stronger than common black pepper

Use:
Use SPARINGLY.
Use at BEGINNING or END of cooking, depending upon tolerance. It will get hotter the longer it cooks or if it is frozen. Use with beans, meat, cooked cheese, chili, Mexican dishes, seafood, sauces, soups and stews.

> **Red pepper flakes** are dried pieces of various red peppers that can range in "hotness." They can be used as a cayenne substitute.

Mix with:
⌁Curry Powder ⌁Saffron ⌁Tomato

Color & Form:
Red chile pepper; most often a red ground powder

⌁ Historical Remedies ⌁

Internally:
Arthritis
Colds
Arteries-improves circulation
Memory inducer

Externally:
External contact can burn skin.
Stops bleeding on an open wound

⌁ Origin ⌁
Cayenne is from the flesh and seeds of a cayenne chile. It is native to the town of Cayenne in French Guiana, South America.

⌁ Folklore/History ⌁

Known to Europeans since the discovery of America, cayenne is from the Greek word meaning *to bite*. The name came from the Cayenne River and the same-named city upon it in French Guiana. In fact when Spanish explorers saw natives eating peppers, they later adopted the name Ginnie peppers.

The actual peppers used to make cayenne can be any cayenne or any red pepper, with a certain degree of hotness, that is, 8 on a scale of 1 to 10, 10 being the hottest.

Cayenne is rich in vitamins and iron.

Celery Seed

Flavor/Taste:
Celery-like, slightly bitter

Use:
Use SPARINGLY, ½-1 tsp for 2 servings. More can be bitter.
Use with poultry, dressings, eggs, potato salads, sauces, stews
and tomato juice.

Mix with:
- Dill
- Honey
- Onion/Scallion
- Tomato

Color & Form:
Brownish whole seeds or ground powder

. . . .

❧ Historical Remedies ❧

Internally:
Gout
Hives
Insomnia
Kidney stones
Reduces fevers
Increases urination
Drunk in a tea combined with peppermint.

❧ Origin ❧
Celery Seeds come from lovage, a distant
relative of celery. It is native to the salt
marshes of the Mediterranean.

❧ Folklore/History ❧

Popular in French cooking, celery seed was first
cultivated by the Italians in the 17th century. At
that time the celery that was used was a plant
known as smallage or lovage.

The celery must be left unharvested in order
for the white flowers to bare the seeds.

High in calcium and sodium.

Cheese

Flavor/Taste:
Creamy, tangy and/or salty, depending upon variety

Use:
Use GENEROUSLY, allow ½ lb for 2 servings.
Use low heat and slow cooking just enough to melt; high heat causes curdling, toughness or stringiness. If shredding, add it in the last 5-10 minutes. If baking, cut it into same size pieces for even melting. If microwaving, cook a few seconds on high. Use with fruit, eggs, meat, pastas, pizza, salads, sauces and vegetables, or as an appetizer.

Mix with:
- Caraway Seed
- Cumin
- Fennel
- Garlic
- Mustard
- Onion
- Sage
- Wine

Color & Form:
White, golden yellow or blue-veined in curds, creamy, shredded or solid blocks, spheres or wedges.

4 oz cheese = 1 cup = ¼ lb shredded

Soft cheeses (toss if moldy) do not last as long as hard ones (cut off mold and eat the rest).

Cheese will absorb flavors close to it.

Serve at room temperature for the best flavor.

Grease cheese grater to keep it from sticking.

❧ Cooking with Cheese ❧

Melting Cheeses:
Munster
Cheshire/Cheddar
Goat cheeses

Cooking Cheeses:
Mozzarella
Bel Paese
Emmental
Gruyére

❧ Origin ❧
Cheese comes from animal milk, usually cow, sheep or goat.

❧ Fat Content of Cheeses ❧

Blue	high	Edam	medium
Brie	high	Feta	medium
Camembert	medium	Gouda	high
Cheddar	high	Mozzarella	medium
Cottage	low	Parmesan	high
Colby	high	Ricotta	low
Cream	high	Swiss	high

Folklore/History of Cheese

The origin of cheese was in the Near East. Its invention is tied to the domestication of animals around 5000 BC and the first use of pottery. No doubt someone tasted curdled milk that had been sitting in a container for a while and liked it.

Cheese is milk that has had bacteria added to it. The milk thickens and separates into curds and whey. From drained curds come the unripened cheeses, such as cottage, cream cheese and ricotta. Curing the curds by heating, adding more bacteria, soaking, spicing and coloring leads to the ripened or aged cheeses.

Actual proof of cheese making in Europe was found circa 2800 BC. As early as 2500 BC there were over 20 different cheeses being made in Babylon.

During the Dark Ages (400-1000 AD), the European monasteries perfected cheese production and became the centers of agriculture. Frequent invasions disrupted this agriculture and resulted in a general decrease in population. The monasteries persevered, however, and by 1100 they had become centers for travellers, who were fed on cheese. Thus, the word about cheese production spread.

The One Hundred Years War (1337-1463) further deteriorated the ability of most people to make cheese. Few could afford to own a cow. Thus, cheese became a symbol of prosperity. Goats, which took care of themselves, became the source of dairy products for the poor.

The discovery of the New World (1492) and the spice trade (1600-1750) meant the introduction of spices and, thus, more flavorful cheeses. With the advent of the railroad in the mid-1800's, the most fragile cheeses could be transported long distances and still retain their flavor. Thus, all of Europe was exposed to the various cheeses of the continent and cheese became an essential part of the economy.

Some feel that the flavor of cheese has been hurt, because of the changes caused by the industrialization of its making. Changes in agriculture have resulted in flavor erosion: animals no longer graze on organic grassland; antibiotics given to dairy cows pass through to the milk; and pasteurization alters the acidity or pH balance and destroys the organisms necessary to give cheese flavor. Europe continues to make some of its cheeses locally. So if you are travelling, make sure you try the local cheese.

Only about 60% of the world's population eats cheese. It is often considered the wine of foods. Cheese, and its  infinite varieties, is to milk what wine, in its infinite varieties, is to the grape.

Chervil

Flavor/Taste:
Mild licorice with a peppery aftertaste

Use:
Use ½ tsp dried leaves for 2 servings.
Use at the END or last minute of cooking. Do not boil.
Use in cream soups and sauces, dressings and green salads,
eggs, seafood, chicken, sweet vegetables and French dishes.

Mix with:
- Basil
- Chives
- Leeks
- Lemon Juice
- Marjoram
- Parsley
- Saffron
- Shallot
- Sorrel
- Tarragon
- Thyme

Color & Form:
Fresh green leaves are better than dried

Historical Remedies

Internally:
Ancient hiccup cure

Externally:
Eyewash (boil in water, steep and let cool)

Origin
Chervil is an annual plant in the parsley family. It is native to southern Russia and the Middle East.

Folklore

Chervil is often connected with Easter in Europe, where it is eaten as part of the Easter ceremony. This is probably because of its similarity to the odor of myrrh, one of the three gifts of the wise men to baby Jesus.

It is one of the seasonings used in a French blend called **fines herbes**, which also includes chives, tarragon and parsley.

Chervil is also known as **sweet cicely**.

Chili Powder (blend)

Flavor/Taste:
Can be hotter than black pepper; can dominate

Use:
Use at the END of cooking. It gets more potent as it cooks.
Some varieties should be used SPARINGLY.
Use in eggs, mushrooms, Indian, Cajun and Mexican dishes,
especially with beans, chili, beef and in dips and stews.

Mix with:
- Coriander
- Cumin
- Garlic
- Onion/Scallion
- Tomato

Color & Form:
Red to brown ground chile peppers and other spices

Historical Remedies

Internally:
Colds
Fever
Flu
Hypothermia
High in vitamin A

Origin
Chile Powder is the dried blend of chile peppers and other spices. Its origin is American.

Folklore/History

The word *chilli* came from the Aztecs. They used a blend similar to that found in today's chili powder. The American chili powder flavoring was derived from an Englishman living in Texas in the 1850's. He was trying to copy the taste of curry, which he had grown fond of while in India. It is made up of chile peppers, cumin, oregano, garlic and salt. Tastes vary, based on color–bright red or brownish red powder. The latter tends to be more bitter or stronger in flavor. When cooking Mexican dishes use the redder Mexican chili powder.

Chives

Flavor/Taste:
Similar to sweet mild onions with less sulphur

Chive blossoms are also edible, but can be potent.

Use:
Use ½ Tbsp fresh chopped stems for 2 servings.
Use it at the very END of cooking.
Use in dips, eggs, baked potatoes, soups, salads and white sauces.

Mix with:
- Cheese
- Chervil
- Dill
- Marjoram
- Parsley
- Sage
- Tarragon
- Thyme

Color & Form:
Green fresh stems; dried have little flavor

- -

✾ Historical Remedies ✾

Internally:
Reduces cholesterol
Rich in vitamins A, C and riboflavin.

✾ Folklore/History ✾

Gypsies used chives to tell fortunes and drive away evil spirits.

Chives have been cultivated since the Middle Ages.

✾ Origin ✾
Chives is a perennial plant in the onion family. It is native to Europe.

Chocolate

Flavor/Taste:
Can be bitter or sweet depending upon form

Use:
Use in the BEGINNING of cooking or baking.
Easily burns at low temperatures. Use a double boiler or microwave at half power. Do not cover while cooking.
Use in desserts, drinks, pastries, Mexican meat dishes and sauces.

Mix with:

- Chili Powder
- Cinnamon
- Cloves
- Coffee
- Garlic
- Onion/Scallion
- Mace
- Tomato
- Vanilla

Color & Form:
Brown powder, chips, squares and extract

1 oz unsweetened chocolate = 3 Tbsp unsweetened cocoa + 1 Tbsp butter

12 oz chips = 2 cups

Dark chocolate has less sugar than **milk chocolate**.

White chocolate has no cocoa in it. When substituting white for real chocolate use more white and more butter.

❧ Historical Remedies ❧

Internally:
Releases endorphins to make you feel better emotionally
Stimulant due to caffeine

❧ Origin ❧
Chocolate is from the fermented seeds in the beans of a tropical tree. It is native to Mexico, Central and South America.

❧ Folklore/History ❧

Chocolate was unknown to Europeans before Columbus supposedly discovered it in the cargo of a boat in the Gulf of Honduras. It was not brought to Spain, however, until 1520 by Cortez.

It comes from an Aztec word meaning *food of the gods*— no argument there.

Mexican chocolate has sugar, almonds, salt and cinnamon in it. Thus, it is grainier than other chocolates.

Cilantro

Flavor/Taste:
Faint licorice flavor or a mix of sage and orange

Use:
Use ½ Tbsp of fresh leaves for 2 servings.
Use at the END of cooking. If you like cilantro, the tendency is to overuse it, which can be overwhelming to others.
Use with meats, salads, Mexican and Indian dishes, salsas, sauces, soups and stews.

Mix with:
◦Curry Powder   ◦Nuts-coconut   ◦Lemon Juice

Color & Form:
Green leaves, smaller are better; looks like flat-leaf parsley

---

◦ Historical Remedies ◦

Internally:
Makes medicines taste better
High in protein (20%+)

Externally:
Makeup
Perfumes

◦ Origin ◦
Cilantro is the leaf of the coriander plant, a member of the carrot family. It is native to Southern Europe and the Middle East.

◦ Folklore/History ◦

The Romans used the coriander plant to preserve meat.

Although associated with Mexican salsas and Asian dishes, the coriander plant and its cilantro leaves originated in the Southern Mediterranean region and is a latecomer to America.

Cilantro is also known as **Chinese parsley**.

Cinnamon

Flavor/Taste:
Pungent, slightly sweet

Use:
Use ½ tsp for 2 servings. Use at the BEGINNING of cooking. Use in desserts, drinks, pastries, vegetables, pork and Mexican dishes.

Mix with:

- Allspice
- Cardamom
- Cloves
- Curry Powder
- Fennel
- Ginger
- Nutmeg
- Onion/Scallion
- Pepper, Chile
- Vanilla
- Wine

Cinnamon/Sugar Blend: Add 5½ tsp cinnamon to 1 cup sugar and put in a shaker for cereal, toast or pancakes.

Warm old ground cinnamon in a skillet until you can smell it.

4" stick = 1 tsp ground

Color & Form:
Brown curled sticks (bark), ground powder or extract

☙ Historical Remedies ❧

Internally:
Altitude sickness
Antibacterial
Congestion
Diarrhea (1 tsp per cup of liquid)
Gas
Menstruation symptoms
Sedative

☙ Origin ❧
Cinnamon comes from the inner bark of a fast growing evergreen tree. It is native to Sri Lanka and India.

☙ Folklore/History ❧

It was included in Egyptian embalming mixes, and magicians found it essential for "love potions."

The Arabs kept a monopoly for centuries by telling scary stories about flesh-eating birds and monsters that attacked anyone eating it.

The Chinese (2700 BC) referred to it as the Tree of Life. A person who ate the tree's fruit, located in Paradise, would become immortal.

Cinnamon in most stores is really cassia, a darker and stronger-flavored bark from an Asian tree in the same family.

Cloves

Flavor/Taste:
Strong, pungent, aromatic

Use:
Use SPARINGLY, ¼ tsp for 2 servings.
Use in the BEGINNING of cooking. Heat creates more flavor.
Use in cookies, chocolate, fruit, pastries, marinades, pork,
stuffings and sweet vegetables.

Mix with:
- Cinnamon
- Garlic
- Ginger
- Honey
- Nuts-almonds
- Nutmeg
- Onion
- Parsley
- Thyme

Color & Form:
Brown nail-like buds or ground powder

❧ Historical Remedies ❧

Internally:
Aphrodisiac when combined with milk
Diarrhea and Nausea
Painkiller
Toothaches

Externally:
Earaches

❧ Origin ❧
Cloves are tree buds picked and dried
before flowering. It is native to the Moluccas
(Spice Islands) in Southeast Asia.

❧ Folklore/History ❧

In the 3rd century BC China used whole
cloves as mouth sweeteners.

On the Spice Islands a clove tree was planted
in honor of a child's birth. If the tree died it
foretold the death of the child.

Cloves were an essential commodity with the
early European spice traders and second
only to pepper in the American spice trade.

It comes from a Latin word *clavus* meaning
"nail" and was known for hundreds of years
as the black rose.

Coffee

Flavor/Taste:
Bitter to mild depending upon kind, form and blend of beans

Use:
Use at the BEGINNING of cooking.
The instant or freeze-dried form is good for baking.
Use as a beverage or beverage flavoring, in desserts, especially with ice cream.

Spiced Coffee:
Grind 8 Tbsp of French roast coffee beans with a 3" length of cinnamon stick and 8 whole cloves. Makes 8 cups. Or place a bag of spiced tea on top of the grounds.

Mix with:

~ Chocolate ~ Cloves ~ Nuts
~ Cinnamon ~ Cream ~ Vanilla

Color & Form:
Brown beans, ground, freeze-dried, instant and decaffeinated

~ Historical Remedies ~

Internally:
Coffee contains the stimulant caffeine, which relieves headaches. However, withdrawal from caffeine can also create headaches.

~ Origin ~
Coffee beans come from the hulled ripe berries of a coffee tree. It is native to Ethiopia, Congo and Liberia.

~ Folklore/History ~

Coffee drinking started in Arabia, reached Europe by 1660 and became preferred in America after the Boston Tea Party.

Beans start out green and turn various colors depending upon the heat of the roasting. They turn brown at over 400° F. Their gloss comes from sweating oil at high temperatures.

Both chicory and dandelion roots have been used as coffee substitutes.

Coffee is also known as **mocha**.

Coriander

Flavor/Taste:
Seeds are citrusy, sweet and tart

Use:
Use GENEROUSLY, ¾ tsp for 2 servings.
Use at the END of the cooking cycle.
Use in dips, eggs, lamb, Mexican and Indian dishes, mushrooms, pork, cream soups, sausages, rice and puddings.

Mix with:
- Anise
- Cheese
- Cumin
- Curry Powder
- Onion/Scallion
- Orange
- Pepper, Chile

Color & Form:
Light brown seeds with roots attached are best; ground powder

---

❧ Historical Remedies ❧

Internally:
Arthritis
Cramps
Gout
Prevents gas
Reduces cholesterol
High in vitamin C

❧ Origin ❧
Coriander are the roasted seeds from a fruit of a plant in the carrot family. It is native to Egypt and the Middle East.

❧ Folklore/History ❧

From the Greek *coris*, a bad-smelling bug, the seeds do smell, but last forever, even those buried in ancient Egypt.

During the Han Dynasty (270 BC-220 AD) in China, it was mixed in liquor for an aphrodisiac. The seeds are still used to flavor gin.

Sugarplums were actually coriander seeds coated in colored sugar. During WWII in Europe these candies were called confits (confections). Tossed to audiences at parades, they were later replaced with paper, thus *confetti*.

Cream & Milk

Flavor/Taste:
Sweet and rich, depending upon fat content

Use:
See **Equivalency Chart: Baking** for other Dairy Equivalents.
Use cream with at least 30% milk fat or it will curdle when boiled.
Use cream over pastas, potatoes, rice and vegetables or as a
base for dips, gravies, sauces and soups.
Use whipped cream for pies, dessert and drink toppings.

Mix with:
- Burnet
- Chives
- Horeseradish
- Lovage
- Paprika
- Mace-whipped
- Nutmeg
- Parsley
- Sorrel

1 cup cream + 1 tsp coconut extract = 1 cup of **coconut milk**.

Half & Half Substitute: Pour 1½ Tbsp melted butter plus enough whole milk to make 1 cup. Or use an equal amount of evaporated milk.

Milk is **scalded** by heating (not boiling) until a thin skin forms.

Color & Form:
White to creamy liquid or solid (butter); classified by milk fat

Whipping Cream (at least 20% fat content)
Cream doubles in volume when whipped.
Chill cream, bowl and beaters 30 minutes.
Add ¼ tsp unflavored gelatin per cup and
a few drops of lemon juice to avoid
separating. Flavor it with 1-2 Tbsp sugar
and 1 tsp instant coffee or ½ tsp
peppermint extract after it is foamy. Stop
beating if the cream turns yellow. Use a
cold can of evaporated milk as a substitute.

❖ Origin ❖
Cream is milk fat that rises when unhomo-
gonized milk is allowed to separate naturally.

❖ Milk Fat Content ❖	
Skim Milk	0%
Buttermilk (commercial)	2%
Whole Milk	4%
Evaporated Milk (canned whole milk minus water)	4%
Sweetened Condensed Milk (canned whole milk minus water plus lots of sugar)	4%
Half & Half (milk & cream)	10-12%
Light cream (used in coffee)	18-30%
Common whipping cream	30-36%
Heavy (whipping) cream	36-40%
Butter (US)	80%

Whipped toppings are not made from milk fat.

Cream, Sour

Flavor/Taste:
Tangy, tart and creamy

Use:
Use at the BEGINNING of cooking, if cooking for a short period and at low temperatures. Do not boil.
Use in desserts, dips, dressings, sauces, soups and with baked potatoes.

Use ⅞ cup plain soy milk + 2 Tbsp lemon juice as a substitute for buttermilk when baking.

Mix with:
- Horseradish
- Lemon Juice
- Lovage
- Mustard
- Paprika
- Pepper-all kinds

Color & Form:
White gelatinous cream

❧ Buttermilk ❧

Buttermilk, which you can get in powdered form, has an acidic, tangy flavor and is used mostly as a beverage. It is good in breads, pancakes and smoothies, especially with cherries or pears. Its acid acts like yeast or baking powder and helps dough rise. For baking, 1 cup buttermilk = 1 cup milk + ½ tsp baking soda less 2 tsp baking powder.

❧ Origin ❧
Sour cream is milk with bacteria added (lactic acid culture) for tang and kept at a specific temperature.

❧ Sour Cream & Fat Content ❧

Kind	Fat Content
Regular	18-20%
Light	10-12% made with Half & Half
Nonfat	0%

Sour cream keeps for about a week. Do not use it if mold forms.

In many instances you can substitute nonfat yogurt for sour cream.

Cumin

Flavor/Taste:
Strong, bitter peppery flavor with an equally strong odor

Use:
Use SPARINGLY, ¼ tsp for 2 servings at the BEGINNING of cooking. Do not combine with sweet flavorings.
Use with beans, chili, cabbage, deviled eggs, meats, Indian and Mexican cooking and sauces.

Mix with:
- Caraway Seed
- Chili Powder
- Coriander
- Curry Powder

Color & Form:
Brownish gray seeds like caraway; ground powder

❧ Historical Remedies ❧

Internally:
Antiviral
Stomach cramps

Externally:
Arthritis
Rheumatism

❧ Origin ❧
Cumin is the dried fruit of an annual plant of the parsley family. It is native to Egypt, Western Asia and the Mediterranean.

❧ Folklore/History ❧

Cumin is interchanged with caraway seed in German cooking.

The Romans used it as a pepper substitute.

One of the earliest spices, cumin is mentioned in the Old Testament.

Europeans used cumin in breads and cakes.

Curry Powder *(blend)*

Flavor/Taste:
Mild to hot blend of spices; pungent

Use:
Use SPARINGLY, ¼ tsp for 2 servings.
Use at the BEGINNING of cooking. Heating does increase aroma.
Use in Indian and Asian dishes and with cheese, eggs,
mushrooms, poultry, soups, sauces, stir-frys and vegetables.

Mix with:
- ❧Butter/Margarine
- ❧Cayenne
- ❧Nuts-coconut, cashew
- ❧Paprika
- ❧Onion/Scallion
- ❧Tomato

Color & Form:
Golden ground blend of seasonings that may or may not
include the leaves of the curry plant

❧ Historical Remedies ❧

Internally:
Poisonous venom
Rabies
Seizures
Traumatic shock

❧ Origin ❧
The Curry plant is a relative of the lemon
tree. It is native to southwest Asia and India.

❧ Folklore/History ❧

Curry comes from a Hindu word, *turcarri*,
meaning "sauce."

Curry is a blend of 10 to 20 spices, including
turmeric, nutmeg, cardamom, mustard,
coriander, cumin and peppers. Its hotness is
determined by the amount of cayenne used.

Curry is used in East Indian cooking where
it is called **garam masala**. It is also used in
Southeast Asia without the sweeter spices
and with a heavy dose of basil.

Dill (Seed & Weed)

Flavor/Taste:
Seeds like sweet caraway; leaves less pungent

Use:
Use leaves at the END of cooking, just before serving.
Use seeds at the END, but they can take more cooking than leaves.
Use leaves in soft cheeses, white meats, eggs, salads,
mushrooms, mustard sauces and vegetables.
Seeds are used with apples, breads, cabbage, fish and stews.
Most of us associate dill with pickles and sour dishes.

Mix with:
- Chives
- Mint
- Mustard
- Onion/Scallion
- Parsley
- Tomato

Color & Form:
Light brown seeds with lighter outline, ground powder or salt
Green feather-like leaves

⤳ Historical Remedies ⤳

Internally:
Breath freshener
Colic
Insomnia
Gas and Stomach cramps
High in vitamin C, calcium, protein (20%+)

⤳ Origin ⤳
Dill is a hardy annual plant related to
parsley. It is native to the Mediterranean
and is grown in India.

⤳ Folklore/History ⤳

Dill comes from the Norwegian *dilla*,
meaning "to lull." It has a history of being
used for soothing or curing insomnia.

The presence of dill was an indication of
prosperity to the Greeks. In the 8th century,
Charlemagne used it at banquets to relieve
hiccups. It was used as a love potion in the
Middle Ages and to keep witches away.

Fennel

Flavor/Taste:
Mild nutty-like licorice; aromatic

Use:
Use ¼-½ tsp for 2 servings. Use at END of cooking cycle.
Crush seeds for more flavor.
Use with apples, bread, eggs, meat, especially fish, sauces and green vegetables.

All but the fibrous stalks of this plant can be eaten, the seeds and dill-like leaves are used for flavoring.

Mix with:

- Curry Powder
- Oregano
- Parsley
- Rosemary
- Sage
- Thyme

Color & Form:
Light brown seeds, green leaves or stems, white bulb

ꙮ Historical Remedies ꙮ

Internally:
Breath freshener
Congestion
Mild stimulant thus good for headaches
Stomach cramps
High in vitamin A

Externally:
In large doses for fleas and ticks on animals

ꙮ Origin ꙮ
Fennel is a bulbous perennial plant of the carrot and parsley families. It is native to the Mediterranean.

ꙮ Folklore/History ꙮ

Fennel was good for eyesight and used as a symbol of success in battle. Roman and Greek soldiers would "fennel load" before battle, like we might carbo-load today. They would flog students with fennel to literally beat some sense into them. It was a cure for obesity, helped mothers give more milk and even allowed snakes to shed their skins.

Fennel is the Greek word for *marathon*, which meant "to grow thin." The Battle of Marathon was fought in a field of fennel. Fennel was thought to be an appetite suppressant.

Fenugreek

Flavor/Taste:
Slightly bitter, celery-like; nutty

Use:
Use SPARINGLY. Heat releases the flavor.
Use as a thickener for meats in stews, stir-frys, curries and tea.
Use as a marinade for vegetables.

Mix with:

◦Cardamom   ◦Garlic

Color & Form:
Light green leaves, brownish-yellow seeds, white ground powder

---

◦ Historical Remedies ◦

Internally:
Lowers cholesterol
Congestion
Laxative
Substitute for quinine and cod liver oil
Prevents gas (as a tea)
Sore throat
Ulcer

◦ Origin ◦
Fenugreek is an annual legume in the pea family. It is native to Western Asia.

◦ Folklore/History ◦

Fenugreek means "Greek hay."

The ground seed is used for artificial maple extract. The oil is extracted from fenugreek and used in perfumes.

Ancient Egyptians used it for embalming.

Recent studies indicate an association between fenugreek and increased milk production in lactating women.

Five-Spice Powder (blend)

Flavor/Taste:
Sweet, aromatic, light licorice flavor

Use:
Use GENEROUSLY.
Although sweet, it makes hot flavors seem hotter.
Use with pork, poultry, beef, stir-frys and Asian dishes.

Mix with:

- Cilantro
- Coriander
- Curry Powder
- Honey
- Shallot

Color & Form:
Yellowish red to brown powder

Historical Remedies

See individual flavorings that make up this blend in this section.

Folklore/History

This spice blend is also known as **Chinese Five-Spice Powder**.

It consists of two parts each of star anise, Szechuan pepper and fennel and one part each of clove and cinnamon.

Origin
Five-Spice Powder is a blend of star anise, Szechuan peppercorns, cinnamon, cloves and fennel. It is native to China.

Flowers to Eat

Flowers are more commonly used for decoration than flavor. Here are some common edible flowers with a brief description on use. Several herbs have edible flowers, such as thyme and chives. The best-flavored blossoms are chamomile, hibiscus, lavender and violas. Use dressings before adding the flowers to avoid discoloration. Rinse and use flowers right away. *Be aware that the leaves or other parts of these edible flowers may be toxic and may trigger allergic reactions.*

Bee Balm-Its leaves are used for TEAS, and they have a citrusy flavor of orange and lemon. The flowers are used as a red garnish.

Borage-Available in liquid capsules as a fatty acid, the leaves and flowers are not readily available. *The flowers are toxic in quantity.* They are used as an accent in PUNCH bowls. Leaves taste like cucumber and are used in POTATO and FISH SALADS, SOUPS, TEAS and VEGETABLES.

Clove Pink-The petals of these perennial dianthus are edible. They taste like cloves and are used in LIQUEURS and VINEGARS. They are also eaten as CANDY and in SOUPS and SAUCES.

Geranium-Use the fresh leaves on ice cream, puddings and other DESSERTS. It is also used to make jellies. The flavor (nutmeg, coconut and lemon) varies with the kind of geranium.

Marigold/Calendula-Once considered a cheap substitute for saffron, the marigold petals (without pistil, stamen and heel) have an aromatic, slightly bitter flavor that is good in BEEF, EGGS, CREAM CHEESE, RICE, SALADS, SOUPS, STEWS and VEGETABLES.

Nasturtium-A flower with a peppery flavor, it is used in EGGS, CREAM CHEESE, DIPS, PASTA and TEA. Add it at the end of cooking and use it with lemon juice, tarragon and olive oil. The leaves are used in SALADS and SANDWICHES. Once used as a scurvy preventative, it is rich in iron and vitamin C.

Pansy/Violas-Remove the pistil, stamen and heel of this flower before adding them to SALADS. They add a vibrant color against green salads. Johnny jump-ups are good with PEACHES.

Rose (hip)-The ripe fruit of the rose, it is used to make TEAS, SYRUPS and JELLIES. Although they are too tart to eat raw, they are used in powder form and are rich in vitamin C.

Violet-Violets are used as a garnish in SOUPS, PUNCHES, PASTRIES, JAMS and PUDDINGS. Their leaves are used in SALADS. The flowers are usually candied.

Other Edible Flowers

Bachelor Button	English Daisy	Lilac
Carnation	Fuchsia	Mint Blossom
Chamomile	Hibiscus	Snapdragon
Chive Blossom	Hollyhock	Squash Blossom
Chrysanthemum	Honeysuckle	Yucca
Dandelion	Impatiens	
Daylily	Lavender	

Edible Flower Dressing

½ cup safflower oil
¼ cup honey
2 Tbsp lemon juice

Whisk for 1 minute.

Garlic

Flavor/Taste:
Strong, oniony; nutty if roasted

Use:
Use 1 clove for 2 servings. Use it at the END of cooking.
It becomes more pungent as it cooks and bitter if overcooked.
Garlic's flavor becomes stronger the smaller you chop it up.
Use in Italian dishes, in stews, sauces and gravies.

Mix with:
- Fennel
- Olive Oil
- Oregano
- Thyme
- Ginger
- Onion
- Rosemary
- Tomato

Color & Form:
Light beige whole garlic with white tissue-thin skin, a clove,
minced, garlic powder (better than salt), extract and oil

1 medium clove =
¾ tsp minced =
¼ tsp garlic powder

For a milder taste,
oven roast a whole
garlic by wrapping it
in foil at 300° for 1
hour or boiling it
whole for 20 minutes.

Use cardamom to
neutralize garlic odor.

To store fresh garlic
puree 12 cloves with
½ cup olive oil.

❧ Historical Remedies ❧

Internally:
Antibacterial
Lowers cholesterol and blood pressure
Lowers blood sugar for diabetics
Reduces water retention
High in vitamins and minerals

Externally:
Rub on corns, bunions, warts, bites

❧ Origin ❧
Garlic is a perennial plant of the lily family
related to onions. It is native to Central Asia.

❧ Folklore/History ❧

Muslims were afraid of garlic because of its
association with the devil. When Satan left
the Garden of Eden after the fall of Adam,
garlic grew from his left foot print and onion
from his right.

The American Indians used garlic in their
diet both directly and indirectly. They would
spread cloves of garlic on the ground for
birds. The birds would weaken after eating
them and thus became easier to catch.

Ginger

Flavor/Taste:
Peppery and citrusy

Use:
Use ½ tsp for 2 servings. Use in the MIDDLE or END of cooking.
Use to reduce gas in beans and fattiness in pork.
Use in breads, cookies, pies (baked fruits), meats, sauces,
soups, yellow vegetables and as a tea.

Refrigerate peeled and sliced ginger after storing it in a jar with 1 inch of white wine. Frozen fresh ginger also lasts for months.

Mix with:
- ✤Cheese
- ✤Curry Powder
- ✤Garlic
- ✤Onion/Scallion
- ✤Soy Sauce

Color & Form:
White to cream root, crystallized root or ground powder

✤ Historical Remedies ✤

Internally:
Antibacterial
Improves circulation
Diarrhea
Headaches
Prevents gas
Good for lymph glands
Reduces motion sickness

✤ Origin ✤
Ginger is the one-year-old root of a tall lilylike perennial plant. It is native to Egypt and Greece.

✤ Folklore/History ✤

When Marco Polo's travels were published in the 1300's, he said he'd seen ginger growing in China. This helped start the search for a sea route to the Orient.

Theme birthday cakes may have originated from a gingerbread modeled in the shape of the Kremlin. The cake was for Peter the Great in honor of his birthday. It weighed 150 pounds. That's a lot of ginger!

Ginger was used as medicine against the plague during the Black Death.

Honey

Flavor/Taste:
Sweet, rich

Use:
Use at the BEGINNING for baking; END for glazing or coating. Easier to digest and healthier than sugar. *Not for small children.* Crystallizing is normal, warm to liquefy it and keep 1 year. Use for breads, soft cheeses, chicken (with almonds), ham and pork, spicy sauces, pastries, stir-frys and fruit or as a spread.

⅔ cup honey + ¼ cup flour = 1 cup of sugar

Lessen heat 25° and cook a little longer when using honey instead of sugar to avoid browning too quickly.

1 cup honey = 1¼ cups sugar + ¼ cup water

Mix with:
- Cinnamon
- Ginger
- Mustard
- Nuts-chestnuts
- Orange
- Thyme

Color & Form:
A thick liquid from yellow to dark brown, the darker has more flavor

⚜ Historical Remedies ⚜

Internally:
Cough syrup
In hot teas for colds

⚜ Origin ⚜
Honey is from the nectar of flowers mixed with bee saliva. Honey is native to where ever bees and flowers are found.

⚜ Folklore/History ⚜

Only in the last 200 years has sugar been affordable as a sweetener. Honey was used prior to that.

There are 200-300 kinds of honey.

Cane sugar is in flower nectar, but bee's saliva changes it to glucose and fruit sugar.

Honey in the US contains an average of:
38% fruit sugar/fructose
31% glucose
7% malt sugar

Horseradish

Flavor/Taste:

A peppery, pungent taste similar to mustard

Use:

Use SPARINGLY raw and use immediately. Use for its crisp texture or with cream or mayonnaise as a relish.
Use with meats, especially seafood, cream cheese, dips, eggs, especially hard-boiled, sauces, salads and stir-frys.

Grate 2 cups horseradish root and add a little white vinegar to blend. Measure out 1⅓ cups. To this add ¾ tsp salt and ⅔ cup white vinegar. This is tastier than prepared.

Mix with:

↜Cream-to sweeten ↜Vinegar-to add sourness
↜Lemon Juice-to add sourness

Color & Form:

Light yellow fresh roots better than dried; relish, ground powder

↜ Historical Remedies ↜

Internally:
Antibiotic
Coughs, congestion and sore throat
Kidney stones
Water retention

Externally:
Arthritis and Rheumatism
Poultice for infections

↜ Origin ↜

Horseradish is the root vegetable of a perennial plant of the mustard family. It is native to Eastern Europe.

↜ The Red Radish ↜

Milder than horseradish, red radishes are used as a garnish and are rarely cooked. They are good in salads and slaws, adding both texture and color. (Their leaves are also eaten in salads.) Soak them in ice water to crispen. Like horseradish, they come from the mustard family, but are native to southern Asia.

Daikon-a mild peppery radish, that looks like a carrot, is peeled and used for its texture. It comes pickled in soy sauce and sugar. It is used in soups and with pork and fish.

Wasabi-a Japanese horseradish with a fierce aroma and a biting taste. It is used in BBQ sauces and dressings.

Hyssop

Flavor/Taste:
Bitter taste with a hint of mint

Use:
Use SPARINGLY, ½ tsp for 4 servings.
Use in fruit, especially cranberries, pasta, rice, green salads, soups, stews and stuffings.

Mix with:
- Cheese
- Tomato
- Sage

Color & Form:
Fresh or dried leaves and flowers; less potent in sauce form

- -

❧ Historical Remedies ❧

Internally:
Antiseptic
Arthritis
Coughs
Fever
Sore throats

❧ Origin ❧
Hyssop is a perennial shrubby plant of the mint family. It is native to the Mideast and southern Russia.

❧ Folklore/History ❧

From the Greek, *hyssopos*, meaning "holy". Because of its aroma, it was used to purify holy places.

Hyssop was also dropped on floors. When people stepped on it, it would release an aroma that would clean the air.

The American Indians used hyssop as a treatment for respiratory illnesses.

Juniper

Flavor/Taste:
A bitter gin taste

Use:
Use SPARINGLY, 3-4 berries crushed in a roast or stew.
Use with cabbage, game meats, marinades, pork, salmon, sauces and stuffings.

Mix with:
- Anise
- Bay Leaf
- Cumin
- Fennel
- Garlic
- Marjoram
- Parsley
- Thyme
- Wine

Color & Form:
Purplish, usually dried whole berries; crush for flavor

☙ Historical Remedies ☙

Internally:
Hard on kidneys

Externally:
Arthritis
Hives
Sore throat

☙ Origin ☙
Juniper comes from the cones or berries of an evergreen bush. It is native to Europe.

☙ Folklore/History ☙

Juniper comes in separate male and female bushes. Females bare the berries.

Extensive use can cause kidney damage.

Gin, which is made from juniper berries comes from the French word *genievre*, which means both juniper berry and gin.

Ask your nursery whether you can use the berries off the juniper bush you buy from them for drying and eventual eating. When in doubt, do not eat!

Leeks

Flavor/Taste:
Onion and peppery flavor, milder than scallions

Use:
Use at the BEGINNING and cook immediately after cutting.
Trim all but 1½" of the green leaves.
Use as you would an onion.
Use with white meats, starches, green salads and soups.

Buy small leeks and wash them carefully. It is best to slice them down the middle and cut the root end off to wash away the sand.

Mix with:
- Butter/Margarine
- Oils & Fats-olive
- Tomato
- Cream & Milk
- Paprika

Color & Form:
Like a giant green and white scallion

◦ Historical Remedies ◦

Internally:
Rich in minerals

◦ Folklore/History ◦

The Romans were responsible for leeks spreading throughout Europe.

They have been very popular with the Welsh for over 1,000 years. In fact, the Welsh wore leeks in their hats during battle to distinguish themselves from their enemies.

◦ Origin ◦
Leeks come from a biennial herb of the lily family. Its earliest record was in Egypt at the time of the Pharaohs.

Lemon Grass

Flavor/Taste:
Subtle, citrus or lemony flavor

Use:
Use GENEROUSLY at the END of the cooking cycle.
Use with meats and stews, stir-frys, fruit salads, soups and in tea.

Lemon Verbena can be substituted and is easily grown, though not readily available. It can have a soapy flavor if used too heavily.

Mix with:
- Coriander
- Garlic
- Ginger
- Onion/Scallion
- Parsley
- Pepper, Chile
- Sage
- Tarragon
- Turmeric

Color & Form:
Brownish dried and needle-like with a bulbous base

✤ Historical Remedies ✤

Internally:
Diarrhea
Good for intestinal blockage
High in vitamin A

✤ Origin ✤
Lemon Grass is a grass with citric oils. It is native to Southeast Asia.

✤ Folklore/History ✤

In ancient Malaysia a tea was made with lemon grass to alleviate depression. It is still used as a tea and relaxes the stomach muscles.

Lemon grass is very popular in Thai cooking.

Lemon grass is also known as **citronella**.

Lemon Juice

Flavor/Taste:
Citrus fruit juice of lemon; sour

Use:
Add at the BEGINNING.
Use to add tanginess, to keep fruit from discoloring or as a vinegar substitute. Use in beverages, with meats, seafood, pastas, desserts, pastries, salads, stir-frys and hot vegetables.

2½ Tbsp juice = 1½-2 Tbsp zest

Zest is only the yellow outside layer of the lemon; **peel** is the white bitter layer under the yellow zest.

To get more juice from lemons or limes microwave for 10-15 seconds before squeezing.

Mix with:
- Cardamom
- Ginger
- Onion
- Parsley
- Sage
- Tarragon

Color & Form:
Clear to yellow juice bottled or squeezed from the fruit

❧ Historical Remedies ❧

Internally:
Congestion (with honey and tea)

Externally:
Lemon has long been used as a cleaning agent and a fragrance.

❧ Origin ❧
Lemon Juice comes from the lemon, a fruit of a small spiny citrus tree. It is native to Southeast Asia and Malaysia.

❧ Folklore/History ❧

Common citrus fruits include grapefruits, kumquats, lemons, limes, oranges and tangerines. Most are tart and high in vitamin C. Although originally from Asia, they are grown in Central and South America and in California, Florida and Texas.

Lime

Used almost as much as lemon juice for flavoring beverages, gelatins, candies and to add a tart taste to any food.

Liquid Smoke™

Flavor/Taste:
Meaty, woody and smoky outdoor flavor

Use:
Use GENEROUSLY toward the END of cooking.
Use in sautéing, in browning meats and mushrooms and for grilling.
Use with Cajun dishes, chili, dips, marinades, meats, sauces, stews
and vegetables.

Mix with:

•Caraway Seed	•Cayenne	•Oils & Fats-olive	•Thyme
•Cardamom	•Garlic	•Pepper, Bell	

Color & Form:
Brown liquid, patented and sold in a jar

. . . .

❧ Meat Flavor Enhancers ❧

There are many meat flavor enhancers on the
market. They include **steak sauces** and a
huge variety of **barbeque sauces**. Many can
be used as a marinade before cooking, as well
as a basting agent during grilling. Try adding
them to canned or cooked beans, chili or
stew.

❧Origin ❧
Liquid Smoke is man-made liquefied smoke
derived from flavored wood chips.

❧ Folklore/History ❧

First patented in the early 20th century by
S.E. Colgin. Today this company uses
hickory, mesquite, apple and pecan wood
chips. It is smoldered at high temperatures.
The smoke and associated gases are
chilled quickly to liquefy the smoke. It is
then filtered and bottled without any other
additives.

Lovage

Flavor/Taste:
Strong lemony, celery-like

Use:
Use at the BEGINNING of cooking.
Use SPARINGLY. It can overwhelm other flavors.
Use in eggs, soups, starches, stews and salads.
Seeds are used in breads and cakes.

Mix with:
- Cheese
- Fennel
- Marjoram
- Mustard
- Tarragon
- Thyme

Color & Form:
Green or dried brown leaves, seeds or roots

❧ Historical Remedies ❧

Internally:
Digestive
Diuretic
Heartburn
Memory

Externally:
Poultice for boils

❧ Origin ❧
Lovage is a large perennial plant grown from celery seed or root divisions. It is native to southern Europe.

❧ Folklore/History ❧

Large quantities can harm kidneys and should not be used by pregnant women.

It was used in Greek and Roman times to get rid of or cure freckles and as a love potion, thus its alias "love parsley".

During the Middle Ages the leaves were often placed in shoes to freshen feet.

Lovage, also known as **smallage**, is a very tall plant that produces the familiar **celery seed**.

Mace

Flavor/Taste:
Like nutmeg, but stronger and more pungent

Use:
Use ¼ tsp for 2 servings. Use at the BEGINNING of cooking.
Use as a substitute for nutmeg.
Use with beans, vegetables, cheese, meats, pastries, fruit salads
and soups.

Mix with:
- Allspice
- Cardamom
- Cinnamon
- Cloves
- Curry Powder
- Ginger

Color & Form:
Light reddish brown to brown lacy strands pressed flat; ground

✧ Historical Remedies ✧

Internally:
Diuretic
Fevers
Hypothermia

✧ Origin ✧
Mace is the lacy cover of the fruit pit or
nutmeg of the nutmeg tree. It is native to the
Moluccas (the Spice Islands).

✧ Folklore/History ✧

In the 17th century mace brought a better
price than nutmeg. The Dutch ordered half
the nutmeg trees destroyed and replaced by
planting more mace trees. They both come
from the same tree!

Mace and nutmeg were two of the spices
that started the European trade competition
for the Spice Islands in the East Indies. The
competition benefited the US also. Many
shipbuilders along the northeast became
rich from the trade, and Connecticut
became *The Nutmeg State*.

Marjoram

Flavor/Taste:
Like oregano, but sweeter and more subtle

Use:
Use ¼ tsp dried for 2 servings. Add at the END of cooking. Use with beans, cheese, eggs, meats, mushrooms, pizza, potatoes, sauces, soups, stews and vegetables.

Mix with:
- Basil
- Bay Leaf
- Chives
- Garlic
- Lovage
- Oregano
- Savory
- Thyme
- Tomato

Color & Form:
Green fresh or dried leaves; ground powder is more bitter

❧ Historical Remedies ❧

Internally:
Arthritis
Asthma and Colic
Indigestion
Vericose veins (as a hot tea)

Externally:
Arthritis
Vericose veins

❧ Origin ❧
Marjoram is related to oregano and is from the mint family. It is native to Southwest Asia and the Mediterranean.

❧ Folklore/History ❧

A servant was told to carry an urn to the King of Cyrus. He dropped it on the way. Fearing the king's fury, the servant died of fright in the puddle made by the spilled "perfume." On his grave grew a plant with the same fragrance. The plant was marjoram. A later tale stated that if marjoram grew on a grave it meant that the departed was happy.

It was also said that if you bathed in marjoram before going to bed, you would dream of your future spouse.

Mint

Flavor/Taste:
A cool, sweet taste; peppermint is more pungent and peppery

Use:
Use at the BEGINNING, SPARINGLY, ¼- ½ tsp for 2 servings.
Use Peppermint in sweets, teas, sauces, salsas and jellies.
Use Spearmint in fruit, salads, sauces, stews, sweets, tea and vegetables.
.

Use chocolate mint with berries, lemon mint with potato salad or fish, orange mint with salads and pineapple mint with cucumber or fruit salads. Or add any of these mints to flavor your cookie batter.

- Basil
- Cilantro
- Dill
- Nuts-coconut
- Onion/Scallion
- Parsley
- Pepper, Chile
- Rosemary
- Tomato

Mix with:
Color & Form:
Peppermint: Bright green leaves, extract or oil

❧ Historical Remedies ❧

Internally:
Colic (spearmint)
Cramps (with warm milk)
Headaches (peppermint)
Kidney stones (spearmint)
Peppermint has menthol used in medicines

Externally:
Insect repellent (peppermint)

❧ Origin ❧
Mint is an intrusive perennial plant that grows by runners. It is native to the Himalyan Mountains and Greece.

❧ Folklore/History ❧

A poor couple were eating their last food when they invited two unexpected visitors to dine with them. Embarrassed, they rubbed the table with mint to make the room smell better. As thanks the guests, who were Jupiter and Mercury, transformed the couple's home to a temple and had servants wait on them for the rest of their lives.

Pluto fell for the lovely nymph Minthe. His wife jealously turned her into a plant. Pluto could not undo the spell, but made it so that the more Minthe was walked on the sweeter she smelled. Minthe became Mentha, the genus name of mint.

Mustard

Flavor/Taste:
A strong, pungent, bitter, peppery taste

Use:
Use ¼ tsp for 2 servings. Mix equal amounts cold water and dry mustard. Let stand for 10 minutes before using.
Add at the END of cooking, cook gently and do not boil.
Seeds are used for pickling, in sauerkraut and salads.
Use with beans, cheese, eggs, meats, sauces, soups and vegetables.

Mix with:
- Basil
- Garlic
- Lemon Juice
- Marjoram
- Onion/Scallion
- Rosemary
- Sage
- Tarragon
- Thyme

1 tsp dried mustard =1 Tbsp prepared

Mustard: Mix 2 Tbsp dry mustard to 1 tsp sugar. Add hot water or vinegar to desired thickness.

Chinese Mustard: Stir ¼ cup boiling water into ¼ cup dry mustard and 2 Tbsp cooking oil. Add salt or soy sauce to taste.

Color & Form:
Yellow seeds, ground (dry) powder, or prepared

❧ Historical Remedies ❧

Internally:
Congestion

Externally:
Arthritis-poultice, mixed with warm wine
Bronchitis
Sore throat

❧ Origin ❧
Mustard is an annual from the cabbage family. It is native to the Middle East and the Mediterranean.

❧ Folklore/History ❧

The Romans mixed unfermented grape juice, known as *must* with crushed seeds of the mustard plant. They called it mustard, *ard* meaning "to burn."

Buddha, sympathizing with the loss of a woman's child, told the woman that the child would be restored if she got mustard seeds from a house where no one had died. She never found such a house and realized that no one was immune from death and its accompanying sorrow.

Nutmeg

Flavor/Taste:
Sweet, nutty

Use:
Use at the END of cooking, but the BEGINNING for baking.
Use SPARINGLY and do not use with cumin or anise.
It can be poisonous in large quantities.
Use with eggs, custards, fruit, mushrooms, pastries, white sauces, vegetables, especially potatoes, spinach and squash.

Mix with:
- Allspice
- Cheese
- Cinnamon
- Cloves
- Honey
- Lemon Juice
- Onion
- Vanilla

Color & Form:
Brown small egg-shaped seeds; ground powder

❧ Historical Remedies ❧

Internally:
Diarrhea
Digestive
Fevers
Hypothermia
Insomnia

❧ Origin ❧
Nutmeg is the seed of the fruit pit of an evergreen tree. It is native to the Moluccas (Spice Islands).

❧ Folklore/History ❧

Ancient Rome fumigated streets with nutmeg.

In Europe, people carried nutmeg graters with them to restaurants as a status symbol. The graters became elaborate, depending upon the wealth of the individual.

Connecticut is *The Nutmeg State* because early merchants substituted wooden nutmegs, that had been soaked in nutmeg extract, for the real thing.

In 1955 40% of the world's nutmeg was lost to a hurricane on the island of Grenada.

Nuts

Flavor/Taste:
Oily, rich, sweet

Use:
Use at the BEGINNING or END of cooking.
It adds richness, texture, protein and calories to foods.
Toasting 2-3 minutes on low enhances flavor, so you can use less.
Use in cookies, pastries, salads, stir-frys, pestos and stuffings or over pancakes.

Refrigerate nuts out of their shells up to 4 months in an airtight container. Nuts in their shells will last twice as long. Refrigerating avoids spoiling due to high levels of fat.

Mix with:
◦Beer   ◦Cinnamon   ◦Curry Powder   ◦Pepper, Chile

Color & Form:
Brown to white nut inside a shell; Out of the shell: whole, halved, sliced, slivered, diced, salted, candied or as an extract or oil

◦ Historical Remedies ◦

Internally:
Chestnuts were thought to cure hiccups
Lowers cholesterol
Good source of vitamin E and fiber
Walnuts were used to lubricate the large intestine and maintain kidneys and lungs.

◦ Origin ◦
Nuts generally come from trees. They are more often seen in hot, humid areas.

◦ Folklore/History ◦

Peanuts were buried by Peruvians with their dead to sustain them on their journey in the afterlife. Peanuts are really a bean not a nut.

Peanut butter was invented in 1890 and considered a health food. It is easy to make by just simply putting peanuts in a blender.

Nut-producing trees are one of the few edible plants existing on more than one continent. They were around before Europe and North America separated about 60 million years ago.

Nut Varieties

Most nuts add a great crunchy texture and a richer flavor to foods. They are high in monounsaturated "good" fat (1 oz = 180 calories and 17 grams of fat) and contain calcium, vitamin B, magnesium, potassium, zinc, iron and lots of protein. As an appetizer, try them with a medium to full-bodied Cabernet Sauvignon or choose the white wines mentioned below. Increase the flavor of nuts by dry toasting them in a pan, stirring constantly until they turn golden.

Combine 2 cups of nuts that are in their shells with 1 cup of water and micro-wave for 4-5 minutes. The meat of the nut will come out whole from the shells.

Almond-From an Eastern Mediterranean tree related to the peach, it can be found in stores either whole, slivered, sliced or as an extract. Almonds mix well with a light Chenin Blanc, a fruity Fume Blanc or a sweet Riesling wine. Mix with butter, coriander, olive oil or paprika. Toast them in sugar for a sweet crunchy addition to Asian salads. They go well with BEANS, CHICKEN, LAMB, RICE and SEAFOOD (crab). They can turn bitter if cooked too long. Blanch in boiling water and let stand for 5 minutes to remove skins. Use GENEROUSLY. Almonds contain lots of calcium.

Brazil Nut-Actually a seed from a wild tree in Brazil, they have a rich flavor. They are wonderful with chocolate, mint and fruits and are used in BREADS, DESSERTS, RICE and STUFFINGS.

Cashew-A kidney-shaped seed from a South American tree. They have a sweet flavor and when ground are used to thicken curries or sauces (grind them with 1-2 tsp of olive or canola oil). They mix well with curry and are especially good with ASPARAGUS, CHEESE, CHICKEN, INDIAN VEGETABLE DISHES and in SALADS. They are 48% fat, the lowest of any nut except chestnut. They tend to get soggy in baked items.

Chestnut-The fruit of a fast-growing tree in the Mediterranean, the shell should be slit and the nut roasted in hot oil before using. It mixes well with anise, celery seed and lemon juice and is good in MEAT SAUCES, DESSERTS and STUFFINGS. *Do not confuse the chestnut you eat with the non-edible horse chestnut or buckeye.*

Coconut-The nut of a Malaysian palm tree, the coconut comes whole, shredded, in flakes and as an extract. Its sweetness balances with hot spices and is good with chili powder, chile pepper, curry and black pepper. Although used mostly in DESSERTS, it goes especially well with SPICY CHICKEN and SEAFOOD, FRUIT SALADS and STIR-FRYS. A coconut contains lots of iron, potassium and protein. Unfortunately, it is also high in saturated "bad" fat and in calories.

1 cup coconut = 3 oz
2 cups dried unsweetened coconut + 2½ cups hot water (or milk) = 3 cups coconut milk.

Nut Varieties continued

Hazelnut (filbert)-The fruit of the hazel tree, hazelnuts are sweet and about grape size. Remove the brown skin by baking at 350° F for 12 minutes or until they flake, and then rub off while still warm. They come whole, chopped, as an oil (imported, expensive and strong in flavor) or syrup. They add flavor and texture and are used in COFFEE, PASTRIES, SAUCES, VEGETABLE SOUPS and STEAMED or BOILED VEGETABLES.

Macadamia-Native to Australia, the macadamia nut became known after the 1890's. It goes well with Riesling or a medium, spicy White Zinfandel. It is high in fat and is used mostly in DESSERTS.

Peanut-(goobers, ground nuts) Originating in Peru, a peanut is a bean not a nut. It is used whole or as an oil, especially in Vietnamese and Thai foods. It goes especially well with curry, pepper and onions with a light-bodied, spicy White Zinfandel. Peanuts are good in DESSERTS, SALADS, STIR-FRYS and accompanying SAUCES. Peanut oil contains both mono- and polyunsaturated (good) fats and is good for frying.

Pecan-A type of hickory nut from South America, it has the highest fat content of all the nuts and comes either whole, halved or chopped. It is also high in iron and calcium. They are used mostly in COOKIES, SALADS, STIR-FRYS, STUFFINGS and, of course, PECAN PIE. Sprinkle them over pancakes and waffles with fruit. They go well with a full-bodied Chardonnay.

Pine Nut-(piñon) Pine nuts come from a pine cone and are labor-intensive, and thus, expensive, to obtain. They are high in iron, thiamine and magnesium and used in ITALIAN DISHES (pesto), RICE, SAUCES and COOKIES. There are two varieties: the Italian and the stronger-flavored Chinese.

Pistachio-A shelled green seed from a Middle Eastern tree, it is high in iron and potassium. It goes well with a medium to full Chardonnay or a light Chenin Blanc. For cooking it goes well with ginger and honey and is used with CHICKEN, PASTRIES, RICE, STIR-FRYS, STUFFINGS and VEGETABLES. Pick the greenest ones. They may contain large amounts of pesticides, so buy organic.

Walnut-A large tree from Asia, the walnut is used whole, as an oil or an extract. It has a slightly bitter taste, which increases with age. It is best to pick nuts with the lightest-colored shells. They go well with a Chardonnay wine. For cooking, combine walnuts with Parmesan cheese, pepper and shallots. Use them with APPLES, CHICKEN, COOKIES, SALADS, SAUCES and STUFFINGS or as a topping over PANCAKES or WAFFLES.

Oils & Fats

Flavor/Taste:
Varies depending upon the source

Use:
Add at the BEGINNING of cooking.
Use on salads with vinegar, in baking to help make dough expand, in frying to crispen, and in coating to prevent burning and/or sticking.

Heating a pan before sautéing or cooking makes the oil expand, requiring less oil.

Remove fat from soups, stews or sauces by wrapping ice cubes in a paper towel and dragging it over the surface. Fat will stick to the towel.

Mix with:
- Garlic
- Leek
- Onion/Scallion
- Pepper, Bell
- Pepper, Chile
- Shallot
- Tomato
- Vinegar

Color & Form:
Light-colored due to bleaching, oils are liquid and fats are solid

· ·

❧ Historical Remedies ❧

Internally:
Carry fat-soluble vitamins (A,D, E and K) throughout the body

Insulate and cushion organs

Supply essential fatty acids and a concentrated form of energy

Limit fat to 15 grams a day (135 calories)

❧ Origin ❧
Oils come from various nuts, seeds, vegetables, beans and fruits. Many are native to the Mediterranean.

❧ Fats: Good or Bad? ❧

Saturated fats are "bad" fats that increase cholesterol, a factor in heart disease. These include butter, margarine, coconut oil, lard, suet and vegetable shortening. **Unsaturated** fats come from plants and are "good" for you. **Monounsaturated** fats include olive, canola, almond, hazelnut and peanut oils. **Polyunsaturated** fats include safflower, soybean, corn, sunflower, walnut, cottonseed and sesame oils. Polyunsaturated oils found in fish, such as sardines, tuna and salmon, can be destroyed by high heat.

Oil & Fat Varieties

Below is a list of oils and fats used in the kitchen and an explanation of how each oil is used, whether for baking, frying, cooking or for salads. The saturated "bad" fat content of the following oils and fats is noted by the number in parenthesis. Read the total fat content on the packaging or label of butters, margarines, fats and oils that you buy. Use at least 60% fat content when baking cookies and pastries. Nut oils are flavorful, especially when used as a butter substitute over vegetables. Buy nut oils in small quantities and refrigerate them.

Butter/Margarine (80%)-Butter has more flavor than margarine, especially in BAKED GOODS and some FRIED FOODS. Little flavor comes from deep-fried foods no matter which oil you use.
Canola (6%)-Common in Canada, canola has the lowest percentage of saturated fat than any other oil. It is second only to olive oil in monounsaturated "good" fat. Do not use for deep frying.
Coconut (89%)-This oil is used mostly for FRYING and BAKING. See Nut Varieties.
Corn (13%)-Corn oil is polyunsaturated. It is used for NON-DEEP FRYING, BAKING and to make margarine. It is too heavy for salads.
Cottonseed (26%)-Usually used in conjunction with other oils, it is a good all-round FRYING and SALAD oil. Yes, it does come from the cotton plant.
Lard-Lard is pork fat good for making flaky PASTRIES and BISCUITS.
For baking, 1 cup lard = I cup butter
Olive (14%)-It has the highest monounsaturated "good" fat of all the oils and can be used in SALADS, COOKING and FRYING. The darker the color the more intense the flavor. Extra virgin is best unless using high heat, which will kill the flavor, then the less expensive olive oil is better. Do not use olive oil for baking.
Palm (83%)-This oil is used mainly to make margarine and "whipped cream" toppings.
Peanut-(18%)-Peanut oil is used for SALADS and FRYING, especially in ASIAN DISHES.
Poppyseed-This oil is used mainly as a SALAD or COOKING oil.
Safflower (9%)-The most concentrated polyunsaturated fatty acids are in safflower. It is used mainly in diet SALAD dressings and will not solidify when refrigerated. The taste is bland.
Salad-This is a blend of olive, soybean or cottonseed oils used in SALADS, for COOKING and FRYING.
Sesame Seed (18%)- An oil used mostly for its flavor. It is added at the end of low heat cooking in ASIAN DISHES. It is also used in SALADS and MARINADES.
Shortening-This fat is made up of saturated (from hydrogenation) vegetable fat, animal fat or a combination. Good for BAKING, but less ideal for frying.
Soybean (14%)-used in COOKING, especially in CHINESE DISHES, SALADS and in margarine.
Suet-Suet is the solid fat around the kidneys and tender cuts on beef, sheep and other animals. Once used to make candles, the British use it in PASTRIES, PUDDINGS and STUFFINGS.
Sunflower(12%)-a polyunsaturated oil, good for LOW-HEAT COOKING and in SALADS.

Onion/Scallion

Flavor/Taste:
Sweet: red (Italian) and pearl
Peppery: yellow (Spanish), white (Bermuda) and green (scallions)

Use:
Use just after cutting or they become stale. Like garlic, the smaller the piece, the stronger the flavor. Cooking in butter sweetens them. Boiling makes them less pungent. Cooking scallions too hot makes them taste bitter. Use with everything, but sweets.

Mix with:
- Cilantro
- Cloves
- Garlic
- Oregano
- Parsley
- Pepper, Bell
- Thyme
- Sage

1 small onion =
1 Tbsp minced =
¾ cup chopped =
1 Tbsp onion powder

An onion in recipes means a yellow one.

Adding parsley to onions lowers gas.

Use the white and green parts of the scallion. 9 scallions with green tops =
1 cup sliced

Color & Form:
Fresh whole, flakes, powder, salt, canned and pickled

❧ Historical Remedies ❧

Internally:
Antiseptic
Asthma and Coughs
High blood pressure

Externally:
Burns
Hives and Venomous bites

❧ Origin ❧
An onion is a bulbous plant of the lily family. A scallion or green onion is an onion pulled before the bulb forms. It is native to central Asia, Egypt and the Middle East.

❧ Folklore/History ❧

In accounting for expenses to build the Great Pyramid of Cheops, there was inscribed on the pyramid so many pieces of silver for onions, garlic and radishes to feed the slaves.

Egyptians felt that the various layers of the onion signified various levels of heaven, earth and hell.

In England onion was used instead of mistletoe. A girl would cut onions from a doorway and whisper the name of her beau.

Orange

Flavor/Taste:
Citrusy, tangy, sweeter than lemon

Use:
Use it mostly for eating and as a beverage.
Use at the END of cooking, unless baking.
Use mainly with meat and meat sauces, stuffings and desserts.

⅓ cup juice =
1½-2 Tbsp zest

Zest is only the orange-colored outside layer; **peel** is the white bitter layer under the orange zest.

Mix with:
- Bay Leaf
- Honey
- Saffron
- Thyme

Color & Form:
Orange fruit, liquid or frozen concentrate, juice, zest and peel

❧ Kinds of Oranges ❧

Sweet-(Navels) used for eating and juices.

Loose-skinned-(Mandarins, including tangerines) used in orange-flavored liqueurs. They are easy to peel and can be sweet or tart.

Bitter-(Sevilles) used for marmalades and sauces. Peels are used for cooking and liqueur.

❧ Origin ❧
An orange is the fruit of a citrus tree. It is native to southern China and Vietnam.

❧ Folklore/History ❧

Orange comes from the Sanskrit *naranga,* meaning "fragrant." It is said that no word in English rhymes with orange.

It is a citrus fruit with lots of vitamin C.

They are often associated with fertility and weddings.

❧ Substitutions ❧

Grand Marnier, an orange-flavored liqueur or an orange-flavored honey or extract

Oregano

Flavor/Taste:
Stronger than marjoram, zesty

Use:
Use during the last hour of cooking if cooking over an hour.
Otherwise use it at the BEGINNING of cooking.
Use twice as much fresh as dried, instead of the usual 4 to 1 ratio.
Use with beans, cheese, eggs, meats, mushrooms, pasta, pizza,
salads, sauces, Italian dishes and vegetables.

Mix with:
- Garlic
- Leek
- Marjoram
- Olive Oil
- Onion
- Parsley
- Rosemary
- Sage
- Thyme
- Tomato

Color & Form:
Green leaves, whole, dried or ground powder

❧ Historical Remedies ❧

Internally:
Bronchitis
Cramps
Lowers Cholesterol
Insomnia

Externally:
Poultice for swelling

❧ Origin ❧
Oregano is a perennial wild marjoram of the
mint family. It is native to the Mediterranean. A
stronger-flavored version is native to Mexico.

❧ Folklore/History ❧

Oregano comes from the Greek, *oros,*
meaning "mountain" and *goros,* meaning
"joy."

The Greeks let their cattle graze in oregano
fields, thinking it made the cows tastier.

It was unknown to most Americans until
the veterans brought it back from Italy after
World War II.

Paprika

Flavor/Taste:
Mild to pungent sweet pepper

Use:
Use GENEROUSLY, 1 tsp for 2 servings.
Use at the BEGINNING of cooking.
Use soon after purchase as it looses its flavor quickly.
Use with chili, dips, eggs, meats, mushrooms, soups, cream
sauces, seafood, starches and vegetables.

Mix with:
❧Caraway Seed   ❧Cheese   ❧Marjoram

Color & Form:
Red ground powder; brown means it is stale

❧ Historical Remedies ❧

Internally:
Canker sores
Colds
Colic
Gas
Kidney infection

❧ Origin ❧
Paprika is pulverized from the dried pods of
red peppers (pimentos). It is native to
Mexico and the Carribean.

❧ Folklore/History ❧

Paprika arrived in Europe via the explorers
who went to the Americas. It was grown in
Turkey, where the Hungarians liked it and
gave it its name, *paprika*, meaning "Turkish
pepper."

The Nobel Prize was given to Albert Szent-
Györgyi for discovering vitamin C. His
research in finding it was done with paprika.

The **pimento** used to stuff a green olive is the
same red pepper used to make dry powdered
paprika.

Parsley

Flavor/Taste:

Light sweet licorice (flat-leaf more flavorful than curly)

Use:

Stir in fresh leaves at the END of cooking. Wash and dry parsley before chopping to slow down the loss of flavor when cut. Flat-leaf (Italian parsley) is good for cooking. Use with everything, but sweets.

Mix with:

- Basil
- Bay Leaf
- Butter
- Chives
- Dill
- Garlic
- Mint
- Shallot
- Thyme

Color & Form:

Green leaves, fresh; dried parsley is tasteless

Add an equal amount of fresh parsley to dried herbs for a few minutes before adding to salads. It makes the dried herbs taste fresh and stretches the salad further.

Historical Remedies

Internally:
Breath freshener
Eyesight
Kidney stones and liver problems
Menstruation symptoms
Protein content (20%+)

Externally:
Dandruff
Venomous bites

Origin

Parsley is a biennial plant of the carrot family. It is native to Southern Europe.

Folklore/History

Dead bodies were once seasoned with parsley to deodorize them.

Greek legend has it that parsley grew where the blood of Archemorus was spilled, when he was eaten by snakes. Greeks used parsley to make funeral wreaths and looked at it as a symbol of death.

In England, parsley was associated with black magic rituals.

It is high in vitamins and minerals.

Defining the Peppers

There are two kinds of peppers. One family is known as capsicum peppers and are from South America. The other family is represented by peppercorns that grow on vines and are from rainy, tropical Asia. Exploration to find pepper and other spices resulted in the discovery of the New World and its many new flavorings.

Capsicum Peppers-Other designations for capsicums are chile peppers, red peppers, sweet or bell peppers, paprika, pimento, cayenne and red pepper flakes. South American peppers are best grouped by use. Chiles come in a wide variety from short to long and from pungent to blistering. They are a digestive and have a lot of vitamin C. The outer skin has a milder flavor than the seeds and the lighter-colored fleshy insides, which are hot.

Green chiles are unripened peppers. Ripe chiles are red, yellow, orange or brown and are used to make Tabasco, chili powder, cayenne and red pepper flakes. In Latin and South America chili powder is made from dried roasted chiles that are ground and deseeded. In the US chili powder is usually a blend of spices and chiles. Cayenne is a specific type of ground red chile, while red pepper flakes are a variety of hot, red chile peppers. Generally, the larger the chile, the sweeter and milder it is.

Bell or sweet peppers are larger than chile peppers and are not pungent. The most common sweet peppers are red, orange, yellow or green. Red bell peppers will not last as long as green, as they are a more mature version of the same vegetable.

Paprika, the powdered dry flesh of a specific variety of sweet pepper or pimento, is mostly mild, with a more pungent variety used in Hungary. Paprika should be bright red. It is meant to be used generously and before it turns brownish red. Pimentos come canned and are used in sandwich spreads, salads, olives and dips.

Peppercorns-It is best to buy whole peppercorns, since ground pepper looses its flavor so quickly. Peppercorns themselves will last indefinitely. White pepper is from the same plant as black pepper, but is less aromatic and used mostly in white sauces. **Muntok** is a kind of white peppercorn, while black varieties include **tellicherry, lampong** and **java**.

Pepper (from peppercorns)

Flavor/Taste:
White pepper is milder and less pungent than black

Use:
Use immediately after grinding at the END of cooking.
Use with everything, but sweets.

Mix with:
⭗ Any flavoring

Color & Form:
Black and white (color based on maturity) whole peppercorns;
ground pepper looses flavor quickly

- -

⭗ Historical Remedies ⭗

Internally:
Arthritis
Digestion
Motion sickness & Nausea
Sore throat gargle (with lemon juice)

Externally:
Insecticide

⭗ Origin ⭗
Black Pepper comes from dried unripened berry clusters from a perennial vine. It is native to the East Indies. White pepper is a ripe version of the same berry clusters.

⭗ Folklore/History ⭗

Pepper is one of the oldest spices known.

The Visigoths called off their siege of Rome in exchange for gold, silver and pepper.

In Medieval times it was used as a money exchange for paying taxes and in dowries.

Elihu Yale went from Boston to London to learn the spice business. He was appointed governor of Madras, India and amassed a fortune from the spice trade. He founded Yale University with his profits without ever coming back to the US to see the college.

Pepper, Bell

Flavor/Taste:
Sweet depending upon ripeness; light, not pungent

Use:
Add at the BEGINNING or END depending upon the desired texture; they soften with cooking.
Use to add texture and color or for stuffing.
Use in Mexican foods, pasta, pizza, salads, stews and stir-frys.

Mix with:
⋄Cheese   ⋄Oils & Fats-olive   ⋄Tomato

Color & Form:
Red, orange, yellow or green hollow fruit

A red pepper is a fully ripened green pepper, is sweeter and does not keep as long.

Avoid peppers with soft spots. Firm peppers that are shiny-skinned and heavy for their size are the best choice. Store 1 week.

⋄ Historical Remedies ⋄

Internally:
Helps fight infections
Green peppers have silicon, which is good for healthy hair, skin and teeth.
Excellent source of vitamins C and A.

⋄ Origin ⋄
Bell Peppers, like hot peppers, are from an annual plant. It is native to Latin America.

⋄ Folklore/History ⋄

Bell peppers come from the same family as the hot chile peppers. Because they are not hot they are considered sweet. Another relative includes **paprika**, which comes from the sweet **pimento** pepper.

Natives ate bell peppers raw like fruit. The idea of cooking it came from Europe. The Spanish roasted them and introduced them to olive oil—thus the Spanish olive. The Turks were the first to stuff them, and the Hungarians were responsible for grinding the dried red bell peppers into paprika.

Pepper, Chile

Flavor/Taste:
Hotter than black pepper, can overwhelm

Use:
Use SPARINGLY at the END of cooking. It is more potent as it cooks. Roasting brings out the flavor and helps remove the skin. Scoop out the seeds and veins. *Use gloves and cut them under cold water, since the fumes and juices can burn the skin.*
Use in Cajun and Mexican foods, beans, mushrooms, dips and stews.

Mix with:
- Coriander
- Cumin
- Garlic
- Onion/Scallion
- Tomato

Color & Form:
Red to yellow to green fresh, dried, canned, in flakes or ground

1 Tbsp powdered chile = 1 large chile (ancho)

⅛ tsp cayenne = 1 small chile

Avoid shriveled or soft spots on chiles. Mix varieties for better flavor.

Eating bread, sugar or milk will help get rid of the sting.

Red pepper flakes are dried red pepper pieces that can range in "hotness."

❧ Historical Remedies ❧

Internally:
Arthritis
Hardening of arteries
Memory

Externally:
Backache (with peppermint)
Stops bleeding without stinging

❧ Origin ❧
Chile Peppers are from the pods of a bush. They are native to the Caribbean.

❧ Folklore/History ❧

Thought to be the earliest cultivated flavoring, chiles were found at 9,000 year old Mexican and Peruvian burial locations and were originally used for decoration. They were unknown in Europe until Columbus came to the New World.

Chiles are high in vitamins A, C and E, have no cholesterol, are low in sodium and produce endorphins, which create a sense of well being. So eat up!

Chile Pepper Varieties and Hotness Rating

There are over 100 varieties of chiles from Mexico. Generally, the smaller the chile, the hotter it is. This is because by volume, smaller chiles contain more capsaicin, the agent creating "heat." Below are the most commonly used chiles with their hotness rated from 1-10, ten being the hottest. Roast and remove seeds and veins before using fresh chiles. Dry-roast dried chiles in a pan 3-4 minutes and then soak them 20 minutes in enough not-quite-boiling water to just cover them. Blend and use them in cooking sauces, dipping salsas and soups. Do not store chiles in a plastic bag.

Anaheim (2.5)-This mild pepper is common in the US and is green, long and narrow. The dried red variety is bunched together on strings (**ristras**). Poblano is a hotter substitute.

Cascabel, Chile bola (4)-This small round brownish red chile rattles when you shake it. It has a smoky, nutty flavor and is medium hot. When dried it tastes like dried plums.

Cayenne (8)-One of the best known peppers, it is long, narrow and bright red when ripened. It is ground to make cayenne and is usually sold in that form.

Chilaca (4)-A long, dark green to brown, medium hot chile, that when dried are called **pasillas** or **chile negros**. They are medium hot and are brownish black in color.

Fresno (6.5)-This chile is equal to jalapeño in hotness and is bright green to red.

Guajillo or Travieso (8)-This dried chile is deep red and hot. It is a variety of the cayenne.

Güero or Caribe (6)-These chiles are substitutes for the California or banana pepper. *Güero* means blond and is yellowish green and 5" long. Among the yellow chiles are the **Hungarian Wax** (medium hot) and the **Santa Fe Grande** (small and cone-like, running mild to hot).

Habanero or Scotch bonnet (9)-This very hot yellow to maroon chile has fruity-flavored undertones. It is roundish or acorn-shaped, although larger on top.

Jalapeño (5.5)-They are quite hot if preserved in oil. Fresh ones are dark green and about 2½" long. Dried, smoked ones are reddish brown **chipotles** and are very hot.

Jamaican Hot (9)-This green to red chile has an odd shape and is as hot as the habanero.

Pepperoncini (4)-These thin, red, wrinkled peppers are pickled and presented as a garnish.

Mulato (3)-This dried poblano variety is used in mole and is fruitier and smokier than the **ancho.**

Pequín (8)-These are smokey, hot and tiny reddish to orange oval-shaped chiles.

Poblano (4)-These long green to black chiles are rich in flavor and popular for cooking. Dried ones are called **anchos**, look like prunes and taste like dried plums. Anaheim, although milder in flavor, is a substitute. **Anchos** are used in chili con carne.

Serrano (7)-Commonly used in hot sauces, salsas and guacamole and particularly good with tomatoes and cilantro, they are green when fresh and red to orange when dried. Dried serranos are called **japonés**. Use **pulla** or pequín chiles as a substitute.

Thai Chile (9)-Just ¼" wide, this green to red chile is very hot and used in Asian dishes. They are derived from the cayenne. They should be shiny and can be dried.

Pepper, Szechuan

Flavor/Taste:
Hot pepper, stronger than cayenne

Use:
Use at the END of cooking, it gets hotter the longer it cooks.
Use SPARINGLY.
Use in Asian cooking with meats, mushrooms and stir-frys.

Mix with:
- Curry
- Ginger
- Honey
- Onion/Scallion

Color & Form:
Dried red berries, ground powder or flakes

- -

❖ Historical Remedies ❖

Internally:
Anesthetic
Antibacterial
Stimulant

❖ Origin ❖
Szechuan Pepper comes from the dried berry of a prickly ash tree. It is native to China.

❖ Folklore/History ❖

At one time it was used as a flavoring in both food and wine and then offered to the gods.

It is named after the province of the upper Yangtze River in China. It is not related to black pepper.

Szechuan is also known as **anise pepper**, **fagara** and **sansho**.

Until recently, true Szechuan pepper was banned from the US because of a bacteria harmful to citrus fruits.

Poppy Seeds

Flavor/Taste:
Sweet, nutty, like walnuts

Use:
Use GENEROUSLY, 1 Tbsp for 4 servings.
Lightly toast before using to bring out the flavor.
Use with breads, cookies, eggs, Indian dishes, salads,
starches, sauces and vegetables.

Mix with:
- Cheese
- Curry Powder

Color & Form:
Blue-black, gray or white to yellowish small seeds

Historical Remedies

Internally:
Appetite stimulant
High in phosphorus
Protein contents (18%+)

Origin
Poppy Seeds are from the opium poppy
flower, but contain no opium. It is native to
the Middle East.

Folklore/History

Poppy Seeds were included in the diets for
trainees of the original Olympic Games.

It takes 900,000 seeds to make one pound.

Poppy seeds were used for cooking oil by
Egyptians circa 1500 BC.

They are popular in Slavic and Hungarian
baked items.

Raisins

Flavor/Taste:
Goldens are sweeter than brown

Use:
Use at the BEGINNING of cooking.
Use GENEROUSLY.
Use in desserts, cereals, cookies, salads, stuffings and stir-frys.

Soak in hot water for 5 minutes to plumpen. Store in a jar with red wine and a cinnamon stick. Or refrigerate raisins in an air-tight container for 6 months or longer.

Mix with:
- Allspice
- Cloves
- Nuts
- Cinnamon
- Nutmeg

Color & Form:
Brown or yellow whole, dried grapes.

⚜ Raisin Varieties ⚜

Three main type of grapes are used to make raisins: Thompson, Muscat and Zante. Currants, from the Zante grape, originated in Corinth, Greece and are used in baking. Another currant in black, red and white varieties are used for jams and sauces.

⚜ Origin ⚜
Raisins are dried grapes, which come from a vine. Grapes are native to the Middle East and the Mediterranean.

⚜ Folklore/History ⚜

Brown raisins are sun-dried grapes, thus their dark, shriveled look. Golden raisins are mechanically dried and chemically treated to prevent darkening and are larger and moister than the brown ones. All are high in vitamins and minerals.

California now produces about half the world's raisins.

Muscat grapes are also used to make Muscatel wine.

Rosemary

Flavor/Taste:
Piny, with a slight ginger taste

Use:
Use ½ tsp for 2 servings. Use at the BEGINNING of short term cooking. Flavor fades with long cooking. Crush before using. Use with bread, eggs, fruit, Italian foods, meat, mushrooms, potatoes, soups, stews and vegetables.

Mix with:
- Bay Leaf
- Chives
- Fennel
- Sage
- Tomato
- Chervil
- Garlic
- Olive Oil
- Thyme
- Wine

Color & Form:
Greenish needle-like leaves, fresh, dried or ground

⁕ Historical Remedies ⁕

Internally:
Breath freshener
Circulation
Coughs
Headaches
Liver or kidney problems
Menopause
Rheumatism

⁕Origin ⁕
Rosemary are the leaves of a woody, pine-scented evergreen bush of the mint family. It is native to the Mediterranean and Spain.

⁕ Folklore/History ⁕

When fleeing Herod, Mary and infant Jesus hid behind some rosemary bushes. The flowers on them turned from white to blue because of Mary's blue cloak. The flowers were then called the roses of Mary.

The Queen of Hungary bathed daily in rosemary essence. She was so lovely by age 72 that the Polish King proposed. Hungary Water is the oldest perfume still being made.

Rosemary is best known as a symbol for friendship, love and remembrance. In Greece wearing garlands of it in you hair helped your memory.

Saffron

Flavor/Taste:
Bittersweet, like medicine

Use:
Use SPARINGLY, ⅛ tsp for 2 servings. Soak threads (stigmas) and add toward the END of cooking (last 10 minutes).
Use more in starches like rice, less in meats.
Use with cheese, chicken, eggs, Indian dishes, pasta, rice, soups and stews.

> Saffron is the most expensive spice because it is picked by hand. It takes 75,000 plants to make a pound.

Mix with:
- Allspice
- Anise
- Cayenne
- Cheese
- Curry Powder
- Fennel
- Garlic
- Onion
- Orange
- Sage
- Tomato

Color & Form:
Maroon colored, dried thread-like stigmas; powder has no flavor

- -

✷ Historical Remedies ✷

Internally:
Bronchitis
Fevers

Externally:
Gout
Hangovers (to sleep on saffron-stuffed pillows cured hangovers)
Varicose veins

✷ Origin ✷
Saffron comes from the dried stigmas of a crocus flower. It is native to Greece or Asia.

✷ Folklore/History ✷

Greeks used saffron's golden color to dye the royal robes, although it was water soluble. In Europe (1300-1700) Henry VIII forbade its use to tint a lady's hair, fearing a shortage for his food.

In Kashmir, exportation of it was punishable by death. During Edward III's reign a traveler disguised as a monk, hid a crocus bulb in a hollow staff and planted it near London. This area is still known as Saffron Walden, although it is no longer grown there. The Arabs believed saffron kept away both melancholy and a dreaded lizard.

Sage

Flavor/Taste:
Slightly bitter (smaller plants are sweeter) and lemony
Pineapple sage can be used as a pineapple flavoring

Use:
Use SPARINGLY, ½ tsp for 4 servings, at the END of cooking.
Use with bread, cheese, meat, especially pork, starches, sausage, soup,
stuffing and vegetables.

Mix with:

- Bay Leaf
- Chives
- Garlic
- Onion
- Oregano
- Paprika
- Parsley
- Thyme
- Rosemary
- Wine-white

Color & Form:
Greenish-gray fresh leaves, dried and ground powder

Historical Remedies

Internally:
Antiseptic
Canker sores
Cold and fever
Epilepsy
Menstruation symptoms
Slows aging

Externally:
Insect repellent

Origin
Sage is one of hundreds of plants in the mint
family. It is native to Syria and the North
Mediterranean coast.

Folklore/History

Sage meaning *wise* comes from ancient times,
when sage was believed to help with memory
retention. Sage also comes from the Latin
salvus, meaning safe, referring to its healing
powers. It is a member of the salvia family.

Arabic doctors in the 10th century said that
sage would extend your life to immortality.

England made use of sage for infusions,
before tea became popular.

The herb sage should not be confused with
Western American folklore and sagebrush.

Salt

Flavor/Taste:

Salty, one of the four basic tastes

Use:

Use SPARINGLY, 1 tsp or 2400 mg is the daily requirement.
Add to boiling water to reduce cooking time. Add to boiled
vegetables, so minerals are not lost. Add to onions to prevent
browning. Add to items that are too sweet.
Adding salt when microwaving toughens the food.
Saltiness increases when items are chilled.

Mix with:

All but salty flavors: bouillon cubes, capers or soy sauce

Color & Form:

White ground sea salt is best

If you salted too much, add a cut raw potato to the dish before serving (works for other spices also); or add 1 tsp cider vinegar + 1 tsp sugar to absorb the salt.

Brine is a heavily saturated salt solution used in pickling.

Historical Remedies

Internally:
Excesses can cause high blood pressure and
hypertension. However, it is one of the
essential minerals needed to maintain life.

Externally:
Sore throat gargle
Epsom salts for aches

Origin

Salt is a chemical mix of sodium chloride
mined from ancient dried up sea beds. It is
native to the sea and from mineral deposits.

Folklore/History

Used mainly as a preservative, salt slows
bacterial growth by draining their cells of water.

Roman soldiers were paid a fee known as
salarium to buy salt, thus the word salary and
being worth one's salt.

A revolt against a salt tax played a part in the
French Revolution.

Herb Salt

Bake iodized salt with chopped herbs in a
325°F oven for 10 minutes. Break up lumps and
bake 10 more minutes. Blend and store in a jar.

Savory

Flavor/Taste:
Strong peppery taste, milder than thyme

Use:
Summer savory is more common and milder.
Use winter savory SPARINGLY.
Use with beans, eggs, meats, pizza, rice, salads, soups, stews, stuffings and vegetables.

Mix with:

❧Basil	❧Fennel	❧Mint	❧Sage
❧Bay Leaf	❧Garlic	❧Onion	❧Thyme
❧Chervil	❧Honey	❧Rosemary	

Color & Form:
Green fresh leaves better than dried

❧ Historical Remedies ❧

Internally:
Congestion
Diarrhea
Gas
Nausea

❧ Origin ❧
Winter savory are leaves from the perennial shrublike plant of the mint family. Summer savory is an annual. They are native to the Mediterranean and Egypt.

❧ Folklore/History ❧

Summer savory is more popular than **winter savory**. For hundreds of years it was considered an aphrodisiac, while winter savory was thought to decrease sexual desire.

In the Middle Ages, savory was used to flavor cakes, pies and puddings.

Sesame Seeds

Flavor/Taste:
Almond-like; sesame oil adds an Asian flavor

Use:
Use ½ tsp for 2 servings.
Dry roast in a pan 3-4 minutes until light brown to release flavor.
Use with beans, bread, cakes, cookies, meat, pasta, salads, stir-frys and vegetables.

Mix with:

↝Anise	↝Cilantro	↝Fennel	↝Shallot
↝Cheese	↝Curry Powder	↝Saffron	↝Soy Sauce

Color & Form:
Small white seeds, oil

Calcium in 1 Tbsp of sesame seeds is equal to that in 1 cup of milk.

Tahini is a paste or butter made of sesame seeds. It is used in hummus, sauces and dressings.

↝ Historical Remedies ↝

Internally:
Germ resistant
Spleen
Stress
High in calcium
Protein content (26%+)

↝ Origin ↝
Sesame Seeds are an annual dried fruit picked before the pods burst. It is native to India.

↝ Folklore/History ↝

Thousands of years BC, Assyrians believed their gods drank sesame wine before creating earth. It is one of the oldest spices.

Ali Baba opened the treasure-filled den of thieves by saying "Open sesame!" probably because of the way the plant bursts open its pod and scatters the seeds.

India ink comes from the black residue from using sesame oil in lamps. Fragrant flowers were dipped in sesame oil and used for bathing and hair dressing in India.

Shallot

Flavor/Taste:
A mix of mild onion and garlic; bigger ones are stronger

Use:
Use in the MIDDLE of cooking. Browning turns them bitter.
Use as an onion or garlic substitute, when a milder taste is desired.
In recipes, 1 shallot is the entire bulb-like item that you peel.
Use with chicken, salads, buttery sauces, halibut, cod and stews.

Mix with:
- Butter/Margarine
- Garlic
- Oils & Fats-olive
- Thyme
- Vinegar
- Wine-red

Color & Form:
Purplish red skin over onion-like rings or garlic clove-like clusters

❧ Historical Remedies ❧

Internally:
Appetite enhancer
Stimulant

Externally:
Relieves burns
Relieves insect bites

❧ Origin ❧
Shallots are an onion variety forming bulb clusters. It is native to Turkestan.

❧ Folklore/History ❧

The name shallot comes from the Greek, *askalon*, a trading port in Southern Palestine associated with the plant.

Both the Greeks and Romans ate the plant. The Romans thought it was an aphrodisiac.

It was introduced to Europe by crusaders, who came back from the Near East in the 18th century. It is still popular in France.

Sorrel

Flavor/Taste:
Acidic, tangy like lemon, slightly bitter; French variety is best

Use:
Use SPARINGLY at the END of cooking.
Do not use in an iron skillet.
Use with dips, eggs, marinades, meat, cream sauces and seafood. Use raw in salads and sandwiches.

Mix with:
- Butter/Margarine
- Cream
- Mustard
- Vinegar

Color & Form:
Fresh green young arrow-shaped leaves

❧ Historical Remedies ❧

Internally:
Diuretic
Laxative
Rich in potassium
Rich in vitamins A and C

❧ Origin ❧
Sorrel is a perennial plant with wide leaves. It is native to Europe and Asia.

❧ Folklore/History ❧

Ancient Egyptians used sorrel as a digestive.

During planting season farmers from the 1790's would eat sorrel when they were low on water and got thirsty.

Also called sheep's sorrell, it should not be used by people with kidney stones.

Soy Sauce

Flavor/Taste:
Salty

Use:
Use toward the END of cooking, like a condiment.
Use to salt or enhance flavor, do not mix with red pepper.
Use with beans, carrots, marinades, meats, tomato sauces,
soups, stews and stir-frys.

Mix with:
⚮Anise   ⚮Curry Powder-mild

Color & Form:
Brown to black thin liquid sold in jars

⚮ Soy Sauce Varieties ⚮

Tamari is a thicker Japanese version of soy
sauce with no wheat, less sodium and a
milder flavor that holds up well under
prolonged cooking.
Light Soy Sauce-means that it is *thinner and
saltier* and lighter in color than the dark soy
sauces, including a **Chinese Soy** that is very
dark and contains molasses. Do not confuse
this with "lite" in the sense of less salt!

⚮Origin ⚮
Soy sauce is fermented soybeans and roasted
wheat or barley flour, usually in equal amounts.
It is native to China and Southeast Asia.

⚮ Folklore/History ⚮

Soy sauce is an Asian condiment often used
instead of salt.

Commodore Perry introduced soybeans to
America in 1854. Now the US produces
about 75% of the world's soybeans. Because
of its high protein content, it is used mostly
for stock feed. When cooked, mashed and
filtered it becomes **tofu**. When fermented,
added to brine, filtered and pasteurized it
becomes soy sauce.

Star Anise

Flavor/Taste:
Like anise or licorice, but with more bitterness and intensity

Use:
Use at the BEGINNING of cooking.
Use as a substitute for anise.
Use with breads, candies, fruit, sauces and stir-frys, especially with duck or pork.

Mix with:
‑❖Five-Spice Powder   ❖Ginger

Color & Form:
Brown oval seeds contained in an 8-pointed, star-shaped pod

❖ Historical Remedies ❖

Internally:
Breath freshener
Diuretic
Reduces gas

❖ Origin ❖
Star anise is from a star-shaped fruit of an evergreen (magnolia family) tree. It is native to China.

❖ Folklore/History ❖

The bark of the tree, from which star anise comes, is used as an incense.

The Japanese variety of the tree is considered sacred and is planted near grave sites.

Another Japanese variety of the tree is poisonous and smells like turpentine.

The Chinese name for the spice translates "eight-horned fennel."

Sugar

Flavor/Taste:
Sweet, one of the four basic tastes

Use:
Use at the BEGINNING of cooking.
The darker the sugar the easier it burns when baked.
To cut sweetness, add 1 tsp cider vinegar.
Use sugar to combat acidity, especially in tomato recipes.
Use mostly in baking, beverages, cookies, pastries and desserts.

To **glaze** means to give cooked items a shiny surface or coating, sometimes with sugar.

If brown sugar hardens, microwave it in an open container near a cup of hot water for 2 minutes per pound. Brown sugar is good for about four months.

Mix with:
•Butter •Cinnamon •Cloves •Nutmeg •Vanilla

Color & Form:
White refined, superfine, powdered/confectioners (ground with 3% cornstarch), light or dark brown, cubes and raw.

• Sugar Varieties •

In the order of sweetness, highest first:
> Fructose (fruit sugar) sweeter than sucrose
> Sucrose (cane sugar) household white sugar
> Glucose (grape sugar) corn syrup
> Maltose (malt sugar) keeps items moist
> Lactose (milk sugar) least sweet of sugars

White sugar is chemically the same, whether it is made from sugar cane or sugar beets. Brown sugar and molasses are less refined cane sugar. Other sugar sources are maple trees (syrup), palm trees and sorghum plants.

• Origin •
Sugar comes from sugar beets or sugar cane. It is native to Asia and the West Indies.

• Sugar Equivalencies/Substitutes •

2 cups sugar = 2¼ cups packed brown sugar = 1 lb
2 cups sugar = 3½ cups powdered sugar = 1 lb

1 cup sugar = ⅔ cup honey + ¼ cup flour
1 cup sugar = ⅔ cup maple syrup + ¼ cup flour
(In baking, reduce heat 25° F and cook a little longer when using honey or syrup for sugar)

1 cup corn syrup = 1 cup sugar + ¼ cup water
1 cup honey = 1¼ cups sugar + ¼ cup water

To reduce sugar in a recipe, replace up to half of it with nonfat dry milk. To increase sweetness add fruit. To add sweetness without calories, double the amount of extract, whether vanilla, maple or other.

Syrups & *Extracts*

Flavor/Taste:
Sweet, aromatic to strong and smoky, depending upon kind

Use:
Use at the BEGINNING of baking.
Use mostly for breakfasts, in beans, BBQ sauces,
beverages and in baking cookies and desserts.

> Grease the cup before measuring syrups and it will come out clean.
>
> Syrups are good for up to one year.

Mix with:
- Cinnamon
- Cloves
- Coffee
- Cream & Milk
- Nuts
- Nutmeg
- Raisins

Color & Form:
Syrups: clear liquid **corn**, brown **maple** or dark brown **molasses**;
also, fruit-flavored and nut-flavored syrups and extracts

❖ Syrups ❖
Syrups are used in baking and by pouring over other foods, such as pancakes, or mixing in with other liquids, such as coffee, milk or smoothies.

❖ Extracts ❖
Extracts are formed by removing essential oils from barks, nuts, seeds, berries and other plant parts and dissolving it in alcohol, thus creating a concentrated flavor in liquid form. If you increase the use of an extract in a recipe, use less sugar. Use maple as a substitute for vanilla in beans, breads, cookies, ham, pastries, sweet potatoes and yogurt.

❖ Folklore/History ❖

Before the honey bee came to the New World in 1625, natives used **maple** as a sweetener. **Corn syrup** is interchangeable with granulated sugar, but it does not crystallize as sugar does. The darker the **molasses,** the less sweet it is. **Blackstrap**, the darkest, is close to bitter.

❖ Syrups as Sugar Substitutes ❖

1 cup sugar = ⅔ cup maple syrup + ¼ cup flour
(In baking, reduce heat 25°F and cook a little longer when substituting maple syrup or honey for sugar)

1 cup corn syrup = 1 cup sugar + ¼ cup water

Tabasco™

Flavor/Taste:
Hot chile peppers

Use:
Use at the END, since it gets hotter the longer it is cooked.
Use SPARINGLY and with a bit of sugar to neutralize its acidity.
Use with Cajun dishes, chili, dips, eggs, marinades, meats,
Mexican foods and stews.

Mix with:
❧Cheese ❧Garlic
❧Pepper, Bell ❧Tomato

Color & Form:
Red liquid sauce

❧ Other Liquid Pepper Sauces ❧

Cholula-a hot sauce imported from Mexico containing vinegar, red peppers, pequín peppers, salt and spices.

Green Tabasco-is made with vinegar, water, jalapeño peppers and salt. It is a milder version of the red Tabasco sauce.

Check your grocer for many other varieties.

❧ Origin ❧
Tabasco is a red pepper sauce made from chiles. The peppers are native to Mexico.

❧ Folklore/History ❧

The name Tabasco, means "damp earth" and comes from a river of the same name in Mexico.

Tabasco is a trade marked name from the McIlhenny family. Created in the 1860's, it contains the fermented Tabasco pepper, (used only to make Tabasco sauce), vinegar and salt. Fermentation takes 3 years and is done in oak barrels.

Tamarind

Flavor/Taste:
Sour, fruity flavor with a pleasant odor

Use:
Use at the BEGINNING of cooking and use SPARINGLY.
Use with beans, Indian dishes (curries), fruit drinks, meats, rice,
soups and stews.

Mix with:

- Cayenne
- Curry
- Ginger
- Nut-coconut
- Orange
- Worcestershire Sauce

Color & Form:
Brownish pulp in jars, dried ground pods, canned paste, syrup

---

❧ Historical Remedies ❧

Internally:
Laxative

❧ Origin ❧
Tamarind comes from the pod fruit of a large
tree. It is native to Northeast Africa.

❧ Folklore/History ❧

Tamarind is used to flavor Indian and
Middle Eastern foods the way we might use
lemon juice.

Tamarind is an important ingredient in
Worcestershire Sauce and is used in many
chutneys and condiments.

Sailors mistakenly used it to prevent scurvy,
but it does not contain Vitamin C.

It is also known as **Indian date**.

Tarragon

Flavor/Taste:
A slightly peppery licorice and mustard flavor

Use:
Use SPARINGLY, ½ tsp dried for 4 servings.
Use at the END of cooking. It diffuses quickly and becomes bitter.
Use with cheese, dressings, eggs, meats, mushrooms, starches,
salads, cream sauces, soups and vegetables. Don't use with sweets.

Mix with:
- Chervil
- Chives
- Garlic
- Lemon
- Lovage
- Mustard
- Onion
- Orange
- Parsley
- Tomato

Color & Form:
Green fresh or dried leaves; ground powder

❧ Historical Remedies ❧

Internally:
Antifungal and Antioxidant
Breath freshener
Insomnia
Protein content (20%+)

Externally:
Venomous bites

❧ Origin ❧
Tarragon are the leaves of a tall perennial
bushlike plant from the aster family. It is
native to Europe (French version).

❧ Folklore/History ❧

There is a **Russian tarragon**, which has a
coarser leaf and is not as popular. It was
introduced by the Moors to Europe in the
13th century.

Tarragon comes from the Arab word
tarkum (dragon) possibly because the
roots of the plant are twisted like a snake.

In France it is called *herbe au dragon*
because of its ability to cure serpent and
mad dog bites.

Thyme

Flavor/Taste:
Mint-like, aromatic, slight clove aftertaste

Use:
Use SPARINGLY, ½ tsp dried for 2 servings.
Use at the BEGINNING of cooking.
Use with beans, Italian dishes, cheese, dressings, eggs, meat,
pizza, potatoes, salads, soups, stews and vegetables.

Mix with:
- Basil
- Bay Leaf
- Garlic
- Lemon
- Lovage
- Marjoram
- Mustard
- Onion
- Parsley
- Rosemary
- Tomato

Color & Form:
Green leaves, fresh or dried; ground powder

❖ Historical Remedies ❖

Internally:
Arthritis
Coughs, sore throats and fevers
Cramps
Digestion of fatty foods

Externally:
Burns
Dandruff

❖ Origin ❖
Thyme comes from the leaves of perennial
bushy plants in the mint family. It is native to
Greece and the Mediterranean.

❖ Folklore/History ❖

Recorded use of thyme goes back to 3000 BC
when the Sumerians used it as an antiseptic.

The Egyptians used it in mummification.

Thyme comes from the Greek word, *thymon,*
meaning "courage." It was a symbol of
courage and strength in the Middle Ages.
Women would put it on the clothing of
crusading knights.

The Scottish felt that thyme tea warded off
nightmares.

Tomato

Flavor/Taste:
Slightly acidic, fruity moist taste

Use:
Use at either the BEGINNING or END of cooking.
Use GENEROUSLY, adding a little sugar to lessen acidity.
Use with cheese, chili, eggs, meats, pasta, pizza, salads,
sandwiches, sauces, spaghetti and stews.

Mix with:

- Basil
- Cheese
- Garlic
- Olive Oil
- Parsley
- Rosemary
- Thyme

Color & Form:
Fresh: Red whole, small red cherry or grape-sized
Canned: whole, stewed, minced, sauce, juice and paste

⋄ Tomato Varieties ⋄

Beefsteak-common sandwich tomato
Cherry/Grape-small whole salad tomato
Plum, Italian, Roma-small, oblong-shaped tomato with more pulp, used in canning
Sun-dried-a dried, very sweet and tangy tomato, used in pastas, salads and soups
Tomatillo-a small green firm tomato relative with an onion-like skin used in salsas and sauces. It tastes better when cooked.

⋄ Origin ⋄
Tomatoes are the fruit of an annual plant in the eggplant and potato family. It is native to Peru and Ecuador.

⋄ Folklore/History ⋄

Tomatoes were considered poisonous to Northern Europeans, unlike other New World foods. Southern Europeans, though, discovered its affinity to olive oil. It was ketchup that turned the tide. The idea of adding tomatoes to make a **ketchup** (any sauce made with local ingredients, an idea the British copied from the East Indies and brought to the New World) was actually an American idea. And so the tomato, also known as the love apple, became acceptable. This fruit, because of its wide use, qualifies as both a flavoring and a food.

Turmeric

Flavor/Taste:
Musky; a mild, starchy ginger

Use:
Use 1 tsp for 4 servings.
Use at the END, do not boil it. It turns bitter if burned.
Use as a saffron substitute and as a curry spice.
Use with beans, cookies, Indian dishes, salads, deviled eggs,
meats, potatoes, rice, sauces and vegetables.

Mix with:
⚬Butter/Margarine   ⚬Mustard

Color & Form:
Yellow to orange dried root; ground powder

⚬ Historical Remedies ⚬

Internally:
Antioxidant
Reduces cholesterol
Indigestion

Externally:
Inflammations

⚬ Origin ⚬
Turmeric comes from the roots of a
perennial plant in the ginger family. It is
native to Cochin, China.

⚬ Folklore/History ⚬

Asians have been using this flavoring since
600 BC in religious ceremonies, perfumes
and as a dye.

It is also used as a preservative to help extend
the shelf life of fats and oils.

In the Middle Ages it was known as Indian
saffron and was used as a saffron substitute.
It was and still is used as a yellow-orange
dye for fabrics, in dairy products and for
prepared mustards.

Turmeric is a large ingredient of curry powder.

Vanilla

Flavor/Taste:
Sweet and aromatic

Use:
Use at the BEGINNING.
Use SPARINGLY.
Use with chocolate, cookies, ice cream, pastries, lobster, puddings and yogurt.

> Extracts allow you to use less sugar in your recipe. See also Syrups & Extracts in this section.

Mix with:

- Chocolate
- Coffee
- Maple
- Nuts-coconut
- Saffron

Color & Form:
Brown thin dry beans, powdered, syrup or extract

❧ Extract Varieties ❧

Extracts are long-lasting, concentrated flavor enhancers used in baking cookies, breads and deserts. They will not change the consistency of what is cooked and very little is needed. **Maple** is a good substitute for vanilla and nut flavors. For icings use a **butter** extract. There are also fruit and spice (garlic) extracts.

❧ Origin ❧
Vanilla comes from the fermented bean pod of a climbing orchid. It is native to Southern Mexico.

❧ Folklore/History ❧

Extracts are the essential oils of a plant distilled by steam or by soaking in water and alcohol. Extracts will keep indefinitely. Any alcohol content evaporates with cooking.

Vanilla was used by the Aztecs to flavor chocolate.

It was unknown to Europeans before Columbus came to the New World in 1492.

Vinegar

Flavor/Taste:
Sour wine, acidic

Use:
Use to bring out the flavor of other spices.
Use with cabbage, deviled eggs, marinades, mushrooms, potato salads, tomato sauces, spaghetti, stews and stuffings. It is essential in making pickles, mustards and salad dressings.

If items are too sweet, add 1 tsp cider vinegar.

Add 1 Tbsp of vinegar to spaghetti to kick in the spices already added.

Boil vinegar in a new frying pan to prevent foods from sticking.

Mix with:
- Basil
- Cumin
- Mint
- Onion
- Tarragon
- Bay Leaf
- Garlic
- Oils & Fats
- Rosemary
- Thyme

Color & Form:
Varieties: cider; red, white and rice wine; white "clear" liquid

✤ Vinaigrettes ✤

Basic Vinaigrette: Combine 1 cup vinegar, 2 cups oil, ½ tsp sea salt and ½ tsp black pepper. To this add garlic, basil, cilantro or your favorite spice.

Vinaigrette Sauce: Combine 1 tsp salt, 1 tsp sugar, ½ tsp dry mustard, a pinch of pepper, 2 Tbsp water and 4 Tbsp wine vinegar. Cover and shake. Add 1 cup olive oil and shake again.

✤ Origin ✤
Vinegar comes from the oxidation of wine, via the grape. It is native to China.

✤ Folklore/History ✤

Vinegar comes from the French *vin aigre*, meaning sour wine. It was originally used as a preservative, but has become more of a condiment.

Salad Dressing Base: Add a clove of garlic to a pint of cider vinegar and let stand for eight days. Remove garlic and use the vinegar for making salad dressings.

Making Herbed Vinegars

Vinegar ranges in strength from mild (4%) to strong (6+%), depending upon the amount of acetic acid. Malt (from barley) and cider vinegars (from apples) are milder than wine vinegar. For consumption, white, red, cider and rice vinegars are best. Distilled white vinegar (a grain-alcohol mix), contrary to its name, is the strongest of all. Vinegars keep indefinitely and will preserve fresh herbs and spices.

Following are three ways to make herbed vinegars and to the right are herb combinations you may want to try. You may do single herbs. Try basil, dill, tarragon or garlic by themselves. Crushed or chopped herbs help distribute the flavor.

Quick, Boiled Vinegar: If you are in a hurry, bring crushed or chopped herbs and vinegar to a boil and simmer 20 minutes. Strain, pour it into a clean bottle and serve. Add fresh herb leaves or sprigs for appearance.

Heat and Age Vinegar: To make an herbal vinegar, heat the vinegar without boiling. Add it to a sterilized glass jar of fresh herbs. Use 3 leaves or a sprig, a clove or a chile for each cup of vinegar. Let it cool, then cover and store in a dark place for a couple of weeks, shaking occasionally. It will remain good for a year.

Sun Vinegar: You may also empty out about ¼ cup of vinegar from a full pre-packaged glass bottle and add herbs to it. Set it in the sun 3 weeks and strain. This lasts about six months. Use cheesecloth over the top to pour out the flavored vinegar without the herbs.

The popular Balsamic vinegar is made from Trebbiano grapes and is aged in barrels over several years.

Cider Vinegar
Chiles
Garlic
Oregano

Red Wine Vinegar
Parsley
Sage
Shallot

Rice Vinegar
Cilantro
Garlic

White Vinegar
Cardamom
Honey
Mint

White Vinegar
Garlic
Orange peel
Raisins
Rosemary

White Vinegar
Burnet
Dill Weed
Shallot

Wine

Flavor/Taste:
Various, depending upon grape, additives and aging

Use:
Use at END of cooking to maximize flavors. Use for cooking after it has been open for 5 days. Store at a constant 55-60° F on its side. Serve red wines at room temperature; chill whites 2 hours before serving. Wine intensifies other flavors. Use less salt when cooking with wine. Use to marinade or tenderize meats, with mushrooms and in sauces.

Mirin-a syrupy rice wine, good in stir-frys with shrimp, scallops and vegetables.

To keep cooking wine from going sour, pour a little cooking oil on the surface.

Mix with:
⤷ See listing of spices paired with wines following.
⤷ Avoid chocolate desserts when serving wine.

Color & Form:
White to pink (blush) to burgundy liquid

....

⤷ Historical Remedies ⤷

Internally:
Acts as a depressant
Lessens inhibitions

Externally:
Antiseptic

⤷ Origin ⤷
Wine comes from fermented grapes. It is native to the Mediterranean and Middle East.

⤷ Folklore/History ⤷

The search for a way to prevent wine from turning to vinegar happened just prior to finding a cure for bacterial infections. Napoleon III sought out Louis Pasteur on behalf of French wine makers. By 1866 Pasteur had published a book on the bacteria in wine. From that came the solution for bacterial infections.

Only red wines have tannin, which is contained in the skin of the grape. Tannin allows for aging and also provides color.

Have a glass while you cook!

Cooking and Choosing Wine

A wine adds its own flavor to foods, whether nutty, fruity, tart or tangy. It can also blend the flavor of other ingredients already in the food you are cooking. The alcohol content, whether cooking with wine or other liquors, evaporates when cooked.

Use 1-2 Tbsp wine for each serving.
Use 1-2 cups wine as a meat marinade.

There are four kinds of wine used in cooking:

- *Appetizer*, or aperitif, like sweet sherry or vermouth;
- *Red table wines* like burgundy or members of the claret family;
- *White table wines* such as Sauterne and the Rhine families; and
- *Dessert wines* such as Port, Muscatel and Cream Sherry.

I rarely cook with wine and prefer picking a wine to drink with the meal or with an appetizer. For those of you who love to dabble, however, included is a little information on pairing wines with foods. There is also a list of seasonings to go with particular wines, one list each for reds and whites. Because the flavors of wines vary even from Chardonnay to Chardonnay, the wine list is not fool-proof, but it can be a guide to get you started. I leave it to you to do further research in this area.

Pairing Wine with a Meal

Wines that are high in acidity, tannin (that dryness that puckers your mouth) or sweetness can overpower or clash with the taste of your food. It is better to start with light and medium-bodied wines until your palate becomes more discriminating. Then you may use the following guidelines:

- The heartier the dish the more full-bodied the wine should be. Rich fatty foods, such as beef, lamb or cheese are best paired with oaky Chardonnays or young red Cabernets or Zinfandels.
- Oily dishes can tame tannins and make your wine taste smoother and fruitier. Sparkling wines are good with oily foods.
- Sweet, light wines can cool off the spiciness in foods.
- Sweet foods are best paired with wines that have a similar level of sweetness.
- Salty foods go well with Riesling, Gewurztraminer, White Zinfandel or Chenin Blanc.
- Highly acidic foods (citrus, tomatoes, vinegar) are best suited to highly acidic wines, such as Sauvignon Blanc.
- Great combinations come from either matching taste components or contrasting with them.
- Match the wine used in cooking with the wine served with the meal.

Cooking with Wine and Food

Soups	Wine	What to Do
Cream soup	Marsala, Sherry	Add 1 Tbsp wine
Minestrone	Burgundy	for each 1½ cups
Tomato soup	Red wine	soup just before
Vegetable	Chablis	serving.

Meats		What to Do
Beef	Burgundy, Chianti, Sherry	Add ¼ cup wine
Game meat	Red wine	per pound after
Ham	Burgundy, Madeira, Marsala, Sherry	browning (½ cup
Lamb	Burgundy, Red or White wine, Sherry	for game meat).
Poultry	dry Marsala, Rhine, Sherry, White wine	Baste ham with 1-2
Pork	dry Marsala	cups of wine. Baste
Seafood	dry Vermouth, White wine	poultry or seafood
Veal	White wine, dry Marsala	with equal parts wine and butter.

Sauces		
Spicy sauces with cayenne, capers, paprika, shallot, tarragon	White wine	Do not combine white wines with cream, ham or mushrooms. Add
Sauces with bay leaf, cream, garlic, mushrooms, onion, savory or thyme	Red wine	1-2 Tbsp wine per cup of other liquids.

Vegetables		
Beans	Red wine (full-bodied)	Add 1 Tbsp wine
Carrots	White wine	per cup after
Mushrooms	Marsala (or dry Sherry)	vegetables are
Peas	White wine	cooked.
Tomatoes	Red wine (full-bodied)	

Fruits and Desserts		
Apricots	Madeira	Add 1 Tbsp per cup
Ice cream	Marsala	before serving and
Nuts-almonds, pistachios	Marsala	let stand a few
Pudding	Marsala	minutes.

White Wine Seasonings

Seasoning	White Wines to Go with Seasoning (body type = light medium or full, flavor)
Allspice	Riesling (light or full, sweet)
Bay Leaf	Chardonnay (medium to full), Sauvignon Blanc
Basil	Fume Blanc (light to medium, fruity), Riesling (sweet), Sauvignon Blanc (light to medium)
Cardamom	Chardonnay (medium), Riesling (sweet), White Zinfandel (light to medium, spicy)
Chervil	Chenin Blanc (light, melon-like), Fume Blanc (light to medium, fruity)
Chives	Chardonnay (medium), Fume Blanc (light to medium, fruity), Sauvignon Blanc (light)
Cinnamon	Gewurztraminer (light), Grenache (medium), Muscatel (full, fruity and sweet)
Cloves	Riesling (light or full, sweet)
Cilantro	Gewurztraminer (light), Sauvignon Blanc (light to medium)
Cumin	Chenin Blanc (light, melon-like), Riesling (sweet), Sauvignon Blanc (light to medium)
Curry	Chenin Blanc (light, melon-like), Gewurztraminer (light)
Dill	Chardonnay (medium), Sauvignon Blanc (light to medium, fruity), Riesling (sweet)
Fennel	Chardonnay (medium to full), Grenache (medium), Riesling (sweet)
Garlic	Chardonnay, Sauvignon Blanc (light to medium)
Ginger	Chardonnay (medium to full), White Zinfandel (spicy), Riesling (sweet)
Leeks	Chardonnay (medium), Chenin Blanc (light, melon-like), Fume Blanc (medium, fruity)
Lemon Juice	Chardonnay (medium), Chenin Blanc (light, melon-like), Fume Blanc (medium, fruity)
Marjoram	Fume Blanc (light to medium, fruity), Sauvignon Blanc
Mint	Gewurztraminer (light), Grenache (medium), Riesling (sweet), Sauvignon Blanc
Mustard	Chardonnay, Fume Blanc (light to medium, fruity), White Zinfandel (medium, spicy)
Nutmeg	Chardonnay, Fume Blanc (light to medium, fruity)
Onion	Chardonnay (medium to full), Fume Blanc (light to medium, fruity), Grenache (medium)
Orange	Chardonnay (medium to full), Fume Blanc (light to medium, fruity), Grenache (medium)
Oregano	Chardonnay (medium to full), Sauvignon Blanc (light to medium)
Pepper, Bell	Grenache (medium)
Pepper, Black	Sauvignon Blanc
Pepper, Chile	Chenin Blanc (light, melon-like), Gewurztraminer (light), Riesling (sweet)
Rosemary	Sauvignon Blanc
Sage	Chardonnay (medium to full), Sauvignon Blanc (light to medium)
Savory	Sauvignon Blanc
Scallion	Chenin Blanc (light, melon-like)
Sesame Seeds	Fume Blanc (light to medium, fruity)
Shallot	Chenin Blanc (light, melon-like)
Sorrel	Fume Blanc (light to medium, fruity)
Tarragon	Chardonnay (medium to full), Riesling (sweet), Sauvignon Blanc (light to medium)
Thyme	Chardonnay (medium to full), Sauvignon Blanc
Tomato	Chenin Blanc (light, melon-like), Fume Blanc (light to medium, fruity)
Turmeric	Fume Blanc (light to medium, fruity), Grenache (medium)

Red Wine Seasonings

Seasoning	Red Wines to Go with Seasoning (body type = light medium or full, flavor):
Allspice	Cabernet Sauvignon (medium to full), Merlot, Pinot Noir
Anise	Merlot, Syrah (medium), Zinfandel (medium to full)
Basil	Beaujolais (light), Cabernet Sauvignon (medium to full), Madeira (full, sweet), Merlot, Zinfandel
Cardamom	Syrah
Chives	Cabernet Sauvignon (medium to full), Merlot (medium to full), Muscatel (full, sweet)
Cinnamon	Chianti (medium), Pinot Noir, Syrah (medium), Zinfandel (medium to full)
Cilantro	Cabernet Sauvignon (medium to full), Zinfandel (medium to full)
Coriander	Cabernet Sauvignon (medium to full), Zinfandel (medium to full)
Cumin	Syrah (medium), Zinfandel (medium to full)
Curry	Zinfandel (medium to full)
Fennel	Syrah (medium), Zinfandel (medium to full)
Garlic	Chianti (medium), Merlot (medium to full), Pinot Noir, Syrah (medium), Zinfandel (medium)
Ginger	Zinfandel (medium to full)
Mint	Cabernet Sauvignon (medium to full), Merlot (medium to full)
Nuts	Cabernet Sauvignon (medium to full)
Oregano	Bardolino (light), Cabernet Sauvignon (medium), Chianti (medium), Merlot, Zinfandel (full)
Parsley	Beaujolais, Bardolino (light), Cabernet Sauvignon (medium), Zinfandel (medium to full)
Pepper, Black	Cabernet Sauvignon (medium to full), Pinot Noir, Zinfandel
Pepper, Chile	Syrah (medium), Zinfandel (medium to full)
Rosemary	Cabernet Sauvignon (medium), Merlot, Pinot Noir (medium), Zinfandel (medium to full)
Sage	Pinot Noir (medium to full), Syrah (medium), Zinfandel (medium to full)
Shallot	Cabernet Sauvignon (medium to full), Pinot Noir (medium to full)
Tarragon	Cabernet Sauvignon (medium to full), Syrah, Zinfandel
Thyme	Cabernet Sauvignon (medium), Merlot, Pinot Noir (medium), Zinfandel (medium to full)

Worcestershire Sauce™

Flavor/Taste:
Like beef bouillon, but spicier

Use:
Use at the BEGINNING and SPARINGLY.
Use as a marinade before cooking.
Use with cheese, eggs, meats, mushrooms, soups and stews.

Mix with:
- Garlic
- Ginger
- Pepper, Black
- Shallot

Color & Form:
Brown liquid mix of the following spices–ginger, shallot and garlic

---

Pronunciation

Unless you are from New England, location names like Worcestershire can be difficult to pronounce. Pronounce it as if it is spelled *Wooster-sure,* with the accent on Woos and Wooster rhyming with rooster.

Origin
Worcestershire Sauce comes from a mix of malt vinegar, soy sauce, molasses, red pepper, meat juices and spices. It was originally a recipe from India.

Folklore/History

In 1837 a retired Bengal governor asked two pharmacists to mix up a recipe he had gotten from India. It did not taste very good and was forgotten until years later when the two druggists found it while cleaning out the cellar. They tasted it and liked it so much that they began making it for local consumption. Within ten years it became so popular that the gentlemen began to export it, and you can still buy it as Lea and Perrins' Worcestershire Sauce.

Other Blends and Flavorings Defined

This section is included for all of those who would ask, "But what about . . .?" The following herbs, spices, blends and condiments were put here to avoid: duplicating flavors already represented, listing blends made up of flavorings already mentioned and talking about items not readily available in stores.

Aspic-a transparent jelly-like mold of meat, tomato or other juice, often found with meat or seafood, and eaten as a relish.

Barbecue Seasoning-usually made with a tomato base with garlic, onion, mustard, vinegar and brown sugar.

Baking Powder-contains cornstarch to keep it dry and sodium bicarbonate, a chemical that reacts with a liquid to free carbon dioxide gas. *Use less in high altitudes, not more!*

Baking Soda-sodium bicarbonate, which gives off carbon dioxide gas when mixed with an acid, thus causing baked items to rise. *Use less in high altitudes, not more!*

Bouquet Garni-French for bundle of herbs, a group of equally-sized fresh sprigs of parsley, bay leaf, basil, savory, marjoram and thyme tied in cheesecloth, cooked or simmered with a dish and removed before serving. It is good in sauces, soups and beef stews. Do your own with a teaball and dried herbs.

Brandy-distilled from wine, this alcoholic beverage is used mostly in French cooking. It includes cognac and armagnac. Apricot or fruit-flavored brandies are called marcs.

Cajun/Creole Seasoning-chiles are the main ingredient of a good Cajun blend. Black pepper, onions, garlic, celery and mustard are also traditional.

Caramel-made by melting sugar in a skillet and adding water. Used for coloring gravies, candies and of course, caramel apples.

Cassia-similar to sweetened cinnamon and cloves, cassia is often what is sold as cinnamon in American stores. It is usually less expensive than cinnamon.

Catnip-once rubbed on roast and used as an herbal tea, it is seldom used in cooking now.

Chat Masala-spice blend of asafoetida, mint, ginger, ajowan, cayenne, black salt, mango powder, cumin and dried pomegranate seeds used in Indian dishes.

Other Blends and Flavorings Defined continued

Chutney-like a spicy, sugared vegetable puree, which includes onions, fruit pulp and raisins marinated in vinegar. It is best served with bland starchy food, such as rice or potato.

Costmary-this lemony pepper-like, slightly bitter flavoring is native to India and Western Asia. Used sparingly it was added to wild game, eggs, soups, seafood (tuna, shrimp) and veal. Not readily available now, American colonists used the broad leaves as a Bible marker. If the sermon was boring just a sniff or nibble would perk up the parishioner, thus its nickname, Bibleplant.

Cream of Tartar-used in baking soda as an acid to release carbon dioxide from the soda. This was used before baking powder was available. It comes from deposits on the inside of wine barrels. *It gives frosting a creamy consistency and egg whites more stability and volume.*

Crème Fraîche-not always available, but always expensive. Make it by adding 2 Tbsp buttermilk (or sour cream) to 1 cup whipping cream. Shake it and leave it out overnight to thicken.

Cubeb Pepper-similar to allspice in flavor and more bitter than black pepper, this spice grows on a vine in Java and the Indonesian Islands. It is good with chicken, rice and vegetables and in marinating ham. It is not used much today and is not readily available.

Dukka-an Egyptian powdered spice blend of ground toasted seeds and nuts, such as hazelnuts, chickpeas, pepper, cumin, coriander and sesame seeds. It is used on vegetables, meats and bread.

Dulse-a coarse-looking red to purple seaweed with a salty flavor. It is high in iron, vitamin A and phosphorus and is used in soups and salads.

Epazote-a flavoring not readily available in stores, used in bean dishes and tortillas.

Filé Powder (See also **Sassafras**)-from the leaves of a sassafras tree used in Creole or Cajun dishes and gumbo. *Small amounts can cause organ damage.*

Fines Herbes-a French blend of basil, chervil, parsley, thyme, marjoram, rosemary and tarragon good with eggs, salads, soups and cheese sauces. It is added at the very end of cooking. Tarragon is used less in this blend because of its dominant flavor.

Galangal-a peppery, ginger-like dried root of a perennial plant. It is native to Southern China and Indonesia. Peel it as you would ginger root. Use with meats, in coconut sauces, seafood, stews and stir-frys and to make curries for Malaysian and Russian dishes. It is cream colored and blends well with curry powder and ginger. It was used at one time to prevent seasickness.

Other Blends and Flavorings Defined continued

Garam Masala-a spice mix of northern India including cumin, coriander, cardamom, black pepper, cloves, mace, bay leaf and cinnamon. It is available as a blend in some stores and is similar to curry.

Gremolada-a garnish blend of parsley, garlic and lemon peel. It is native to Milan, Italy and is used with slow-cooking meat dishes toward the end of cooking. It blends well with orange.

Grenadine-a syrup made from pomegranate juice.

Herbes de Provence-a blend of oregano, marjoram, rosemary, savory and thyme. It is good in stews, baked tomatoes, roast chicken or pizza. Used in Southern France, it is available in stores.

Italian Seasoning-this usually includes oregano, basil, rosemary, thyme, garlic and fennel seed.

Ketchup-originally from the Indonesian *ketjap*, a syrupy chutney with pureed mushrooms. Clean copper or brass by soaking in ketchup for 10 minutes. See also Tomato in spice section.

Kirsch-a brandy used for mostly desserts, especially with fruit, cream and pastries. It is used with cheese in fondues and in some meat dishes. It tastes like sweetened blackberries.

Lemon Thyme-the leaves of a bushy, hardy plant. It goes with ginger and rosemary and is used with chicken, pork, soups, stews, stuffings, as a tea or with vegetables. Although not always available in stores, it is easy to grow.

Licorice-the bittersweet root of a perennial legume (bean) used in sweets, drinks and liqueurs. The black sticks are made from the juice of the root, which is concentrated by boiling.

Marc-a substitute for brandy used when cooking sweets, it comes in various fruit flavors. Apricot brandy is the most commonly used. It is made from the leftover grapes after they have been pressed in the wine-making process.

Mayonnaise-to make this begin with an egg yolk. Alternately add 1 teaspoon of vinegar and 6 drops of salad oil, mixing constantly.

Mincemeat-a blend of cloves, cinnamon and allspice mixed with fruits, nuts and alcohol. Generally no real meat is used, although beef fat can be included. It is good in cookies, pies, puddings and sweet rolls.

Other Blends and Flavorings Defined continued

Monosodium Glutamate (MSG)-sodium salt of an amino acid found in vegetables, grains and sugar beets. MSG is now made from molasses glucose fermented with bacteria. It is a flavor enhancer but has no taste itself. Because it can cause allergic reactions in many people, it is not a flavoring for experimentation. Developed in Japan in the 1920's, it is called **ajinomoto** there and **mi-shin** in Vietnam.

Mulling Spices-including allspice, cinnamon, cloves and nutmeg, they are used to flavor heated beverages such as red wine and cider. Citrus fruit is also used.

Nigella-small tear-shaped seeds with a nutty peppery flavor, used in India on vegetables, legumes (beans) and in breads.

Okra-a small 2"-3" vegetable, native to Africa, with a peppery flavor. It goes well with bell peppers and onion and is used more for thickening gumbo, soups and stews than for flavoring.

Persillade-a mix of parsley and garlic that is sautéed and added at the last. It is good with chicken, beef or vegetables.

Pesto-originally from Genoa, Italy, pesto is fresh basil, garlic, pine nuts, Parmesan and olive oil ground up into a sauce.

Pickling Spice-a blend of spices consisting of dill, peppercorns, red chiles, allspice, bay, cloves, ginger, coriander and mustard seeds. Used to pickle or season meats, fruits, vegetables and sauces.

Pie & Pudding Spice-a blend of cinnamon, cloves, ginger and other spices used in pies, especially pecan, pumpkin and sweet potato, sweet rolls, rice pudding and fruit salad dressing.

Poultry Seasoning-a blend of sage, thyme, marjoram, savory, rosemary and other spices used to season chicken, turkey and other fowl. Use it in hamburgers, stuffings, meatloaf, pork and cornbread.

Pulses-a grouping of mature vegetable seeds, including beans, peas and lentils.

Pumpkin Pie Spice-a blend of sweet spices, including nutmeg, cloves, cinnamon and ginger. It can be used for puddings, cakes, cookies, muffins and, of course, pies.

Quatre Epices-literally four spices, it includes cloves, nutmeg, ginger, cinnamon and pepper. It is used to flavor French items such as roasts, poultry, vegetables and desserts. Without the white pepper it is commonly referred to as pumpkin pie spice.

Other **B**lends and **F**lavorings **D**efined continued

Rue-the leaves of a small bushy plant that has a bad smell when rubbed. It is a perennial evergreen and a stimulant with a bitter taste. It is used on fish, eggs and cream cheese. *Use only a leaf or two, because it is dangerous in large amounts—especially if pregnant (it can cause abortions). It can also cause severe burning and blistering of the skin on contact.*

Sansho-a ground table spice used as a pepper in Japan. It is one of seven spices used to make schichimi, a Japanese spice blend, used with noodles and soups.

Sassafras (Filé Powder)-*as little as a teaspoon can cause organ damage.* From a small deciduous tree native to North America, it was used by the Choctow Indians as a thickening agent and later in Creole dishes and even as a tea. It does offer relief as an antiseptic against poison ivy or oak.

Seaweed (Kelp)-there are many varieties of algae known as kelp or seaweed, the most common being agar. They are rich in minerals, especially iodine, vitamins and protein and are used mostly in soups, salads, sushi and Japanese stir-frys.

Sprouts-germinated seeds.

Sumac-a bush growing in mountainous areas, it is native to the Middle East. The berries are acidic with a fruity sourness. *The leaves cause a skin reaction like poison ivy or oak, thus this flavoring is not readily available in stores.* The berries are good in just about everything. It blends well with onion and olive oil and is used mostly as a replacement for lemon juice or vinegar.

Tabil-a condiment used in Tunisia made by mixing garlic, sweet red peppers, chile peppers, caraway seeds and cilantro into a paste.

Tahini-finely ground sesame seeds used to flavor pureed chickpeas (hummus).

Water Chestnuts-good with curry and cayenne, they are used more for texture (like a juicy raw potato) than flavor. Native to China, use them in cream soups, salads and stir-frys.

Woodruff, Sweet-leaves and flowers are used to make tea. Place sprigs in white wine for 1-2 days.

Zahtar-stronger than thyme, it is a low shrub of the mint family, grown and used in the Middle East and North Africa. It is sometimes substituted by combining sumac, roasted sesame seeds and ground thyme.

The Four Tastes and How to Use Them

There are four taste sensations:

>   **sweet,**
>   **salty,**
>   **sour and**
>   **bitter**.

Little is known about how taste actually "works." What is known is that taste and smell go hand in hand to create flavor. The nose, in fact, shares an airway with the mouth so that we smell and taste food at the same time.

The taste buds are located on the tongue, number a few thousand and decrease after age 45. They indirectly transmit impulses to three areas of the brain.

The nose, on the other hand, contains the "smell cells," which number in the millions! These cells can regenerate, are hot-wired directly to the brain and, thus, are more important in the tasting process than the taste buds. Remember how difficult it is to taste anything when you have a stuffed up nose? Without getting too technical, let's just say that these "smell cells" and the four basic tastes mentioned above can differentiate flavors the way our eyes differentiate thousands of hues by combining just three primary colors.

The importance and preference of tastes, that is, sweet, salty, sour and bitter, follow the location of the taste buds in the mouth. Sweet is at the tip of the tongue, salty on either side of the tip, sour on either edge of the tongue behind the salty taste buds and bitter lies across the back and top of the tongue.

Why such a strong urge for sweet foods? Early humans were nomadic. They went where there was food and water and ate the obvious and showiest of plants, like fruit. Fruits are sweet and because fruits supply sugar and sugar supplies energy, it was natural to crave sweets. Likewise, poisonous plants tend to be bitter and taste unpleasant—sort of a natural early warning device.

It is important to listen to your body, which naturally craves foods that contain minerals and nutrients that our bodies need. It is also important to vary your diet with new flavors in order to keep both the sense of taste and smell finely tuned. So spicing up your food with seasonings can be considered exercise for the senses.

Sweet Flavorings

Most of us are specialists on this taste. When you are wanting to add sweetness to your dish, combine some of the items below. Sweets are not just for desserts. Honey with sweet spices and cracker crumbs over chicken are very tasty. Many people enjoy the sweet and sour flavor, so do not be afraid to combine the two groups.

Here are a few hints on using sweets:

- Sweets are stronger in hot dishes than cold ones.
- Add salt or a teaspoon of cider vinegar to lessen sweetness.
- Add fruit and/or extracts to increase sweetness and decrease sugar usage in recipes.

Allspice	Cream	Poppy Seeds
Angelica	Honey	Raisins
Anise	Mace	Sugar
Butter/Margarine	Mint	Syrups & Extracts
Cinnamon	Nutmeg	Vanilla
Cloves	Nuts	

Salty Flavorings

Many flavoring blends contain salt, such as celery, garlic and onion salts. These are poor substitutes for the powder equivalents. Salt is widely used in canned items (soups, sauces) and in snack items (crackers, chips, candies). Watch for the sodium content on packages. The recommended daily intake is just one teaspoonful. Therefore, you seldom need to add salt when you are cooking. Many foods are naturally high in sodium, such as spinach and celery. When salt is needed, use sea salt for a better flavor. Also try tamari, a less-salty alternative to soy sauce.

Helpful hints on how to use salt in cooking:

- Salty flavors are stronger in cold dishes than hot ones.
- Salt meats after browning.
- To absorb saltiness, add a cut raw potato.
- Do not salt food before microwaving or pressure cooking, as salt will toughen it.
- Salt water before cooking vegetables on the stove to help retain their natural minerals and to lessen the time needed to boil.

Bouillon Cubes	Cheese	Soy Sauce
Capers	Salt	

Sour/Acidic Flavorings

Sourness is always caused by high acid levels. It is theorized that being able to detect the acid level or pH balance was important to humans when we lived in water eons ago.

A few things to know about acids or sour-tasting foods:

- Neutralize acids by adding a little sugar, honey or cream to a recipe.
- Acids are tenderizers, thus good in marinades for meats.
- Acids are stronger in hot dishes than cold ones.
- When adding an acid to a recipe containing baking powder, neutralize it by adding ¼ tsp baking soda and reduce the baking powder by ½ tsp for each ¼ tsp of baking soda added.

Apple-tart	Coffee	Tamarind
Beer	Cream, Sour-Buttermilk	Tomato
Cayenne	Lemon Juice	Vinegar
Pepper, Chile	Orange-any citrus fruit	Yogurt
Chocolate	Syrups-Molasses only	Wine

Bitter Flavorings

We react much more strongly to bitter tasting food than to any other taste, no matter whether it is hot or cold. This may be a primitive reaction to preservation, since so many poisonous plants are bitter tasting.

The bitter flavors below are often eaten with a combination of other flavors. Bay leaf is used for flavoring, but is usually removed before serving and not eaten. Raw dry mustard, unlike prepared mustard in a jar, is bitter enough to be used to induce vomiting in the case of poisoning.

A few things to know about bitter flavorings:

- Bitter flavors are stronger in cold dishes than hot ones.
- Neutralize bitter tastes with sugar, syrups, cream and milk.

Angostura Bitters	Cumin	Mustard
Bay Leaf	Dill Seed	Saffron
Cayenne	Fenugreek	Sorrel
Coffee	Hyssop	Tarragon

Flavor Blends

Use level ground teaspoons or tablespoons as the unit of measurement, depending upon how much you want. Dried herbs are better than ground. Keep extra in jars for future use. Change them to fit your taste.

Try any one of these blends on popcorn.

Beans or Rice Blend
3 Black Pepper
½ Cayenne
1 Celery Seeds
½ Marjoram
1 Oregano
2 Paprika
1 Sage
1 Thyme
1 Turmeric

Beef Blend
2 Black Pepper
¼ Garlic Powder
2 Onion Powder
3 Parsley
2 Rosemary
1 Savory
1 Thyme

Cajun Blend
(Slow cook with chicken , seafood, sausage, bell peppers, bay leaf, rice, celery, okra and tomatoes.)
1½ Cayenne
¾ Garlic Powder
3 Onion Flakes
1 Oregano
¼ dry Mustard
1 White Pepper
½ Thyme

Chicken Blend
1 Basil
1 Dill Weed
2 Marjoram
1 Paprika
1 Parsley
½ Thyme

Chinese Blend
2 Coriander
½ Cayenne
½ Cumin
¼ Five-Spice Powder
1 Garlic Powder
1 Ginger
1 Onion Powder

Curry Powder Blend
1 Allspice
½ Black Pepper
¼ Cayenne
4 Coriander
1 Cumin
½ Ginger
1 dry Mustard
3 Turmeric

French Blend
1 Chervil
1 Chives
1 Parsley
1 Tarragon

Greek Blend
½ Black Pepper
2 Garlic Powder
1 Lemon Peel
1 Oregano

Indian Blend
(Garam Masala)
2 Black Pepper
2 Cardamom
1 Cinnamon
5 Coriander
4 Cumin
1 Nutmeg

Italian Blend
2 Basil
1 Garlic Powder
2 Marjoram
1 Oregano
½ Rosemary
½ Sage
½ Thyme

Lamb Blend
1 Garlic Powder
1 Parsley
2 Rosemary
1½ Thyme

Mexican Blend
½ Cayenne
1½ Cilantro
1 Coriander
1½ Cumin
½ Garlic Powder
½ Ginger
½ dry Mustard
1½ Onion Powder
½ Oregano

Seafood Blend
2 Basil
2 Chervil
2 Marjoram
1 Parsley
3 Tarragon

Soup Blend
1 Basil
1 Celery Seed
1 Chervil
1 Parsley
1 Rosemary
½ Sage
1 Thyme

Thai Blend
½ Cayenne
¼ Cinnamon
2 Coriander
1 Cumin
1 Garlic Powder
1 Ginger
½ Onion Powder

Turkey Blend
1 Ginger,
2 Parsley, flakes
1 Marjoram
1 Oregano
1 Rosemary
⅓ Sage
1 Thyme
⅓ White Pepper

Veggie Blend
1 Basil
½ Celery Seed
1 Chervil
1 Marjoram
½ Tarragon

Foods and Flavorings that Go with Them

This alphabetical list contains the most common foods that we eat in America. Some demanded special attention and more in-depth information as you will see. For example, beans, mushrooms and pasta are divided by specific varieties with descriptions of each kind. Each food includes the following information:

Benefits: Because we want to justify our food habits, I have listed certain benefits of foods, such as low in sodium, ideal roughage and high in vitamins, sometimes naming the particular vitamins or minerals.

Seasonings to use with____ : This is an alphabetical list of flavorings that go particularly well with each food. Certain foods, especially meats, seem to be good with almost any flavoring. However, that does not mean mixing all the flavorings will be good with the meat. Refer to the *Flavor Blends* chart on the preceding page for ideas or look up a particular seasoning in Section 1 and see what other flavorings complement or mix well with it. Generally, salt and pepper can be used with any non-dessert foods and may not be listed.

How to Cook and **Buying Guide:** For those of you new to cooking, use this area to learn more about cooking and purchasing food. Cooking tips and tricks, along with measurement guidelines, definitions and miscellaneous information are under **How to Cook**. The **Buying Guide** includes what to look for when buying each food at the grocery store.

Preparation Ideas: Last, but not least, are actual recipes and meal ideas for dinners, desserts, salads, and so on for each food. An occasional bit of history is also included. Most of the recipes can be cooked in less than 45 minutes. Items that take longer, like spaghetti sauce, lasagna or chili, are best made in bulk and frozen in smaller leftover portions. Unless, of course, you have a husband like mine who can eat spaghetti five days in a row and still asks if he can take some to work for lunch! In that case, take a little more time, make up a large portion on the weekend and serve the same thing several days in a row. *Items in boxes, charts or italics are additional, and hopefully useful, information. All temperatures are in Fahrenheit.*

Apples/Applesauce

Benefits: No sodium, high in vitamins A and B$_2$, helps clean teeth

Seasonings to use with apples and applesauce:

Allspice
Anise
Butter/Margarine
Caraway Seed-cooked apples
Cardamom-baked apples
Cheese-cheddar, Swiss
Chervil-salads
Cinnamon

Cloves
Coriander
Cream & Milk
Dill
Fennel
Five-Spice Powder
Ginger
Mint

Nutmeg
Nuts-walnuts
Onion/Scallion
Raisins
Shallot
Sugar
Tarragon
Wine

How to Cook:

For cooking: Golden Delicious, Fuji Rome Beauty, MacIntosh, Greenings. **For pies:** Jonathan, Winesap, Granny Smith. **For Applesauce:** Golden Delicious, Granny Smith or Jonathan. (Use 8-10 apples with ¾ cup water.)

Apples emit gas that causes potatoes to sprout and lettuce to brown. So store separately in the refrigerator. Browning is the apple's defense mechanism against disease and can be delayed by adding lemon juice.

Buying Guide:

A *smaller* size usually means better taste. Large, bright red, dark green or egg yellow apples may be past their prime.

Tart:	Jonathan, McIntosh, Winesap and Granny Smith
Sweet:	Red or Golden Delicious, Golden Russet and Fuji
Healthy:	Freedom and Liberty (less pesticides used in growing)

1 lb apples = 4 small, 3 medium or 2 large = 3 cups diced
2 lb apples = 9 inch pie

Preparation Ideas:

Grapes and cheese are good with apples as an **appetizer**, especially with a dry red wine.

Smoothie: Make an applesauce smoothie with vanilla ice cream and a bit of cinnamon; or use slices of apples mixed with yogurt and walnuts and make your own smoothie.

Slice apples and cook in butter. Throw in some fennel or caraway seeds. Serve over **pork** topped with cheddar cheese.

Vary that turkey **stuffing** with baking apples, onions, celery, nuts and raisins.

Apples add crunchiness and tanginess to stir-frys and salads. Pair them with walnuts and add toward the end of cooking.

Use applesauce instead of oil to moisten cakes, cookies, or muffins. Add the amount that will give you the same batter consistency (a little less than the oil). It may also take a little longer to cook.

See Fruit or Salad pages in this section for more ideas.

Try apples with sauerkraut or red **cabbage**.

Apples with **fondue** are pretty good, too.

Apple/Applesauce Preparation Ideas continued:

Beer, Beans, Apples & Sausage Casserole: (Do on weekends because of time.) Warm oven to 300°. Put ½ lb or 3 cups cooked pinto beans in a casserole dish. Add 1 cup bean juice (or water), 6 oz beer, 2 small diced apples, ⅛ cup soy or tamari sauce, ¼ cup brown sugar, 2 cloves minced garlic, ½ tsp dry mustard and ½ lb sliced smoked hot sausage. Bake covered 1-1½ hours until liquid is absorbed and it looks moist but not soupy.

Side dish with Pork: Sprinkle a little cinnamon in with your applesauce. Serve with pork.

Waldorf Salad: Mix 2 diced apples, 1½ Tbsp lemon juice, ¼ cup chopped celery, ¼ cup halved green grapes, ¼ cup chopped walnuts and a handful of raisins. For dressing mix ½ cup yogurt, ½ Tbsp sugar and ¼ tsp lemon juice or 1 cup whipped topping.

Stir-Fry: Sauté butter, apples and onions together. Serve with pasta or rice. Add vegetables and/or the meat of your choice.

For a sweet-flavored **stir-fry** add sweet spices like five-spice powder, cinnamon, allspice and fennel that will blend well with apples. Contrast the sweetness with Szechuan pepper or cider vinegar.

Apple Pancakes/Waffles: Cut up apples and sauté a few minutes in butter. Either add them to the batter or sprinkle them over the cooked pancakes or waffles. Nuts and powdered sugar add flavor and an appealing presentation.

Dessert: (1 hour cooking time) Core (leaving part of the bottom) one unpeeled apple per person. Pack with sugar and bake at 400° for 20 minutes. Refill with sugar and 1 tsp of butter on top. Bake 15 minutes, baste with pan juice and bake 25 more minutes. Top with 1 Tbsp brandy. Serve with cream.

Pound Cake: Applesauce (instead of water or milk), allspice and cinnamon added to a pound cake mix is especially tasty.

Dessert: Peel and cut 3 pears and 3 apples (Granny Smith). Place them in a pan with ¼ cup water, ¼ cup orange juice and 1 Tbsp lemon juice. Heat on stove top for 20 minutes, adding 3 Tbsp sugar in the last 10 minutes. Puree and add ¾ tsp vanilla. Serve chilled.

Dessert: Melt cheddar cheese on top of a piece of apple pie.

Dessert: In a casserole dish peel and slice 6 apples. Separately, sift ½ cup brown sugar, ½ cup flour and ¾ tsp cinnamon. Cut in 4 Tbsp butter until crumbly. Add a cup (4 oz) of grated cheddar. Spread the crumbly mix over the apples and bake it for 35 minutes at 350° until apples are tender and crust is golden. Don't forget the ice cream.

Dessert: Cut apples and sauté in butter until soft. Cover with a mixture of plain yogurt, sugar and cinnamon. Try peaches also.

Syrup: Heat applesauce and brown sugar in a pan and serve it over pancakes or waffles as a syrup. Add a little crushed caraway seed to the batter before cooking.

Artichoke

Benefits: Fiber, easy to digest

Seasonings to use with artichokes:

Bay Leaf	Lemon Juice	Parsley
Butter/Margarine	Marjoram	Savory
Cheese-Swiss, cream	Nuts-pine nuts	Tarragon
Chervil	Oils & Fats-olive	Thyme
Coriander	Oregano	Tomato
Garlic	Paprika	Vinegar

How to Cook:

Use immediately. Cut off the top third and tips of leaves. Brush with lemon juice to prevent discoloring and put in a pan with ¼ cup water. Microwave covered on high 6-8 minutes or until base is easy to pierce. Let stand 5 minutes. Boil or steam them in a covered pot full of water for 30 minutes. When you can pull out a center leaf easily, it is done. Cut them with a stainless steel knife and avoid cooking in aluminum or iron pans. Spread leaves and remove center leaves.

Buying Guide:

Pick bright green, small artichokes that are tightly packed. It should be heavy for its size. Spreading leaves indicate age and toughness. Stem should be white and juicy when cut.

Preparation Ideas:

Artichokes are tasty and are used mainly as **appetizers**. Place artichoke hearts on crackers as an appetizer with or without cream cheese. Ambrosia! Did someone mention wine?

Cook artichokes by microwaving and serve with 1 Tbsp lemon juice, ¼ cup melted butter and 1 Tbsp chopped parsley.

Hearts & Eggs: Cut up marinated artichoke hearts and add to scrambled eggs. Also add fresh chervil for color.

Heart Salad: Try artichoke hearts (in glass jars marinated in oil) in your green salads with tomatoes. Include the oil in the jar as a dressing.

Pasta with artichoke hearts and a white or red sauce (see Sauces and Gravies in this section) is very good. Add sun-dried tomatoes for tanginess or pine nuts or sunflower seeds for crunch.

Artichokes are good chilled with French dressing or vinaigrette.

*The **Jerusalem artichoke** or sunchoke (from the Italian, girasole) is actually from the sunflower family and looks like a ginger root. Eat these raw in salads without peeling or cook them in boiling water and add to soup. They are rich in iron.*

Artichoke Heart Pasta Salad: For a tasty summer salad, cut up a bunch of chervil and a bunch of Italian parsley. Add curly pasta and a jar of marinated artichoke hearts including the oil. Cut up some red cabbage for crunch.

Asparagus

Benefits: Low in sodium, very low in calories, blood purifier, high in vitamin A

Seasonings to use with asparagus:

Butter/Margarine	Marjoram	Sage
Caraway Seed	Mustard	Savory
Cheese	Nutmeg (pinch only)	Sesame Seeds
Chives	Nuts-almonds, cashews, walnuts	Soy Sauce
Garlic	Onion/Scallion	Tarragon
Lemon Juice	Orange	Thyme

How to Cook:
Cut off the bottoms and peel the lower part like a carrot.
Microwave a pound with a little water for 6-8 minutes with spears pointed toward the center.
Boil or steam whole spears in a covered pan 8-10 minutes.

Stir-fry for only 2-3 minutes (put them in last).

Asparagus, from the lily family, comes in green, purple and white varieties.

Buying Guide:
Buy asparagus loose. Stems should be firm, with moist, smooth ends. Avoid open tips with seeds.

Store 2-3 days standing up in water with a plastic cover.

Preparation Ideas:

Bacon & Egg Asparagus: Pour warm water over frozen cut asparagus. Fry 2 slices of bacon and crumbled them up. Use the bacon grease to sauté asparagus with chopped onion and add all to an omelet or scrambled eggs. Try this with savory, tarragon and chives with or without the bacon.

Pasta: Sauté 1 lb asparagus. Add 2 cups toasted walnuts, 4 garlic cloves, 1 tsp thyme and 8 oz goat cheese. Serve over fettuccine.

Pasta Sauce: Boil ¾ lb of asparagus tips in water 1-2 minutes. Puree half of the tips with 1 cup heavy cream and ½ cup chicken broth. Simmer until creamy. Add the rest of the tips and serve over pasta (especially tortellini).

In Salads: Cut up cooked asparagus and add to salads. Include some bacon bits. Also try orange slices with asparagus.

Sauce: Melt ¼ cup butter/margarine; stir in ⅓ cup flour and ⅛ tsp nutmeg. Add 1 cup milk and 1 cup broth or stock and simmer. Add ⅓ cup grated Swiss and ¼ cup Parmesan. Pour over cooked asparagus and leftover chicken. Warm in the oven at 350° for 20 minutes.

Stir-Fry: Mix 1 Tbsp warm water with 1 tsp cornstarch and 1 tsp soy sauce and set aside. Slice 1 lb asparagus. Stir-fry them in 1 Tbsp peanut oil with 4, 1" sliced scallions about 4 minutes. Add 1½ cups of sliced mushrooms and cook a minute. Stir in soy sauce mix until thick. Cut into wedges 2 tomatoes and add. Serve over rice or pasta.

Vegetable Side Dish: Frozen asparagus is great when cooked tender. Add butter and lemon juice. Make it go further by stir-frying with mushrooms. Sprinkle with toasted sesame seeds. Try an orange-flavored honey on top.

Avocado

Benefits: High in iron, copper and unsaturated (good) fat (59g of fat per lb), low in sodium

Seasonings to use with avocados:

Cayenne	Lemon Juice	Pepper, Chile
Chili Powder	Oils & Fats-olive, sesame	Tabasco
Cilantro	Onion/Scallion	Tomato
Cream, Sour	Orange	Vinegar
Garlic	Oregano	Worcestershire Sauce

How to Cook:
These are usually served raw. Do not cut into one until you are ready to serve it, since it discolors so quickly. Slow the discoloration by adding lemon juice and/or wrap it with plastic wrap.

Avocado comes from an Aztec word meaning *tree testicle* and is also known as **alligator pear**. To ripen, store at room temperature in a closed brown paper bag with a couple of holes in it.

Buying Guide:
Pick unripened avocados that yield slightly. They should be firm, without soft spots and feel heavy for their size. If a leaf squeaks when you rub it, it is tender.

Preparation Ideas:

Appetizer Ideas: 1) Try crackers with avocados and artichoke hearts. OK, with all those calories just make a meal of it! Sprinkle it with one of the flavorings above. Open a bottle of wine ... 2) Combine avocado with cooked shrimp and cocktail sauce. 3) Scoop out part of an unpeeled avocado half, add grapefruit sections over what is left of the half and cover with French dressing.

Authentic Guacamole: Mash 2 ripe avocados. Add 1 Tbsp each lime and lemon juice, 1 crushed garlic clove, 2 chopped scallions, 1 jalapeño chile (or 1 tsp Tabasco), 4 Tbsp chopped fresh cilantro and 1 chopped tomato. Dip away!

Avocado Dressing: Mash a large avocado. Add ¾ cup sour cream, ⅓ cup milk, 1 Tbsp lemon juice and a few drops of Tabasco. Cover and use before discoloring. Makes 1⅔ cups.

Easy Guacamole: Buy the packets usually located near where avocados are sold in the grocery store and/or spice up your own guacamole dip with any or all of the above seasonings. Add tomatoes.

Stuffed: Spice up mashed avocados and stuff it into celery, tomatoes, bell peppers or mushrooms.

Colorful Salad: To ½ cup canola oil add 2 Tbsp lemon juice, 2 Tbsp orange juice, 1 clove crushed garlic, ¼ tsp each of salt, oregano and Tabasco. Shake and pour over 2 sliced avocados, 2 tomatoes cut in wedges and 1 sectioned orange. Let it stand a bit before serving. **Variation:** Use olive oil, a cucumber instead of an orange, more oregano and some feta cheese.

Fruit & Nut Salad: On lettuce arrange wedges of orange, grapefruit and avocados. Grind 1 Tbsp pecans and 1 Tbsp blanched almonds and add 2 Tbsp each lemon juice and sesame oil. Pour over salad.

Bacon

Benefits: Questionable, it is high in cholesterol, animal fat and salt

Seasonings to use with bacon:

Cayenne	Garlic	Pepper, Black
Cheese	Onion/Scallion	Shallot
Cloves	Parsley	Tomato

How to Cook:
Reduce saltiness by rinsing bacon in water. Reduce curling by pricking with a fork before frying or microwaving (4-5 minutes for 6 slices). You can also bake bacon at 400° for 10 minutes.

Although not included as a flavoring, bacon is used to enhance the flavor of foods. The grease is used to add salty or meaty flavor to soups, salads and sandwiches.

Turkey bacon is a leaner alternative.

Buying Guide:
Bacon comes in thin, medium and thick slices or as an unsliced slab. **Canadian bacon** is leaner and closer to ham. Buy bacon that is shiny looking and check the date. Wrap and freeze it according to the size helping you use.

Preparation Ideas:

Breakfast: Cook bacon and eggs for breakfast or have bacon *in* eggs as in an omelette.

Appetizer: Cook up bacon and serve with cream cheese, artichoke hearts or peanut butter on crackers. Or crumble the bacon and add it to dips.

Appetizer: Wrap bacon around an oyster with cayenne and parsley. Hold with a toothpick and cook in a frying pan.

Partially fry up bacon, crumble and add it (and some of the grease) to your favorite **beans**.

Warm Dressing: Use hot bacon grease directly on a spinach salad as a dressing or combine and heat 3 slices of cooked, crumbled bacon with its grease, ¼ cup vinegar and 1 tsp sugar.

Wrap a slice of bacon around **filet mignon** before cooking.

Add bacon to **fried rice**. Use the grease to actually fry the rice after cooking.

Sandwich: Bacon, lettuce and tomato is still a favorite. Add a slice or two of bacon to your **hamburger**.

Re-use the grease. Our dog appreciates our conscientious recycling of grease in her food.

With Sauce: Remember chipped beef on toast? Why not make a white sauce (see Sauces and Gravies in this section), stir in cooked bacon bits instead, with peas or mixed vegetables. Serve on toast, bagels or over pasta.

Sausage or Meat Substitute: Add partially cooked slices of bacon to chili or lasagna, when you don't have sausage.

Skewer small slices of bacon with other vegetables and have a **shish kebab**.

Stir-fry with bacon instead of meat. Slice and cook an apple and onion and serve over rice.

Beans (dry peas, lentils, legumes)

Benefits: High in fiber, protein and iron; stabilizes blood sugar; low in fat

Seasonings to use with beans: (See also Green Beans and Kidney Beans in this section.)

LIMA BEANS:
Basil
Butter/Margarine
Cayenne
Celery Seed
Chervil
Chives
Lemon Juice
Marjoram
Mustard
Onion/Scallion
Parsley
Pepper, Black
Rosemary
Sage
Savory

NEW ENGLAND BAKED:
(white pea beans are best)
Curry Powder
Mustard
Onion/Scallion
Syrups & Extracts-molasses
Vinegar
Worcestershire Sauce

NAVY BEANS (Boston)**:**
Cheese
Garlic
Mustard
Oils & Fats-olive
Onion/Scallion
Syrups & Extracts-molasses

PORK & BEANS
Cayenne
Chili Powder
Liquid Smoke
Mustard
Onion/Scallion
Pepper, Black
Syrups & Extracts-maple, molasses
Thyme

*Beans, beans that musical fruit.
The more you eat the more you toot!*

How to Cook:

Above 3,000 feet, add 25% more cooking time, unless you are using a pressure cooker. See following pages. If you can mash it, it is cooked enough. Use digestive spices (bay leaf, cumin and fennel) to avoid gas.

Water your plants with the *soaking* water. Use water from *cooked* beans for soup, sauce or gravy stock.

Mix beans with grains, seeds, dairy or meat to make a complete protein.

Buying Guide:

Avoid cracked seams, wrinkled and dull beans. Presoaked beans are available, if time is a problem.

Never eat beans raw.

1 cup dry = 2-2½ cups cooked

Preparation Ideas:

Add basil, lemon juice and Parmesan to your cooked beans.

Add molasses, mustard, cayenne, spicy sausage links or hot dogs to beans; for a barbeque flavor, add Liquid Smoke to spice up canned **pork and beans**.

Add celery, onion, orange concentrate and mustard to **baked beans**.

Burrito: Add beans to corn, rice and Mexican spices to make burritos. Add ground beef or shredded chicken for meat.

Put 1 lb **lentils** (3½ cups) into a pot with a large cut up potato, a medium chopped onion, 2 bay leaves and 2 quarts water. Cook covered 3 hours until beans are tender. Add 2 cups milk, 2 cups cream and 2 tsp salt. Add sausage links.

Quick Baked: Combine 1 can (1 lb) baked beans, 2 Tbsp brown sugar, 1 tsp dry mustard and 1 tsp instant coffee. Warm in the oven.

Succotash: Boil 2 cups frozen **lima beans** in water until tender. Add 2 cups frozen corn. Separately, sauté 1 chopped onion and tomato. Add ⅛ tsp nutmeg, pepper and ¼ cup yogurt or cream, keeping the heat low. Add beans and corn and warm throughout. Mix in 2 Tbsp grated Parmesan.

Cooking with Beans (dry peas, lentils, legumes)

Beans are healthy and inexpensive. They have incomplete proteins (adding seeds, dairy, grains or meat will complete it), fiber and most vitamins and minerals, especially iron. Beans absorb water as they pass through the body, thus making you think you are fuller than you are, so you eat less. Their mild flavor lends itself to most seasonings, so you can be creative.

Soak to Avoid Gas: Gas is created by carbo-hydrates (sugars) in beans. Most gas (95%) is odorless, but oh that remaining 5% . . . . To mitigate, soak beans overnight in lots of water, discard or water your plants with the liquid, rinse them well and then cook them in fresh water. Before soaking throw away pebbles and wrinkled or cracked beans. If beans are crunchy, they are not cooked enough to avoid gas. Cook them until you can mash several easily with a fork. *Add bay leaf, cumin or fennel to help with gas. The easiest beans to digest are mung, lentils, black-eyed peas, anasazi and adzuki.*

A Quicker Option: A shorter soaking method that further reduces gas is to cover the beans in cold water by about 2", bring them to a boil and let simmer for 5 minutes. Remove from heat and let stand for 2 hours covered. Drain the water, rinse and cook. To check whether the beans have soaked long enough, cut one in half. The color should be consistent throughout with no white or hard parts. Lentils, mung beans and split peas do not require soaking and take less time to cook.

Spice After Cooking: *Do not add salt, soy sauce, sugar or acidic foods, such as tomatoes or wine until after the beans are cooked.* These ingredients will toughen the bean and slow down the cooking process. Baking soda supposedly speeds up cooking, but, at the same time, it depletes minerals and makes the beans soggy. After cooking add ½-¾ tsp salt for every cup of dried beans and spice generously.

Stove Top Cooking: After soaking, cook the beans in a heavy, covered pan with a ratio of 3-4 units of cold water for every one unit of beans. Let the water come to a boil, then reduce the heat and simmer (boiling will disintegrate them) about 3 hours until tender. Add water during cooking, if necessary, to prevent beans from sticking to the pan.

Baking: After soaking you can boil the beans for 20 minutes and bake them in a covered dish at 350⁰ for 3½ hours.

Fastest Cooking: Cooking beans in a pressure cooker (15 pounds of pressure) with a tablespoon of oil is the quickest option. Allow 8-10 minutes for split peas and lentils, 18-20 minutes for most other beans and 30 minutes for soybeans or garbanzos. See the chart on the next page.

Simmering on the stove top takes longer in higher altitudes, but pressure cooking times remain the same. *Variances will occur depending upon the size of your pressure cooker and the amount and size of the beans being prepared.*

Because of the time involved in cooking beans, cook a lot and store leftovers in freezer bags for up to six months. One pound uncooked beans is equivalent to about six 1-cup cooked servings.

𝓑ean 𝓥arieties: Soaking Required

NAME	DESCRIPTION TASTE	SIMMER	PRESSURE COOK (2 cups dry)	USED IN OR WITH (SW means Southwest)
Adzuki	Light brown; Sweet	1 hr.	8 min	SW cuisine with rice; easy to digest
Anasazi	Mottled red and white; Sweet	1 hr.	8 min	Very digestible; Mexican & SW cooking
Black (Turtle)	Black-skinned, kidney-shaped; Creamy, earthy	1½ hr.	11 min	Soups, Mexican & SW cooking
Cranberry (Roman)	Chubby like cranberries; Sweet, like pinto	1½ hr.	12 min	Also **Borlotti** in Italian cooking; used in New England succotash
Fava (Horse, Broad)	Bright green, large; Creamy, earthy, sweet	1½ hr.	13 min	Mediterranean foods, soups (peel off skins after soaking)
Garbanzo (Chickpea)	Small, tan; Nutty	2 hr.	13 min	Used world-wide, lots of iron; good in minestrone
Great Northern	White, kidney-shaped; Sweet	1½ hr.	13 min	Good with ham
Kidney	Maroon, kidney-shaped; Chalky, nutty, sweet	1½ hr.	13 min	SW dishes, casseroles, chili, soups
Kidney, White (Cannellini)	Long fat kidney-shaped; Tastes like navy beans	1½ hr.	13 min	Bean salads, minestrone, soups
Lima (Butter)	Light green to yellow, oval; Dry, nutty, buttery	1 hr.	8 min	Succotash, soups, stews; hard to digest; good source of protein
Navy (Pea, Marrow)	White; Sweet	1¼ hr.	9 min	Soups, salads, **Boston Baked beans**
Pea, Pidgeon	Grayish-yellow pea; Sweet	¾-1 hr.	10 min	Southern US; cook like a dry bean
Pinto or Pink	Spotted pink and brown; Sweet	1½ hr.	8 min	Mexican and SW dishes, refried beans
Red	Smaller red kidney; Nutty	1 hr.	8 min	Chili, 3-bean salad, Cajun cooking, rice
Soybean	Round with seeds; Nutty, low in flavor	2- 2½ hr.	20 min	As tofu: stir-frys, soups, salads; hard to digest; cooks slowly, high in protein & fat

𝓑ean 𝓥arieties: No Soaking Required

NAME	DESCRIPTION TASTE	SIMMER	PRESSURE COOK (2 cups dry)	USED IN OR WITH
Green (Snap, String)	Long slender pods with seeds; Light, nutty	Microwave See Green Beans		With salty meats, easy to digest, great with roasted almonds or lightly sautéed
Lentils	Green, coral, red or brown; Light flavor	1½ hr.	10 min	Coral: soups, best flavor, cooks fast Brown & Green: salads; easy to digest
Mung	Small; Watery	¾-1 hr.	8 min	Indian curries, Chinese dishes, stews; Sprouts are *bean sprouts*; easy to digest.
Peas, split	Light green or yellow; Sweet	½ hr.	10 min	Cooks quickly, soups
Winged (Goa)	Mix of pinto and green bean	Microwave See Green Beans		Discovered in 1974; Good with nuts; prepare as you would green beans

Beef/Veal (burgers, chili, meatloaf, spaghetti)

Benefits: 18% protein, contains all of the necessary amino acids, 22% fat

Seasonings to use with beef/veal:

Allspice-spaghetti
Basil-meatloaf, spaghetti, veal
Bay Leaf-chili, kabobs, veal
Beer-chili, tenderizer
Bouillon Cubes-soups, stews
Cardamom-chili
Cayenne-chili, spaghetti, tacos
Celery Seed-meatloaf
Chili Powder-chili, meatloaf, spaghetti, tacos
Cloves-chili, meatloaf
Cumin-chili, meatloaf, tacos
Fennel
Fenugreek
Garlic-chili, meatloaf, spaghetti, veal

Ginger-cuts fattiness
Horseradish-corned beef, liver
Leeks
Lemon Juice
Liquid Smoke-chili, meatloaf, spaghetti
Lovage-stew
Marjoram-chili, meatloaf, stew, veal
Mint-ground beef
Mustard-burgers, helps digestion
Onion/Scallion-chili, spaghetti
Oregano- chili, meatloaf, spaghetti, tacos
Paprika-chili
Parsley-meatloaf

Pepper, Bell
Pepper, Chile-chili
Rosemary-meatloaf, veal
Sage-veal
Savory-BBQ, meatloaf, veal
Shallot
Sorrel
Syrups & Extracts-molasses
Tabasco--chili, burgers, steak
Tarragon-veal
Thyme-chili, meatloaf, spaghetti, veal
Tomato-chili, meatloaf, spaghetti
Vinegar-chili
Wine-tenderizer
Worcestershire Sauce-steak

How to Cook:
Fully cooked meats have clear juices. Cook tough cuts with low fat (including veal) slowly and simmer covered. Cook tender cuts fast (broil). Roasting at low temperatures lessens shrinkage and retains juice.

Roast fat side up. Brush with oil, if slow roasting lean meat. Allow ¼ lb per serving without bones, ⅓ lb with bones. Rewrap meats before freezing, since store packaging is good for only 2 weeks. Ground beef can be frozen 3-4 months.

Buying Guide:
The more expensive the cut (that is, *prime* or *choice*), the more fat it has in it. Rump or rounds have the least fat; chuck has the most. Veal is very lean. The whiter the veal meat the more tender it is.

Preparation Ideas:

Burgers: To make burgers more enticing, splurge and purchase a spicy mustard from a specialty store.

Burritos: Ground beef, spiced up with cayenne, salsa, chili powder, onions, cumin and your favorites, a can of pork and beans and a can of corn (cream corn also works) makes good-tasting burritos. Pinto or black beans can be substituted. Melt pepper cheese over it. Add tomato sauce if you want it juicier. Add arrowroot to thicken. Use instant rice instead of beans. How's that for quick, easy and tasty? Don't forget the tortillas.

Do not salt beef until after cooking to retain juices and avoid toughness.

Beef liver *is high in iron, should be light red and should not smell. Tenderize by soaking in milk. Cook quickly on high heat.*

Tripe is the cream-colored lining of a cow's stomach and is precooked. **Menudo** *is tripe soup.*

Beef/Veal Preparation Ideas continued:

Chili: Empty a large can each of pork and beans, tomato sauce and kidney beans in a pot. Add mustard, onion and garlic powder. Take 1-1½ lb ground beef and brown it in a skillet. Add lots of chili powder, garlic and onion powder to taste, drain grease and re-spice. For an outdoor flavor add Liquid Smoke. Mix beans and meat. Warm throughout and serve or let simmer in a crockpot. For a nice touch add 1-2 Tbsp molasses. Add cayenne or chile peppers to make it even hotter. Mom added macaroni to make it go a little further.

Corned Beef: The brisket or stringy chest muscles of cattle require slow cooking to tenderize—great for a crockpot. Soaked in brine and seasonings, today corned beef is less salty and redder than in the past. Combine it with cabbage or make Reuben sandwiches with sauerkraut. The same meat, spiced differently, is used in London broil and in making fajitas.

Meatloaf: The key to a good meatloaf is cooking it slowly to prevent drying it out. An egg or 2 and some oatmeal help to hold it together (which also holds in fat, so buy lean ground beef). Liquid Smoke gives it that outdoor grill taste. Bread or bacon on the bottom keeps it from sticking. Salt after cooking.

Shepherd's Pie: Make mashed potatoes. Cook ground beef and partially cook frozen vegetables. Combine and spice with pepper, cardamom, rosemary and garlic. Put part of it in a bowl and form the mashed potatoes over it. Add grated Swiss cheese and/or make a gravy from the ground beef grease to pour over the top. Cook in the microwave to melt the cheese and warm throughout or bake 15 minutes to brown the top.

Spaghetti: Cook ground beef sprinkling with cayenne and chili powder, drain off grease, add lots of Italian spices: oregano, thyme and rosemary. Add 1-2 cans tomato sauce and 1 small can of tomato paste. Add garlic. A little sugar eases the acidity. A little vinegar makes the hot spices *kick in*. No time to let it simmer? Don't worry it will taste better tomorrow. Add mushrooms if you like. For a quick sauce buy jarred sauce and add mushrooms, onions and/or other spices.

Stuffed Leftovers: Use leftover chili and stuff a tomato or bell pepper with it, bake it and sprinkle with a hot or spicy cheese.

Large pots of stew or chili are good for several days, depending upon the size of your family. With two it can last a week. The prep time is worth not having to cook all week long!

Scaloppine *are thin slices of meat from the loin or leg of a young calf (veal). Larger than ¼" thick refers to a* **cutlet**.

Steak: Broil or grill well. Add barbeque sauce, Liquid Smoke and/or your favorite spices. Wrap a filet mignon with a strip of bacon before broiling.

Stew: Use ground beef or stew meat. Brown it, add chili powder, cayenne and drain the grease. Add more cayenne. Put it in a crockpot. Add tomatoes and/or tomato sauce, onions, garlic, Italian spices and 3 bay leaves. Add 3-4 cut potatoes and 1 lb sliced carrots. The crockpot should be full. Slow cook it while you are at work. If it is too spicy, add a little molasses. Salt to taste. If it is not spicy enough, add pepper or 2-3 Tbsp vinegar. This is incredibly good and makes great leftovers. Include no more than 2 pods of cardamom for a more exotic flavor. Add zucchini in the last 15-20 minutes.

Beverages

Seasonings to use with beverages:

Allspice
Angelica
Anise
Cardamom
Cinnamon
Chocolate

Cloves
Coffee
Coriander
Cream & Milk
Ginger
Honey

Lemon Juice
Mint
Nutmeg
Sugar
Syrups & Extracts
Vanilla

How to Cook:
Always start with cold water when making coffee or tea. Use double the dry coffee to make iced coffee.
Punch tips: Use 4 oz cups for before-dinner drinks or with punch; 8 oz cups with meals.

Pour carbonated fluids along the side of the bowl or glass to maintain carbonation. Remove strong alcohol taste in punch by adding cucumber slices.

Buying Guide:
With store-bought beverages, check the dates, the sugar and caffeine content and decide accordingly.

Beans and leaves are tastier than ground coffee or teabags.

Preparation Ideas:

Apple Cider: Heat apple juice. Add a cinnamon stick.

Cocoa: Peppermint, cream, mint or chocolate-flavored liqueurs in hot chocolate are quite yummy. These go well in coffee, too.

Coffee: Try extracts, syrups, chocolate, cardamom, cinnamon, coriander or cream. **Iced Coffee:** 1 cup cold milk, 4 tsp instant coffee, 2 tsp sugar and 2 ice cubes. Blend until smooth.

Eggnog: Separate 3 eggs. Beat ⅛ cup sugar into each. Add 1½ cups milk, ½ tsp vanilla and ¼ cup bourbon or rum to the yolks. Fold beaten whites into yolk mixture and sprinkle with nutmeg. Warm the milk, if you prefer a hot drink.

Lemonade: Mix 1 cup lemon juice, 3 cups water and 5 Tbsp sugar. Makes 3 cups.

Basic Punch: (Serves 10) Combine ½ cup sugar, 12 sticks cinnamon, ½ tsp whole cloves and ½ cup water in a saucepan. Boil and let simmer, covered for 10 minutes. Toss out spices and chill. Add 3 cups apple juice, 12 oz of apricot nectar and ¼ cup lemon juice. To this add 6 cups dry white wine, 2 cups of brandy, rum or other liquor or if non-alcoholic punch, use 2-28 oz bottles of a fruit-flavored carbonated beverage.

Smoothies: Blend fruit(s) especially peaches, strawberries and bananas. Add ice, plain yogurt and vanilla. Try a different extract/syrup to vary flavor.

Tea: Add allspice, angelica, cinnamon, cloves, ginger, mint, honey or an edible flower. **Sun Tea:** Put 4 teabags and 1½ quarts of cold water in a glass container in the full sun for 2½ hours.

Warm Milk: Drink warm milk with peppermint leaves to calm your stomach, for cramps or insomnia. Add extracts, such as vanilla or coconut, for flavor.

Water: Add 1 cup crushed mint to ½ gallon ice water.

Breads, Muffins, Biscuits (scones, rolls)

Seasonings to use with breads, muffins, biscuits:

Allspice	Cream & Milk	Poppy Seeds
Basil	Cream, Sour-buttermilk	Raisins
Butter/Margarine	Dill	Rosemary
Caraway Seed-rye	Fennel	Sesame Seeds
Cardamom	Ginger	Star Anise
Cheese	Honey	Sugar
Cinnamon	Lemon Juice	Syrups & Extracts-anise, orange
Cloves	Nutmeg	Tarragon-pumpernickel, rye
Coriander	Nuts	Vanilla

How to Cook:

The key is not to stir too much. For moistness use applesauce instead of oil; use equal parts wheat or cake flour with all purpose flour for lighter biscuits and muffins. Biscuits baked closely together will be soft; crispy if spread apart.

Dark pans darken pastries quicker than light pans.
Because quick breads need moisture, place a cup of hot water ⅓ full in a *gas* oven. Place a hot muffin pan on a wet towel to prevent sticking.

Buying Guide:

If buying mixes for muffins, batter should be lumpy— do not over mix. Buy the mix and spice as you like. *A Busy Cook* does not have time to make yeast breads and thus, they are not included.

Preparation Ideas:

Baking Powder Biscuits: Mix together 2 cups flour, 4 tsp baking powder and ½ tsp salt. Cut in 2½ Tbsp margarine the size of blueberries. Make a well in the center. Pour in ¾ cup milk. Mix after all the flour is moistened. Knead on floured board 20 seconds and roll to ½" thick. Cut with a cookie cutter, bake at 450° for 10-15 minutes. Makes about 18-24.

You can make **breakfast sandwiches** by rolling the above to ¼" thick. Stuff them with cheese and either ham or bacon. Press the ends together and brush the tops and sides with milk. Bake at 475°, 10-12 minutes. Or cut in long triangles, add a little cheese or jam and roll them up in a crescent shape.

Buy the little **box muffin mixes** and add cinnamon, allspice, nutmeg or maple extract for fun. Make muffins or a small loaf bread. Throw in an overripe banana in a banana nut mix. Nuts and raisins are good, too.

Since a cup of margarine or butter contains ½ tsp salt, do not add salt to a baking recipe calling for both it and butter.

Add extracts such as anise, butter, orange, lemon, maple or vanilla for a variety in bread flavors. Baking with maple makes your house smell delicious. Use a sprig of herbs as a basting brush with melted butter or olive oil.

Substitute dried fruit, such as cranberries or bananas, if you are out of raisins and want something different. Add nuts for crunchiness.

Breads, Muffins, Biscuits Preparation Ideas continued:

Breakfast Ham & Cheese Muffins: Sift 2 cups flour, ¼ cup sugar, 1 Tbsp baking powder and 1½ tsp baking soda. Combine 1 cup yogurt, ½ cup melted butter and 2 beaten eggs. Add yogurt mix to dry mix and stir. Fold in 1¼ cups shredded cheddar or mozzarella cheese, ½ cup chopped ham and 1 tsp basil. Bake 400° for 20 minutes. Makes 12.

Buttermilk Bread: Mix 4 cups flour, 1 tsp sugar, 1 tsp baking soda and 2 tsp cream of tartar. Add 1 beaten egg and 1½ cups buttermilk. Cook in a greased loaf pan at 350° for 35 minutes.

Cheese Muffins: Mix 2 cups flour and 1 Tbsp baking powder. Add ½ cup (2 oz) of your favorite shredded cheese. Separately, blend 2 eggs, 1 cup milk and 2 Tbsp melted butter. Add liquid to flour mix and stir only enough to dampen the flour. Fill greased muffins ⅔ full. Bake 400° for 15 minutes until golden.

Cheese & Nut Crackers: Mix ¼ lb grated cheddar cheese with 1 Tbsp margarine, ½ cup flour, ¼ tsp cayenne, ¼ tsp sage and ¼ cup finely ground pecans. Form into a small long roll and chill overnight. Slice thin and bake ungreased for 11 minutes at 350°.

Corn Coffee Cake: Beat ½ cup butter with 1 cup sugar until fluffy. Add 3 eggs, one at a time, beating well. Add 1 tsp vanilla. Separately, mix ½ cup cornmeal, 1½ cups flour, 2 tsp baking soda and ¼ tsp salt. Add this to butter mix in thirds alternately with ⅔ cup buttermilk. Stir in 1 cup chopped pecans. Bake 30 minutes at 350° in oiled 9" x 13" pan. Remove and pour ⅔ cup maple syrup on top. Bake 5 more minutes.

Cornbread: Stir 1 cup flour, 1 cup yellow cornmeal, ¼ cup sugar, 4 tsp baking powder and ¾ tsp salt. Add 2 eggs, 1 cup milk and ¼ cup oil (applesauce also works). Beat until smooth. Bake in greased square pan at 425° for 25 minutes.

Stuff **Crescent Rolls** with cream cheese and jam or spice with garlic or rosemary. **Dinner Idea:** Spread rolls open, (2 rows of triangles joined at the wide end). Drain 1 can tuna. Add craisins, celery and frozen peas. Mix with mustard to make 2 cups of filling. Mound this over center of rolls. Wrap triangle tips toward the center. Bake same as rolls.

Sweetbreads *are not what you think. They are glands from the heart and throat of a cow, lamb or pig.*

Add 1 Tbsp of rosemary or cayenne to **cornbread**.

Quick Cinnamon Rolls: Buy biscuits, dunk in egg whites and then into a cinnamon sugar blend. Bake as directions say.

Corn Muffins: Mix 1 cup yellow cornmeal, 1 cup flour, 2 tsp baking soda, ½ tsp salt and ½ cup brown sugar. Separately, beat 1 egg, 2 Tbsp oil and 1-16 oz can of creamed corn. Add to dry ingredients. Add ½ cup raisins (optional). Fill greased muffin pan ⅔ full and bake 20 min at 350°.

Dumplings: Cream 6 Tbsp butter. Add 3 beaten eggs. Add 1 cup fine cracker crumbs, 1½ tsp salt and your favorite flavorings. Stir, shape into balls and drop into 2 quarts boiling, salted (2 tsp) water until they float. Then cover tightly, simmer 13-15 minutes until dry and spongy inside and remove. (If it comes apart, add more crumbs.) Serve with butter or sauce (see Sauces and Gravies in this section).

Breads, Muffins, Biscuits Preparation Ideas continued:

Nut Bread: Beat 2 egg whites, 2 cups skim milk, 1 tsp vanilla and 1 Tbsp margarine. Separately, combine 3 cups flour, 1 cup rolled oats, ¾ cup sugar, 1½ tsp allspice, ½ tsp cinnamon, ⅛ tsp salt, 4 tsp baking powder. Mix this and ⅔ cup chopped walnuts in milk mixture. Bake 325° for 50 minutes in greased loaf pan.

Peanut Butter Tea Bread: Mix 2 cups flour, 4 tsp baking powder, ½ tsp salt and ¼ cup sugar. Separately, blend 1¼ cups milk and ⅔ cup peanut butter. Add dry ingredients and blend thoroughly. Bake in greased loaf pan 350° for 45 minutes.

Popovers: Blend until smooth: 1 cup milk, 3 eggs,1 tsp sugar, 2 Tbsp butter and 1 cup flour. Fill muffin tin by ½, bake 35-40 minutes at 400° until brown and firm to touch. Do not open oven until they are done. Serve hot. Makes 12.

Pumpkin Cake Roll (8): Beat 3 eggs for 5 minutes on high. Beat in 1 cup sugar. Stir in ⅔ cup pumpkin and 1 tsp lemon juice. Separately, mix ¾ cup flour, 1 tsp each baking powder and ginger, ½ tsp nutmeg and 2 tsp cinnamon. Fold into the pumpkin mix. Spread on greased 9" x 13" pan. Top with finely chopped walnuts. Bake 15 minutes at 375°. Turn it onto a towel, sprinkle with powdered sugar and roll towel and cake together into a roll and let cool. **Filling:** Beat 1 cup powdered sugar, 6 oz cream cheese, 4 Tbsp margarine and ½ tsp vanilla until smooth. Spread over unrolled cake and re-roll.

Pumpkin Tea Bread: Stir 2⅔ cups flour, ½ tsp baking soda, 1 tsp cinnamon, ½ tsp nutmeg and ½ tsp allspice. Add ½ cup butter until mealy. Add ⅔ cup sugar. Separately, stir 2 Tbsp corn syrup, 1 cup pumpkin and 1 cup buttermilk. Add the flour mix and blend with a spoon. It will be stiff. Bake in a loaf pan 1 hour at 375°. Cool 30 minutes and remove from pan.

Paula's B&B Scones: Mix 1⅔ cup flour, 4 tsp baking powder, ⅔ tsp baking soda, ⅔ cup sugar and ⅔ cup butter. Add ⅔ cup oatmeal and ⅓ cup cranberries, currants, raisins or dates. Dough is dry and flaky. Add ⅓ cup buttermilk. Knead and flatten with fingers in a 9" x 13" greased pan. Precut before cooking at 375° for 23 minutes.

*A **tart** is a pie with only a bottom crust. They may have been used before dinner plates came along.*

Keep powdered buttermilk to use when you need just a little for baking.

Spoon Bread: To make this custard, mix 2 cups milk, 2 Tbsp butter, 1 Tbsp sugar and ¼ tsp cayenne in a saucepan until bubbles appear. Off the heat whisk in 1 cup cornmeal until smooth and thick. Let cool. Pour half the batter in a casserole dish. Add bacon, ham or leftover chili and add 1 cup cheddar, 1 cup Monterey Jack or ½ cup Parmesan cheese. Then add the rest of the batter. Bake at 350° for 40 minutes until puffy and golden brown.

Shortbread Bars: Sift 1 cup corn starch with 1⅔ cups flour. Cream 1 cup butter and ½ cup sugar. Combine until stiff enough to knead. Press into 12" x 8" pan. Cut almost through with a knife and make holes with a fork. Bake at 325° for 35 minutes until golden. Re-cut. For more flavor add 1 tsp lemon or almond extract. Use this recipe to press into large cookie molds.

Baking: Flour & Baking Powder/Soda

Flour

Wheat is the most common kind of flour used in cooking and baking. Wheat contains gluten, which holds the gases that make baked items rise and yeast stretch. Most of the nutrients in wheat are killed from heat generated in the grinding process, so they are added back later. **Stone-ground** flour retains nutrients because heat is not used.

All-purpose bleached or **unbleached** flours, which can be stored for 15 months, are interchangeable, although bleached is fluffier and unbleached is more flavorful. The flour, that has had nutrients (wheat germ) added back in is labeled **enriched. Whole wheat (also graham) flour** has wheat germ, should be refrigerated and lasts 6 months. For healthier recipes substitute half the **all purpose flour** with **whole wheat flour** and let dough sit for 5 minutes.

Bread flour is high in gluten. You can tell by how much protein is stated on the package. Bread flour has 11-12% protein and is good for yeast bread making. **Pastry flour** is low in gluten with about 8% protein and is better for croissants, cookies, biscuits, pie crusts and light pastries. **All-purpose flour** is a mix of bread and pastry flours. **Instant flour** is used to make "lumpless" gravy.

Watch out for **self-rising flours**. They contain baking powder and salt, which your recipe may also say to add. **Barley, rye and oat flour** must be combined with a gluten flour to make baked items rise.

You can substitute **quick-cooking oats** for **rolled oats** in a recipe. However, quick-cooking is not the same as **instant oats**. Instant oats *should not* be substituted for rolled oats in a recipe. Oat flour is easy to make by just mixing oats in a blender. Oats in most forms are high in vitamins.

There is no need to sift flour since it comes pre-sifted. Just do not tap it down when measuring.

Baking Powder/Soda

Double-Acting vs. Single-Acting Baking Powder. Modern US recipes assume double-acting baking powder, while non-US recipes assume single-acting. Both are made of baking soda, an acid (which releases gas) and cornstarch. Single-acting releases gas as soon as it touches liquid (as does baking soda by itself); double-acting releases gas first when it contacts liquid, and second, when it is heated. Allow 1 tsp of double-acting baking powder per cup of flour in quick breads and muffins (*less at higher altitudes*) and 1½ tsp per cup of flour in biscuits. **Cream of tartar** is actually the acid used in some baking powders to release carbon dioxide gas. Both powder and soda last about 18 months.

*The term **flouring** means lightly dusting the bottom of a pan with flour after first greasing it with a spray or other oil. The flour attaches to the oil. Dust evenly and throw out excess.*

Broccoli & Brussels Sprouts

Benefits: Very low in calories, high in vitamins A and C, calcium and iron

Seasonings to use with broccoli . . .

Basil	Mustard	
Bay Leaf	Nutmeg-pinch only	
Butter/Margarine	Nuts-almonds	
Caraway Seed	Oregano	
Cheese	Paprika	
Curry Powder	Pepper, Black	
Dill	Sesame Seeds	
Garlic	Shallot	
Lemon Juice	Tarragon	
Marjoram	Thyme	

and Brussels sprouts:

Butter/Margarine
Cheese
Cumin
Dill
Fennel
Garlic
Mint
Mustard
Nuts
Tomato

How to Cook:

Broccoli: Remove leaves and peel stalks. Cut into uniform 1" pieces. Cook 1 lb 6-8 minutes in a covered pan in a little boiling water, or 8 minutes for whole spears in a microwave. Steaming takes twice as long, if using whole spears.

Broccoli means *cabbage sprout* in Italian and is related to cabbage.
1 bunch = ½ to 2 lb
Brussels sprouts: Remove outer leaves. Cut an X in base. Microwave 1 lb 8-10 minutes in ¼ cup water. Stir-fry 5 minutes covered. *Add ¼ tsp baking soda to water to cut odor.*

Buying Guide:

Choose **broccoli** that is deep green, avoiding yellowish, wilted flowerets. Also avoid stems that are too thick. The leaves should be crisp.

Select small, firm dark green **Brussels sprouts**.

Preparation Ideas:

Make a mustard or cheese dip for broccoli and eat as an **appetizer**. Add curry powder to the dip.

Try broccoli with sautéed almonds and celery.

Cheese & Broccoli: Melt cheddar cheese with butter and/or mustard and pour over broccoli or Brussels sprouts. Add ham and pasta and you have a casserole. Add croutons or nuts for texture.

Add broccoli to a cold **pasta salad** with almonds and lemon juice.

Brussels Sprouts Casserole: Cook 1½ lb sprouts until tender. Put in a casserole. Cover with 1 cup stewed tomatoes. Separately, mix ½ cup grated cheddar, 2 tsp flour and 1 cup yogurt. Pour over sprouts. Bake covered at 350° for 15 minutes. Garnish with chopped almonds.

Brussels sprouts are not just for Thanksgiving. Cook until tender; they are wonderful with butter.

Soup: Broccoli (2 cups) holds up well when boiled with 4-5 diced potatoes to make a soup. When tender let them cool. Blend half of the mixture in a blender along with the water they were boiled in and then combine with the rest for a chunky soup. Add any of the above seasonings, some diced ham or spicy links. Add 1½ cups milk to thin.

Cabbage (coleslaws)

Cabbage Varieties: Kale, Kohlrabi, Napa, Red (more vitamin C and easier to digest than white) and Savoy
Benefits: High in vitamin C and fiber, low in sodium and calories; good for complexion;
Chard leaves are rich in protein, a natural laxative and sedative

Seasonings to use with cabbage:

Allspice-red cabbage	Fennel	Oregano
Basil	Garlic	Paprika
Bay Leaf	Lemon Juice	Pepper, White
Burnet	Marjoram	Raisins
Butter/Margarine	Mint-spearmint	Sage
Caraway Seed-boiled, salads	Mustard	Savory
Cayenne	Nutmeg	Tarragon
Cumin	Nuts-chestnuts, pecans, walnuts	Thyme
Dill	Onion/Scallion	Vinegar-cider

How to Cook:

Blanch in hot salted water or spice with caraway seed for better digestion. Peel, clean, slice and trim **kohlrabi** ends before cooking high for 13 minutes in microwave. Boil shredded **cabbage** 6-7 minutes in a covered pan. Red takes longer.

1 lb head cabbage = 4 cups

Chard stems taste like asparagus; cooked leaves taste like spinach.

Add lemon juice or vinegar to cooking water to preserve color. Add ¼ tsp baking soda to boiling water to keep it from smelling.

Buying Guide:

Choose small tightly closed **cabbages**. Avoid ones that are strong smelling or have cracked heads. **Kale** has more vitamins than cabbage even after cooking.

Preparation Ideas:

Sal's Coleslaw: Grate 2-3 carrots, 2 scallions and a small head of cabbage. Add 4-5 diced red radishes and salt. Start with a ¼ cup vinegar and 1-2 Tbsp mayonnaise. Try flavored vinegars for fun. The vegetables tend to "sweat" and fluid increases over time—as does the taste!

Mix crushed caraway seeds into your **coleslaw**. Or minced burnet.

Shred **red cabbage**. Add 1 cup boiling water and ¼ cup vinegar. Let stand for 10 minutes. Drain and add 1 Tbsp sugar to the liquid. Brown the cabbage in a pan with butter; add the liquid back with ¼ cup raisins and ½ cup chopped pecans.

Mix **cabbage** with noodles, add bacon, butter and caraway seeds. Add carrots for color and sweetness.

Corned beef and . . .

The meat of choice with the cabbage family is pork, including ham and bacon.

Serve **kohlrabi**, which has a nutty flavor, with white sauces and caraway seed and fennel. It can also be eaten raw in salads and vegetables dishes.

Use shredded Chinese/Napa cabbages in **stir-frys**. They are barrel-shaped and sweet. They also have a shorter life.

Cabbage Preparation Ideas continued:

Cabbage & Apples: Just cover 1 shredded red cabbage, 2 grated apples, 1 grated potato and 3 Tbsp vinegar with water and boil. Reduce heat, cover pan and simmer until cabbage is soft, about 5 minutes. Drain, salt and pepper to taste. Add caraway seed. Or cube the apples, leave out the potato and do not boil, but let simmer for 15 minutes and add a little brown sugar, vinegar and caraway seed.

Cabbage Au Gratin: Put a layer of chopped cabbage into a buttered dish. Sprinkle with grated cheese and your favorite spice. Cover with a white sauce (see Sauces and Gravies in this section). Keep repeating using a total of ½ a cabbage and 2 cups of sauce. Cover with cracker crumbs and butter and bake until browned at 350°.

Cabbage-Cheese Soup: Simmer in a covered pan ½ head shredded cabbage, 1 shredded carrot and 3½ cups milk until vegetables are tender (10 minutes). Mix and then add ¼ tsp crushed caraway seed, 1 cup shredded Swiss cheese, 1 Tbsp cornstarch and black pepper until thickened and cheese melts.

Cabbage & Jicama Salad: Shred 1 lb or 4 cups of cabbage and 1 medium carrot. Chop 3 scallions. Cut 1 small jicama (a zucchini or cucumber will also work) in 2" strips after peeling. Add 1 tsp ginger. Cover with an oil and vinegar dressing. Add nuts for crunchiness. Try adding a little lemon juice or even a flavored honey. A **jicama** is a potato-like vegetable eaten raw or cooked, tasting sweet and watery.

Cabbage with Pecans: Cut a bouillon cube in half, add ¼ cup water and dissolve in a saucepan. Add ½ small shredded cabbage and ½ cup shredded carrots, 4 scallions and pepper. Simmer, covered for 5-10 minutes until tender. Separately, combine 3 Tbsp butter, less than ⅛ cup chopped pecans and 1 tsp prepared mustard and pour over cabbage mix. Serves 4.

Cabbage & Rice Soup: Bring 1 cup of chicken stock to a boil. Add ½ cup rice and 1½ Tbsp minced garlic. Simmer 15 minutes. Blend in a blender with 2 more cups of stock. After blending add 1 more cup of stock and 3 cups of shredded savoy cabbage to the sauce pan. Simmer 15 minutes on low. Add pepper. Pour over croutons in a bowl. Add cut spicy links for fun.

Sauerkraut is salted cabbage that has fermented. It can be eaten raw or cooked.

Cabbage, Fruit & Nut Coleslaw: Mix 1½-2 cups shredded cabbage, ½ cup sliced celery and ⅓ cup raisins. Combine 1 Tbsp lemon juice, ⅛ tsp salt, 1 cup plain yogurt. Pour over cabbage mix. Add 2 tart unpeeled chopped apples and ⅓ cup chopped walnuts.

Irish Colcannon: Boil 5 cut up potatoes. Sauté 3 finely chopped leeks in butter for 5 minutes until tender. Add a small head of green cabbage, coarsely chopped and 1 cup stock or chicken bouillon. Simmer 15 minutes until tender. Mash the potatoes with hot milk. Add cabbage mix to potatoes and mix. Stir in 2 Tbsp fresh chives.

Sauerkraut Casserole: Blend 1 cup sour cream, ½ cup brown sugar and 1 small can tomato paste. Add a 13-oz can of sauerkraut. Bake in greased dish 350° for 30 minutes.

Sweet & Sauerkraut: Sauté 1 chopped onion in 2 Tbsp butter. Add 3 Tbsp brown sugar and a 13-oz can of sauerkraut.

Carrot

Benefits: Low in calories, easy to digest, high in vitamin A

Seasonings to use with carrots:

Allspice	Chives	Mace
Anise	Cinnamon	Marjoram
Basil	Cloves	Mint-spearmint
Bay Leaf	Cumin	Mustard
Butter/Margarine	Curry Powder	Nuts-pecans, walnuts
Caraway Seed	Dill	Savory
Cardamom	Fenugreek	Sugar-brown
Cayenne	Ginger	Syrups & Extracts-maple, orange
Cheese	Honey	Tarragon
Chervil	Lemon Juice	Turmeric

How to Cook:

Carrots have lots of sugar and their flavor lies close to the surface, so do not peel, just wash.

Cook 15-20 minutes in boiling water in a covered pan. Microwave 8 minutes per ½ lb sliced.

Carrots add color and crunch to salads. They are boiled with celery to make soup bases or stocks.

As a garnish, they clean the palate between courses.

Buying Guide:

Look for a little green at the stem; too much green means a tough carrot. Avoid yellowness at top. Check for firmness.

Avoid canned carrots.

Preparation Ideas:

Apples & Carrots: Thinly slice 2-3 carrots at an angle. Add ⅓ cup each of orange juice, lemon juice and water, 2 tsp fresh shaved ginger root, 2 tart peeled apples sliced ¼" thick and 1 Tbsp diced scallions in a frying pan. Cover and simmer until carrots are tender.

Baked Carrots: Quarter 6 carrots lengthwise and boil covered 15 minutes until tender. Place in a buttered baking dish. Drizzle with ¼ cup honey. Sprinkle with 1 cup shredded Fontina cheese. Bake 10 minutes at 400° or until cheese bubbles.

Glaze your carrots with butter, brown sugar, cinnamon and/or cloves. Add pecans for something special.

Carrot Cake: Beat ½ cup margarine, 2 eggs and 1 cup sugar. Add 1¼ cups flour, ½ tsp baking powder, ½ tsp baking soda, 1 tsp cinnamon and ⅛ cup water. Add 1½ cups ground raw carrots and ½ cup chopped walnuts. Bake in 8" x 8" greased pan at 325°, 40 minutes. For frosting beat until smooth 4 oz cream cheese, ¼ cup margarine and ½ lb powdered sugar.

Snack: Dip raw carrots in peanut butter.

Spicy Carrots: Cook 2 cups of thinly sliced carrots with ½ tsp salt and ¼ cup water. In a saucepan, heat 3 Tbsp butter. Add 1 tsp turmeric, ¼ tsp cardamom, 1 tsp fenugreek, 1 tsp mustard seed, 1 clove chopped garlic and ¼ tsp cayenne. Add carrots to spices. Mix 1 cup yogurt with 1 Tbsp flour until smooth. Add to carrot mix. Simmer low 10 minutes.

Carrots are good in slow simmering soups and crockpots.

Cauliflower

Benefits: Low in calories, high in vitamin C and calcium, some iron.

Seasonings to use with cauliflower:

Basil	Curry Powder	Oregano
Butter/Margarine	Dill	Parsley
Caraway Seed	Garlic	Poppy Seeds
Cayenne	Ginger	Rosemary
Celery Seed	Mace	Savory
Cheese	Marjoram	Tarragon
Chives	Mustard	Tomato
Cumin	Nutmeg	Turmeric

How to Cook:
For better flavor, steam or boil the whole cauliflower. Steam 10 minutes for flowerets, 15-20 minutes for whole head. Microwave 13 minutes per lb of flowerets.

Broccoflower is a combination of broccoli and cauliflower, both in the cabbage family. **Romanesca** is a pale green cauliflower, shaped like a pyramid with a lighter flavor than regular cauliflower.

Buying Guide:
Avoid discolored flowerets or grayish leaves. Heads should be closed and tightly packed. Size is not a factor.

Preparation Ideas:

Fried Appetizer: Boil cauliflower for 10 minutes, dip flowerets in beaten egg and quick-fry in hot oil. Another way to do this is to dip flowerets in bread or cracker crumbs, then in a bowl with a beaten egg and then back into the crumbs and fry. Either way use flavored yogurt as a dipping sauce.

Cheesy Cauliflower: Cook it and add a cheddar cheese sauce (see Sauces and Gravies in this section). Mix with broccoli.

With Eggs: Add to scrambled eggs or cheese omelets.

Fondue: Use cauliflower raw in fondues.

You can **bake cauliflower** in a casserole with a cream or cheese sauce (see Sauces and Gravies in this section). Add cheese and buttered crumbs and bake at 350° until crumbs are brown. Try adding ham or crumbled bacon and spice it up with garlic and mustard.

Boil cauliflower as usual, but add broccoli and a diced potato. Blend half of it in a blender for a soup base. Add it back into the non-blended half. Use it as a **sauce** over pasta or thin it by adding milk for **soup**. Add ham or hot sausage links for meat. Add cayenne, garlic and/or onion and rosemary for flavor. Sprinkle with grated Parmesan or other cheese.

Salads: Mix diced tomatoes with cauliflower to add color to a salad or a mixed vegetable plate.

Celery & Celeriac

Benefits: Very high in potassium, cleans teeth, low in calories, good roughage

Seasonings to use with celery and celeriac:

Anise	Cumin	Nuts
Bouillon Cubes	Curry Powder	Onion/Scallion
Cayenne-red pepper flakes	Dill	Paprika
Cheese-cream cheese	Garlic	Poppy Seeds
Chives	Mint	Tomato

How to Cook:

In a crockpot, let celery slow cook in your stew or soup. Add at the end of stir-frying for a crispy texture. Microwave 13 minutes for 4 cups of ½" slices. It contains sodium, so no need to salt much. Whole anise can substitute for celery.

Technically a **stalk** is the whole plant, while a **rib** is just one piece.

Celeriac is a brown root that looks like a turnip, but can be used as a celery substitute. It has a stronger flavor and does not keep as long as celery.

Buying Guide:

Avoid limp celery. Those attached to a base will stay crisper longer than those that are sliced.

Pick smaller celeriac with few eye knobs on them.

Preparation Ideas:

A perfect vegetable for **appetizers**. Stuff with cream cheese and sprinkle with garlic, onion powder or paprika. Or, for you calorie counters, thicken some yogurt with cornstarch or drain yogurt with cheesecloth to thicken and then stuff celery ribs and spice. See Dips in this section for other stuffing ideas. Try stuffing with tuna or chicken salad or guacamole.

In college I would dip celery stalks in peanut butter for a **snack**.

Celery adds a great crunchy texture to **salads**, especially potato salad. It also blends well with nuts and cabbage. Add it to your gelatin mold.

Try it in **stir-frys** for the same crunchy reason.

Add to **soups and stews**; along with carrots, celery is an essential ingredient in soups or broths/stocks. It adds flavor, crunch, sodium and "filler" when you don't know what else to add. It also slow cooks well in crockpots.

You can freeze celery by removing strings and cutting into 1" pieces. Blanch in boiling water for 3 minutes and freeze.

Celery Casserole: Slice thinly 4 cups of celery and cook covered in 2 Tbsp butter for 7 minutes on high in a microwave. Stir midway. After 7 minutes stir in 2 Tbsp flour, 1 cup milk, ¾ cup cheese, 2½ cups sliced mushrooms, 2 Tbsp red bell pepper and 2 scallions. Microwave uncovered another 5 minutes until thick, stirring every minute. Top with more cheese. Almonds add a nice touch.

Cereal & *Oatmeal*

Seasonings to use with cereal and oatmeal:

Allspice
Cardamom-for digesting grains
Cinnamon
Cream & Milk

Honey
Mace
Nutmeg
Nuts

Raisins
Savory
Sugar-brown
Syrups & Extracts-maple

How to Cook:

Cooking cereals include **oatmeal, granola and other grains**. Follow instructions on the package, which may come pre-flavored.

Besides breakfast, use cereal for breading or coating meats, for desserts, cookies and snacks.

If cereal is stale, crispen it by microwaving for 30-45 seconds and then let stand for 1 minute.

Buying Guide:

Cereals are pricey, so look for generic brands. Spend the savings on a fruit topping. Beware of the sugar content, especially with children's cereals. Avoid sugar by reading package labels!

Preparation Ideas:

Use **corn flakes** in place of flour to coat and bake chicken or to "bread" any meat. Mix with a little honey and for a contrast add pepper.

Simple breakfast: Yogurt or soy milk can be used instead of milk in your cereal. Throw in some fruit, especially berries. Mix your cereals if one is too sweet or not sweet enough.

Granola: For a hot breakfast on cold days pour milk over granola and heat it in the microwave. Granola is more filling then light-weight cereals, such as puffed rice. Adding granola to other cereals will also add crunchiness.

Great on a cold day, try spicing up **oatmeal** with cinnamon, honey, brown sugar or fruit. Try maple syrup or your favorite jam on top. Nuts or seeds will add crunchiness.

Use **grits** as a cereal by sweetening it up the way you would oatmeal.

Dessert: Combine crisp or puffed cereals with liquid marshmallow to make bars or sprinkle cereal over ice cream.

Snacks: Mix dry cereals, fruit and/or nuts.

Try graham crackers with hot cereals. It is like getting a cookie with breakfast, but not as sweet.

Add **oatmeal** in place of some of the flour called for in a recipe. Oatmeal tends to be drier and heavier, so try using ⅔ cup oatmeal in place of one cup flour. If the recipe calls for only 1 cup flour, substituting will not work for items that need to rise. It does require some experimentation, but the results are better for you.

Heat leftover **rice** with raisins, milk and allspice for a breakfast cereal.

Mash cereal into small crumbs and use them in place of oatmeal in muffins.

Cheese

Seasonings to use with cheese:

Any Cheese:
Caraway Seed
Cumin
Fennel
Garlic
Ginger
Mint
Mustard
Nutmeg
Onion/Scallion
Paprika
Poppy Seeds
Sage
Sesame Seeds

Cottage or Mild Cheeses:
Anise
Burnet
Cayenne
Chives
Dill
Honey
Marjoram
Sage
Tarragon
Thyme

**4 oz cheese =
¼ lb shredded = 1 cup**

Cream Cheese:
Basil
Chervil
Chives
Coriander
Curry Powder
Dill
Honey
Horseradish
Mace
Mint-peppermint
Nuts-cashews
Parsley
Saffron
Tabasco

How to Cook:
The best **melting cheeses are** Munster, Cheshire (cheddar-like) and goat cheeses. The best **cooking cheeses** are Mozzarella, Bel Paese, Emmental and Gruyère. For **both melting and cooking** try Leicester.

Use cayenne with baking cheeses. Butter chesse edges to keep it from hardening.
Toss soft cheese if moldy. Cut off and discard mold on hard cheese and use the rest. Both soft and hard cheeses can be frozen 4-6 months.

Buying Guide:
Cheese should be free of mold, cracks or discoloration, such as red or grey. Blue (veined) cheeses should look moist. Pre-grated cheeses should be used quickly, since they dry out immediately.

Preparation Ideas:

Appetizers: 1) The classic treat is cheese, eaten with wine and seedless green grapes. 2) Cream cheese on crackers with garlic or onion powder or jalapeño jam is a good appetizer. Add artichoke hearts on top. 3) Cheese and crackers is a great snack when travelling. 4) Mix 3 oz of cream cheese, 3 Tbsp butter, 6 drops Tabasco and 1 Tbsp cream. Make small balls and roll them in chopped pecans.

Dessert: Use cheese as a candy substitute and tell yourself you need the calcium. Melt **cheddar** on apple pie for a treat.

Cheese Rolls: Take cream cheese or grated cheddar and place some inside a store-bought crescent roll. Add spices to suit your meal and bake per package instructions.

Rennin *is an enzyme in the gastric juice of some mammals that causes milk to curdle and is used to make cheese.*

Au Gratin *means topped with a mix of butter and crumbs or cheese and made crisp and brown in an oven or broiler.*

Use **cream cheese** with flour and milk to produce a sauce.

Cheese Preparation Ideas continued:

Beer Cheese: Beat 1 lb cubed sharp cheddar cheese until smooth. Add 1-2 cloves minced garlic, 1½ Tbsp Worcestershire and ½ tsp dry mustard. Add Tabasco to taste. Add 3-4 ozs of a nut brown beer until the texture is smooth and spreadable.

Basic Fondue: The key to fondue is good cheese. Grate, stir and set aside ¼ lb Gruyère, ¼ lb Emmental and 1 Tbsp flour. Rub a pan with a clove of garlic. Heat 1 cup wine and, before it boils, add the cheese and flour mixture. Stir until smooth and melted. Add white pepper, nutmeg and a little Kirsch. Keep under flame or put in a small crockpot. Fruit and bread are good for dipping, but veggies work also.

Gorgonzola: Have it with fruit or bread. Beat together 1 cup diced Gorgonzola with 3 Tbsp heavy cream. Spread it on slices of baguette bread. Place on a baking sheet, drizzle with honey and bake at 400° for 2 minutes or until cheese melts.

Macaroni & Cheese: Cook ½ lb macaroni, mix it with a basic white sauce (see Sauces and Gravies) and ¾ cup of grated cheddar. Bake in buttered dish with ¼ cup cheddar on top for 15 minutes at 400°. Add ham and/or frozen peas for a full meal.

Cheese Soup: Start with a white sauce by mixing 2 Tbsp butter with 2 Tbsp flour and cook low a few minutes. Slowly add 3 cups of milk. Sauté chopped onion in a little butter until soft. Add it to the soup along with ginger, curry powder, mustard, cumin, cayenne, white pepper or your favorite spice. Stir and simmer until it thickens. Add diced ham or tomatoes. Just before serving add ¼- ½ cup of any grated cheese.

Kass' French Onion Soup: Brown 2 thinly sliced yellow onions with margarine and a little sugar. Add 2 cans beef broth (beef bouillon and water will do) to onions and simmer 20 minutes. Line a soup crock with a slice of sourdough and then a slice of Swiss cheese. Fill crock to within ½" of the top with onion soup. Add toasted chunks of sourdough, a slice of Swiss and ½ cup grated Gruyère. Bake at 425° for 20-30 minutes (add another slice of Swiss when cheese starts melting). Broil when done to brown the cheese, if necessary. Serve with sourdough bread.

Use honey with **Parmesan** cheese.

Pork & Cheese: Gouda or cheddar cheese melted on pork chops is wonderful.

Cheese Sauce: A cup of basic white sauce (See Sauces and Gravies in this section) with ¼ cup each Parmesan and Swiss cheeses. Add ¼ tsp dry mustard to each cup of cheese sauce for a tangy alternative.

Sprinkle cheese over green or pasta **salads**.

Add softened cream cheese or yogurt to spicy hot **salsas or dips** to make them go further and neutralize some of the acidity and hotness. Add any of the seed seasonings—celery, poppy, dill or caraway to cheese in dips.

Toasted cheese **sandwiches** are easy. Try using a bagel for variety. My husband dunks cheese sandwiches in ketchup. Add cheese to any sandwich or to burgers.

Melt cheddar in a bowl of hot tomato **soup**!

Perhaps it would be easier to list those items that do not go with cheese. . .

Cheese Tasting

Cheeses are classified in the following ways and can be bought in these groups for cheese tasting:

- by firmness or texture (soft cream cheese, hard cheddars),
- by the look of their rind (outside coating),
- by the animal that the milk came from (cow, goat, sheep, buffalo),
- by where it was made (Swiss, Italian),
- by the kind of milk used (raw, skimmed, pasteurized),
- by similarities in taste and
- by age.

If you are having a cheese-tasting get together, here are a few guidelines:

- Try six or more of the same kinds of cheese, such as cheddars, blue-veined or Swisses to make comparisons.

- Always taste cheese at room temperature. The harder the cheese the longer it takes to bring it to room temperature. Allow for at least an hour.

- Clean the palate with unbuttered bread between cheeses. Avoid flavored crackers or bread as this will detract from the taste.

- Do two tastings of the same group of cheeses in order to distinguish the taste of each cheese. One quarter pound of each is enough for 2 tastings for 2 people.

- Palates are freshest in the morning (no smoking or drinking an hour before tasting).

- Taste the cheese thoroughly throughout your mouth, so that all the taste buds and all four tastes may be detected—sweet, salty, sour and bitter.

- Try to find a dry, light wine (clarets, burgundies) or an unflavored coffee and sip it after eating the cheese. Some beers, strong wines and flavored coffees can distort the true taste of the cheese. Non-herbal tea or tea without flavoring is excellent for cheese tasting.

Cheese Varieties

The following list (by no means complete) should give you a good start on becoming a cheesemonger. In parenthesis are listed how they are used in cooking, where they are from, a description of their flavor or foods they complement. Noticeably absent are brie and camembert cheeses. Many experts feel the only ones worth buying are available only in Europe. You may or may not agree.

Blue-Veined
Cabrales (Spain)
Colston-Bassett Stilton
Danish Blue (fruit, dark breads, red wines)
Gorgonzola (Italian, melted over potatoes, salads)
Point Reyes Gorgonzola
Roquefort (France, dressings, sweet wines)
Stilton (England, port or dry red wine)

Buttery & Mild
Bel Paese (melting, cooking)
Colby (soft cheddar)
Edam (Dutch, nutty)
Fontina (melting, Italian, nutty)
Gervais (soft like cream cheese, fruit)
Gouda (young Dutch, nutty, dark breads or beer)
Havarti (Danish, stronger with age, fruit)
Mascarpone (Italy, fruit)
Monterey Jack (melting, California)
Munster (melting, Europe's version stronger than US)
Port-Salut (France, fruit)

Cheddar & Cheddar Relatives
Caerphilly (ales or port, dark breads)
Cantal (nutty)
Cheshire (melting, Welsh rabbit)
Dunlop (melting, Scotland, breads)
Gloucester (England)
Leicester (melting and cooking, fruit)
Somerset Cheddar (slow-aged)
Tillamook (Oregon)
Vermont Cheddar
Warsawski (American)

Fresh (Unripened)
Chenna (India)
Cottage cheese (fruit, salads)
Cream cheese
Farmer Cheese (drier cottage cheese)
Panir (India, protein source for vegetarians)
Ricotta (Italian, lasagna, cheesecake)

Goat (tangy, sours with age, use in eggs, pasta)
Banon (melting, lemony)
Bucheron (melting, tangy, soft)
Gjetost (also cow, dark breads)
Montrachet (mild)
Ticklemore (England, tangy, semi-hard)

Hard, Spun or Stretched
Mozzarella (cooking)
Parmigiano Reggiano (grating, Italy)
Provolone (aged, cow)

Sheep
Asiago (rich, nutty, also cow)
Feta (Greek, also goat)
Kasseri (Greek, also goat)
Manchego (melting, Spain)
Pecorino Romano (grating, Italy, Parmesan substitute)
Roquefort (France, dressings, sweet wines)
Sardo (grating, Italy, Parmesan substitute)
Vermont Shepherd

Strong
Hervé (Belgium, dark breads, beer)
Liederkranz (NY, dark breads, dark beer)
Limburger (German, onions, dark breads, beer)
Monte Enebro (Spain)
Munster (European)
Roquefort (France, dressings, sweet wines)

Swisses (melting)
Appenzeller (fruity flavor)
Bellelay (like Gruyère)
Emmental (cooking, nutty, good in fondue)
Gruviera (Italian, like Gruyère)
Gruyère (cooking, good in fondue)
Jarlsberg (cooking, Norway)
Raclette (like Gruyère, potatoes, dark breads)
Samsoe (cooking, Denmark, nutty)
Sbrinz (grating, cooking)
Tilsit (cooking, Russia)

Pairing Cheese with Beverages and Fruit

Here is a list of both beverages and fruits that go well with particular cheeses. (Some cheeses are not paired with fruit.) Generally, wine and cheese produced in the same region go well together and simpler wines go with a larger variety of cheeses. Light, sweet wines are better with soft cheeses and reds are better with stronger-flavored, aged cheeses. Always start with the lighter tasting items and move up the hardiness trail. Feel free to eat and sip your way through further research.

Cheese	Beverages	Fruit
Blue-veined	Burgundy, sweet sherry or full-bodied red	Apple, Bananas, Figs, Peaches
Brie	Light-bodied reds; Champagne, Riesling	Green Grapes, Pineapple
Camembert	Light-bodied reds; Champagne, Riesling	Grapes, Pineapple
Cheddar, Cheshire	Light-bodied whites; Cabernet Sauvignon	Apples
Chevre	Sauvignon blanc	Peaches
Danish Blue	Full-bodied reds, burgundies, merlot	Apples, Red Grapes, Pears
Edam	Full-bodied, robust reds	Bananas
Emmental	Light whites	Apples, Bananas, Grapes
Fontina	Riesling, Champagne	
Gorgonzola	Hearty reds, chianti, dessert wines	Apples, Peaches, Strawberries
Goat's milk cheeses	Light, dry, fruity white or rosé; chablis	
Gouda (aged)	Chardonnay, light reds, such as Zinfandel, fruity whites, beer	Apples, Bananas, Pears, Red Grapes
Gruyère	Light whites, full-bodied reds	Apples, Bananas, Grapes
Havarti	Light Chardonnay, Pinot Noir	Figs, Raisins
Limburger	Cold dark beer, hot coffee	Melons
Monterey Jack	Riesling, Champagne	
Parmesan	White chianti, light whites, Bordeaux	Melons, Figs
Parmigiano Reggiano	Dessert wines, cabernets, merlots	Apples
Port Salut	Light, dry fruity red, white or rosé	Pears
Provolone (young)	White chianti	
Roquefort (from sheep)	Sauternes, port, dessert wines	Sweet Plums
Stilton	Port, dessert wines, sherry, dry reds	

Chicken (poultry)

Benefits: Contains 20% protein, skinless is healthier

Seasonings to use with chicken:

Allspice	Dill-pot pies	Oregano
Anise	Fennel	Paprika
Basil	Fenugreek	Parsley
Bay Leaf	Garlic	Rosemary
Beer-marinade, tenderizer	Ginger	Saffron-stews
Cardamom	Honey	Sage
Cayenne	Leeks	Savory
Celery Seed	Lemon Grass	Sesame Seeds
Chives	Lemon Juice	Shallot
Chervil	Marjoram	Tamarind
Cilantro	Mint	Tarragon
Cinnamon	Mustard	Thyme
Coriander	Nutmeg	Turmeric
Cumin	Nuts	Vinegar
Curry Powder	Orange	Wine

How to Cook:

Chicken comes in fryers (2-3½ lb), capons (5-7 lb), roasting (4-6 lb) and Cornish hen (1-1½ lb). Barbecue **bone-in** chicken for 45 minutes; boil/simmer for 2 hours; roast at 350° for 20 minutes per lb if stuffed; 15 minutes per lb if not stuffed; fry for 20 minutes each side.

A quicker, lower fat alternative: microwave 4 **boneless, skinless chicken** breast halves in 8 minutes or cut in small pieces to stir-fry.

Allow ⅔-¾ lb per serving.
5 lb = 3 cups diced cooked meat
1 lb = ¾ cup diced cooked meat

Buying Guide:

Chicken is 5% fat. Look for moist, tender skin and short legs. Avoid dry or bruised skin.

It should not have an odor.

Younger chickens are more tender.

Preparation Ideas:

Do not try all the seasonings at once. Use the Flavor Blends chart to get an idea of which ones to combine.

Mix cracker crumbs in your favorite flavored mustard or in salsa. Pat skinless, boneless chicken breasts, that have been cut in half, dry. Spread the crumb mix as a paste over the breasts and microwave on high 8 minutes.

For an Asian flavor, pat chicken breasts dry, coat with a mix of yogurt, bread crumbs, cilantro and peanut butter and bake.

Chicken with honey and almonds. Pat the chicken dry first.

Rub lemon juice over pierced chicken before cooking.

Sauté boned chicken breast pieces with walnuts. Add tarragon and chives about 5 minutes before they are done.

Cut up leftover chicken and add to white sauce (see Sauces and Gravies). Serve with peas or corn over toast.

Chicken Preparation Ideas continued:

Casserole: Sauté 1 sliced onion, add 3 sliced tomatoes and 1 peeled sliced eggplant. Put all on top of 4 chicken breasts and bake 35 minutes at 350°. Add your favorite spices.

Cajun Chicken: Rinse and pat dry 8 chicken thighs without the skin. In a blender beat ½ tsp of caraway seed, ½ tsp cayenne, ¾ tsp coriander, ¾ tsp cumin, 3 minced garlic cloves, ¼ tsp of thyme, 1½ tsp dry mustard, 4 Tbsp dry white wine and 2 Tbsp lemon juice. Coat the chicken, then place it in foil and bake at 350° for 40 minutes.

Chicken & Rice: Microwave 4 chicken breasts and cook up about 2 cups rice. For color add peas or broccoli. You could also serve this over pasta. Try changing the vegetable, for example, green beans with almonds. Make a basic white sauce (see Sauces and Gravies) and pour it over everything. Warm it in an oven. Sprinkle with crumbs, nuts or cheese.

Crockpot Chicken: Remove the skin of a whole chicken. Cut it to fit in a crockpot with carrots and uncooked rice. Add bay leaf, onions, celery and a little water and cook while at work.

Fried Chicken: *If the oil remains at 365°, the chicken is at room temperature and it is sliced to no more than 1" thick, then it should not soak up much grease and it should cook evenly throughout.* Use as a **batter**: ¾ cup water (milk or beer), 1 egg and 2 Tbsp oil. Add this slowly to ¾ cup flour and 1 tsp salt. Coat meat with the batter and let dry. Dip dry pieces in 1-2 beaten eggs with a little water and then coat with bread, cereal or cracker crumbs. Add your favorite spices in with the crumbs. Let stand 15 minutes before frying.

Indian Flavored Chicken: Microwave 4 boneless, skinless chicken breast pieces cut to 8 pieces for 8 minutes on high. Separately, mix ⅛ cup yogurt and 4 tsp flour. Also separately, boil ⅛ cup water, 1 tsp curry powder, ⅛ tsp each of garlic powder, paprika and lemon pepper. Lower heat and add yogurt mix until thickened. Pour over chicken and top with ⅛ cup chopped peanuts.

Pasta Stir-Fry: Sauté onions, fennel, rosemary and/or garlic. Add stewed tomatoes. Fry up chicken pieces. Serve over pasta.

Stir-fry 1 lb cut up chicken in olive oil. Add 2 cloves of garlic after chicken is cooked and simmer both in ½ cup red wine for about a minute. Add 4 tomatoes, ¼ tsp red pepper flakes and cook 3 more minutes. Add 1 Tbsp flat-leaf parsley or try an Italian blend of spices. Serve over rice or pasta.

Sun Dried Stir-Fry: Stir-fry 1 lb cut-up chicken in a little olive oil. Add 2 cloves garlic and 2 Tbsp diced sun-dried tomatoes. Add 2 Tbsp cracker crumbs or roasted sesame seeds and cook 1 minute. Add 2 cups chopped broccoli or cauliflower (if frozen, microwave partially before adding). Add 2 Tbsp parsley and cooked pasta. Spice with Italian spices or an Asian blend (see Flavor Blends chart).

Sweet Chicken: Mix cracker crumbs, nuts, bread crumbs or even flour with the sweet spices of allspice, cinnamon, nutmeg and/or cloves. Pat chicken dry and dip in honey and then the flour mixture. To contrast with the sweet taste add a little cayenne or black pepper. Microwave.

Cookies & Bars

Seasonings to use with cookies and bars:

Allspice
Anise-traditional pizzelles
Butter/Margarine
Caraway Seed
Cardamom
Cheese-cream cheese
Chocolate
Cinnamon
Cloves
Coffee

Coriander
Cream & Milk
Fennel
Ginger
Honey
Lemon Juice
Mace
Mint
Nutmeg
Nuts

Orange
Poppy Seeds
Raisins
Rosemary
Sesame Seeds
Sugar
Syrups & Extracts
Turmeric
Vanilla

How to Cook:

Bake cookies with rack on top third of oven. Use margarine with at least 60% fat. Use applesauce instead of oil in bars. To prevent toughness use powdered sugar not flour when rolling cookies. Use butter not margarine in rolled cookies to stiffen and chill dough. Dip cutters in oil to prevent sticking. Dark cookie sheets mean darker cookie bottoms. Let sheets cool before adding dough. Oil sheets; butter may burn.Chill dough for chewy outsides and soft insides.

Buying Guide:

Low fat cookies mean you will tell yourself you can eat more of them. Homemade cookies avoid some of the preservatives, sodium and fat that you can control by using substitutions. And doesn't homemade still taste better?

Preparation Ideas:

Substitute allspice for cinnamon to add a little more zing! Try maple extract instead of vanilla for a nuttier flavor.

Quick Cookie Dough: Use a cake mix, but use only enough water to make a dough. Stir, do not use a mixer. Bake at 375° for 10 minutes.

Butter Cookies: Cream 1 cup butter/margarine and ¾ cup brown sugar. Add 1 egg yolk, ½ tsp vanilla, 2 cups flour and ½ tsp baking powder. Cook spoonfuls at 350° for 10 minutes.

Cream Cheese Bars: Cream ¼ cup butter and ½ cup brown sugar. Stir in 2 cups Bisquick and ½ cup chopped walnuts. Should be crumbly. Put 1 cup aside and press balance in pan and bake 12 minutes at 375°. Mix until smooth: 8 oz cream cheese, ¼ cup sugar, 1 Tbsp lemon juice, 2 tsp milk, ½ tsp vanilla and 1 egg. Pour it on the baked layer. Sprinkle 1 cup of crumbs on top. Bake 375° for 40 minutes until center is firm.

There is no need to sift flour since it is packaged pre-sifted.

Add ½ tsp double-acting baking powder per cup of flour.

Grind oatmeal into flour and use it for flouring meats or vegetables. Although healthier, oatmeal can be tricky when substituting it for white flour. You may need to experiment. Add an overripe banana to oatmeal cookie batter to make moister cookies.

Keep cookies moist and soft by storing them with a slice of bread or apple.

Cookies and Bars Preparation Ideas continued:

Crescent Cookies: Cream 1 cup butter/margarine and ¾ cup powdered sugar. Add 2 cups flour, 1 cup chopped pecans, 1 tsp vanilla and 1 Tbsp ice water. Roll with palms of hand into finger lengths. Shape into crescent. Bake on greased sheet at 375° for 20 minutes. Roll in powdered sugar while still hot. Makes 36 cookies. These are like Russian tea cakes and are so popular you may just want to double the recipe!

Annie's Pizzelle Cookies: Cream 1 cup butter, 1⅓ cups sugar, 6 eggs, 3½-4 cups flour, 2 tsp baking powder and 2 tsp maple flavoring. This makes 3 dozen cookies taking about 1 minute each on a hot pizzelle iron. You can vary the flavor extract and use anise, lemon, vanilla or mint. The maple flavoring darkens the cookies, but makes the house smell wonderful. The usual flavoring is anise. Add red or green food coloring for Christmas, but not with the too-dark maple extract.

Cardamom Cookies: Combine 3 cups flour, ¾ cup powdered sugar, 1 cup butter, ¾ tsp almond extract, ½ cup walnuts and ½ tsp ground cardamom. Knead into 1" balls, 2" apart. Bake 20 minutes at 350°. You may roll in powdered sugar.

Criss-Cross Peanut Butter Cookies: Cream 1 cup brown sugar, 1 cup sugar and 1 cup butter. Add 2 beaten eggs, 1 tsp vanilla, 3 cups of flour and 1½ tsp baking soda. Add 1 cup peanut butter. Roll into ¾" diameter balls, spaced 1" apart on greased pan. Criss-cross (press) with floured fork. Bake 400° for 5-10 minutes.

Maple Nut Bars: Beat 3 eggs. Add ¾ cup applesauce, 1½ cups flour, ¾ cup sugar, 1½ tsp baking powder, 1½ cups nuts, ½ tsp salt and 2½ tsp maple flavoring. Pour into a 9" x 13" pan and bake at 350° for 30 minutes. Sprinkle top with powdered sugar.

No-Bake Cookies: Mix in a heated pan ¾ cup sugar, ⅛ cup cocoa, ¼ cup milk and ¼ cup butter. Cook 1 minute after it boils. Add ½ tsp vanilla, 1½ cups oatmeal and ¼ cup chunky peanut butter. Stir well and drop by teaspoonfuls on wax paper until firm. Use a little less oatmeal and a ¼ cup of coconut flakes for variety.

Rosemary Fruit & Nut Bars: Beat 2 eggs and add 1 cup brown sugar. Add 2 tsp vanilla and 1 cup flour sifted with 1 tsp of baking powder, ½ tsp ground rosemary and ½ tsp salt. Fold in ⅔ cup pecans and 1 cup fruit (tart apples, peaches or craisins). Bake at 350° in an 8" x 8" greased pan for 30 minutes.

Shortbread Bars: Sift 2 cups flour with 1 cup cornstarch. Cream ½ cup sugar and 1 cup butter. Combine until stiff enough to knead. Press into 12" x 8" pan (or cookie molds). Cut almost through with a knife and make holes with a fork. Bake 35 minutes at 325° until golden. Recut. For a lemon flavor add 1 tsp lemon extract.

Rich Chocolate Pecan Bars: Melt ½ cup of margarine in a 9" x 13" pan. Sprinkle 1½ cups graham cracker crumbs over it and pour 14 oz sweetened condensed milk over this evenly. Add 1 cup semi-sweet chocolate chips, 3½ oz of coconut and 1 cup chopped pecans. Press down gently. Bake 25-30 min at 350° or until lightly brown. Cool before cutting. Store covered at room temperature. These will not last long!

Corn

Benefits: Very low in sodium, high in carbohydrates

Seasonings to use with corn:

Anise	Chives	Onion/Scallion
Basil	Cream & Milk	Paprika
Butter/Margarine	Cumin	Pepper, Bell-red
Cayenne-red pepper flakes	Curry Powder	Pepper, Chile
Cheese	Garlic	Rosemary
Chervil	Lemon Juice	Saffron
Chili Powder	Marjoram	Thyme

How to Cook:

Soak corn on the cob in its husk for 15 minutes in cool water before grilling; or boil 9 minutes without salt or husk; or microwave 2 cobs without husks in a little water for 6-8 minutes.

Use a clean shoe horn to remove corn from the cob.

3 ears of corn = 2 cups of kernels

Bourbon is corn whiskey that has been aged four years or more.

Buying Guide:

Check for freshness by pricking a kernel to see if it bleeds milky drops. Choose cobs with pale yellow kernels. Dark kernels indicate age and toughness.

Preparation Ideas:

Baked Corn: Add 4 crumbled crackers to 1 beaten egg, 1 cup grated cheese, a pat of butter, ½ cup milk, paprika and 1 can of corn. Bake 30 minutes at 400°.

Spicy Hot Corn Chowder: Stir-fry a diced potato and a diced carrot for 5 minutes in margarine. Add 4 chopped scallions, 2 diced celery stalks and ½ tsp red pepper flakes and stir-fry 10 minutes longer until potato is tender. Add 2 8-oz cans of corn or cooked frozen kernels. Add 3 cups milk, black pepper and marjoram. Add ½-⅔ cup diced ham or sausage. Put half of the mixture in a blender and then return it to the pan. Cook covered on low for 10 minutes stirring occasionally. Add arrowroot to thicken, if needed. Grate cheese over the top. You can also thicken enough to use as a sauce over pasta.

Creamy Cheesy Corn: Sauté 1 medium chopped onion and a diced red pepper and add 2½ cups corn. When heated add ½ cup milk, ½ cup heavy cream and ¼ tsp black pepper. Cook until thick. Cover and cook low 10 more minutes. Add 6 oz grated Fontina cheese. Spice with ½ tsp curry powder.

Cream corn was once a blend of corn, butter and cream. Now there is no dairy and the juice is thickened with starch.

Eat corn on the cob with butter, salt and pepper. Instead of butter, sprinkle each ear with salt, chile pepper and a squeeze of lemon juice.

Corn can be used instead of beans for **burritos**. Cook ground beef, spice it with cayenne, cumin, oregano and lots of chili powder. Drain grease and add cooked rice (instant for speed), salsa and a can of corn. Stuff a steamed tortilla, melt cheese over it with cut tomatoes or lettuce.

Corn Preparation Ideas continued:

Scalloped Corn: Combine in a greased dish, 1 can creamed corn, ½ cup cracker crumbs, pepper, ½ chopped onion and ½ cup milk. Dot with 2 Tbsp butter and top with more crumbs. Bake at 350° for 30 minutes.

Easy Corn & Ham Chowder: Combine 2 17-oz cans of creamed corn, 3 cups chopped cooked ham, ¾ cup grated cheddar cheese, ⅛ tsp black pepper and 1½ cups milk. Garnish with ½ cup chopped sweet red pepper. Flavor with onion or garlic powder. Mustard would also be good.

Corn Custard: Sauté a diced onion, red pepper, celery stalk and carrot. Add 4 cups corn, 2 cups light cream, a little cayenne, black pepper, ¼ tsp salt, ¼ cup sugar and ¼ tsp mace. Simmer 10 minutes and then cool. Beat 2 eggs, stir in 1 Tbsp flour and beat again. Pour into corn mix and blend. Pour the mix into casserole and bake 30 minutes at 350° or until custard is set and top is browned.

Succotash: Boil 2 cups of frozen lima beans until tender. Add 2 cups frozen corn and drain. Separately, sauté 2 tomatoes and 1 onion. Add pepper, ¼ tsp nutmeg and ¼ cup yogurt or cream, while heat is low. Add beans and corn until warmed throughout. Add 2 Tbsp Parmesan and remove from heat.

Corn Muffins: Mix 1 cup yellow cornmeal, 1 cup flour, 2 tsp baking soda, ½ tsp salt and ½ cup brown sugar. Separately, beat 1 egg, 2 Tbsp oil and 1 16-oz can of creamed corn and add to dry ingredients. Add ½ cup raisins (optional). Fill greased muffin pan ⅔ full and bake 20 min at 350°.

Chicken & Corn Chowder: Sauté 2 scallions, 2 Tbsp chopped red pepper, a little cayenne and a chopped celery stalk. Add 2 cups milk. Microwave a boneless, skinless chicken breast for 6-8 minutes in a little water. Cut up the chicken and add it and its remaining juices to the sautéed spices. Add 1 can corn and ½ cup mozzarella and simmer uncovered for 10 minutes. (Try a chopped, spicy sausage in place of the chicken.) Thicken with cornstarch if necessary.

Scrambled Corn: Add a can of corn to 4 scrambled eggs and spice with tomato, basil, oregano or chili powder.

Corn with Rice: Try mixing corn with rice, cooked in a soup stock, and a sautéed onion. Add cilantro for more color and flavor. Add bits of ham or bacon for meat.

Cornmeal Coffee Cake: Beat ½ cup or 1 stick softened butter and 1 cup sugar until fluffy. Add 3 eggs, one at a time, mixing with a blender. Add 1 tsp vanilla. Separately, mix ½ cup cornmeal, 1½ cups flour, 2 tsp baking soda and ½ tsp salt. Add ½ of this to the butter mix, along with ⅓ cup buttermilk. Then add the rest along with another ⅓ cup of buttermilk. Stir in 1 cup chopped pecans and spread batter in 13" x 9" pan. Bake 30 minutes at 350°. Pour over the top ¾ cup maple syrup and then bake 5 more minutes. Cool before serving.

Rejected by Europeans (even today), settlers in the New World were shown corn's versatility and ease of growth by the American Indians.

Cucumber

Benefits: Very low in sodium, low in calories; vitamins and minerals are in the skin

Seasonings to use with cucumbers:

Caraway Seed	Cream, Sour	Oils & Fats-olive
Cayenne	Curry Powder	Onion/Scallion
Celery Seed	Dill	Paprika
Cheese	Garlic	Parsley
Chervil	Horseradish-w/ sour cream	Pepper-black, white
Chili Powder	Lemon Juice	Rosemary
Chives	Mint	Savory
Cilantro	Mustard	Vinegar

How to Cook:
Cucumbers are rarely cooked. They can be coated and fried, however.

Remove the seeds from older cucumbers, since they grow and become bitter with age.

There is no reason to peel a cucumber, since the skin is thin. Smaller varieties are used for pickles.

Buying Guide:
Avoid discolored or wrinkled cucumbers. They should be small, bright green and firm at the stalk end.

Preparation Ideas:

Appetizers: Cut out the insides of a cucumber and stuff with your favorite dip. Or spread cream cheese between 2 slices of cucumber for a sandwich. Flavor with onion, garlic or curry powder. Paprika will add color. Place on round crackers.

Cucumber Stuffed Tomatoes: Discard seeds from 2 large cucumbers and dice. Scoop out the number of tomatoes you'll be serving. Using a blender, blend the tomato's insides, ⅓ of a chopped onion and the diced cucumber. Drain. Add 2 tsp sugar, 4 tsp vinegar and some dill. Stuff the tomatoes and chill. This can be served as a salad. Add cheese if you like.

Cucumber & Feta Salad: Salt 2 sliced cucumbers and let drain in a colander for 10 minutes. Pat dry. For a dressing, blend 2 oz Feta cheese, 4 Tbsp olive oil, 1 Tbsp lemon juice, ½ Tbsp chopped dill, 1 diced garlic clove and black pepper.

Salsa: Thinly dice 1 cucumber. Mix with ¼ cup rice wine vinegar, 1 tsp sugar, ¼ tsp crushed red pepper flakes and salt. Let stand and drain. Use over burgers or with fried rice.

Cucumber & Yogurt Salad: Mince 1 clove of garlic. Add ¼ tsp salt and 2 Tbsp yogurt. Add 2 more cups yogurt and mix with 2 sliced cucumbers. Add dried mint and white pepper to taste.

Sour Cream Cucumber Salad: Stir together ½ cup sour cream, 1 Tbsp vinegar, 1 tsp sugar and ½ tsp salt. Mix in 2 thinly sliced cucumbers. Chill. Sprinkle with chives, cilantro, parsley or cheese.

Use yogurt as a sauce over cucumbers with mustard and/or lemon juice.

Desserts

Seasonings to use with desserts:

Allspice	Coffee	Nutmeg
Angelica	Coriander	Nuts
Anise	Cream & Milk	Orange
Butter/Margarine	Cream, Sour	Raisins
Caraway Seed	Ginger	Poppy Seeds
Cheese	Honey	Sesame Seeds
Chocolate	Lemon Juice	Sugar
Cinnamon	Mace	Syrups & Extracts-maple
Cloves	Mint	Vanilla

How to Cook:

Healthy Substitutions:
Use applesauce or pumpkin instead of oil to moisten a recipe.
Use less sugar and more extracts or add fruit as a sweetener.
Use honey as a substitute for sugar.

Brown sugar, cooked in a cooler oven, is better than white sugar.

If you can, use part oatmeal instead of the full amount of flour called for in a recipe. Oatmeal tends to be drier, so use less.

Buying Guide:

Many desserts are quickly made from mixes, which can be spiced up or added to according to your own taste. Among these are cakes, pies, cheesecake, pudding, ice cream and brownies.

Preparation Ideas:

Apple Cheddar Cobbler: Peel and slice 6 apples in a casserole dish. Separately, sift ½ cup brown sugar, ½ cup flour and ¾ tsp cinnamon. Cut in 4 Tbsp butter until crumbly. Add 1 cup or 4 oz of grated cheddar. Spread the crumbly mix over the apples and bake it at 350° for 35 minutes until apples are tender and crust is golden. Don't forget the ice cream!

Brownies: Add mint flavoring to brownies for a different taste.

Carrot Cake: Beat 1 cup butter, 4 eggs and 2 cups sugar. Add flour mix of 2½ cups flour, 1 tsp baking powder, 1 tsp baking soda, 2 tsp cinnamon and ¼ cup water. Add 2 cups ground raw carrots, ⅔ cup ground peeled zucchini and 1 cup chopped walnuts. This will make 2 layers, so freeze one. Bake in 2, 8" x 8" greased pans at 350° for 40 minutes. Look under Frosting & Icings page for the cream cheese topping.

Cheesecake: Add fresh raspberries or blackberries to your cheesecake mix from the store and blend per instructions. Oh, by the way, you can use soy milk instead of regular milk.

Packaged, frozen and fresh pies are more easily bought than made.

Milk and **cookies** are a favorite dessert. Homemade cookies are especially good. See recipes under Cookies.

Cobbler: Mix ½ cup brown sugar, ½ cup oatmeal and ¼ cup flour. Cut in ¼ cup margarine until crumbly. Cut up 5 cups apples or peaches and place in buttered 9" x 13" pan. Sprinkle with sugar and add crumbly mix on top. Bake at 350° for 40 minutes.

Dessert Preparation Ideas continued:

Baked Gingerbread: Mix 2½ cups flour, 1½ tsp soda, 1 tsp cinnamon, 1¼ tsp ginger and ¼ tsp cloves. Melt ½ cup butter in ⅔ cup boiling water and add 1 cup molasses and 1 well-beaten egg. Add flour mix. Bake in a buttered 9"x 13" pan 25-30 minutes at 350°.

Baked Fruit: Sauté fruit such as bananas, strawberries or peaches in butter and then wrap them in foil with a little sugar and water and bake at 350° for 15 minutes.

Ice Cream: Put fresh cut peaches or strawberries on top of vanilla ice cream. Sprinkle with graham cracker crumbs.

Lemon Cream Cheese Pie: Grease a 9" pie plate with 4 Tbsp of soft margarine. Into this press 4 oz of shredded, separated coconut to form a crust. Separately, beat 12 oz of room temperature cream cheese until light. Add 3 eggs and beat. Add ¼ tsp salt, ⅔ cup sugar and the grated zest and strained juice of 2 lemons. Spoon it onto the crust and bake at 350° for 30 minutes. Cool and then chill 3 hours.

Lemon Custard: Combine ¼ cup sugar, ½ tsp lemon peel and 1 Tbsp cornstarch. Add 1 cup half & half. Microwave until it boils and thickens, stirring every 30 seconds. Blend a small part into 2 beaten egg yolks, then add the egg mix to the sauce. Microwave 1 minute. Add vanilla and chill. Good with pears.

Easy Lemon Meringue Pie: Use store-bought pie crusts and follow directions on the lemon pudding box. Cook per instructions. Let the pie cool before putting it in the refrigerator or you will get little droplets forming on the meringue. My aunt puts vanilla wafers along the edge to form the sides. It makes it seem like it was made from scratch!

Coffee Pudding: Blend instant coffee and powdered sugar with ricotta or cream cheese to make coffee pudding.

Add spices to pre-packaged instant **pudding** mixes. Extracts, such as mint, will add sweetness, so you may want to counter with a little salt.

Pudding Pie: Make instant chocolate pudding and place it in a graham cracker crust with whipped cream on top! Add mint for flavor. Freeze it if you like, but eat it before it gets runny or before the rest of the family gets it.

Rice Pudding: Try making pudding from leftover rice or grits. Add milk or cream, an extract for flavoring and sweetness and maybe some fruit or nuts.

Shortcake Substitute: The next time you make waffles, make extra and serve them with strawberries or other fruit, a little sugar to make a sauce and top it off with whipped cream.

Tapioca: Follow instructions on the box, but add lemon, honey or maple for more flavor. Eat it warm. Add fresh fruit, especially peaches.

Yogurt Pudding: For a healthier pudding to fool the kids: take plain yogurt add vanilla or lemon extract for both flavor and sweetness. Add nuts or raisins for chewiness. Sprinkle with cookie sprinkles. Could the kid in *you* resist it?

Dips, Salsas, Spreads

Seasonings to use with dips, salsas and spreads:

Basil
Burnet
Caraway Seed-sour cream
Cayenne-salsa, avocado, sour cream
Celery Seed
Chervil-avocado, cheese dips
Chili Powder-avocado dips
Chives-sour cream dips
Cilantro-salsas
Coriander
Cream, Sour

Cumin-sour cream dips
Curry Powder
Dill-cheese, sour cream dips
Garlic-sour cream dips
Horseradish-sour cream
Lovage-sour cream dips
Marjoram-cheese, sour cream
Mint
Mustard-sour cream dips
Nuts-cheese balls
Onion/Scallion-sour cream dips

Oregano-avocado, sour cream, cheese dips
Paprika-sour cream dips
Parsley-avocado, sour cream, cheese
Peppers, Bell-container for dips
Peppers, Chile-salsas
Rosemary-sour cream dips, salsas
Savory-cheese dips
Tabasco
Thyme
Worcestershire Sauce

How to Cook:
Most white dips involve mixing mayonnaise, sour cream, cream cheese or yogurt with spices. Homemade red salsas, bean and cheese dips often require cooking.

If stale, crisp potato chips or crackers by microwaving 30-45 seconds and let stand for 1 minute.

Buying Guide:
Check the fat and sodium content of prepared mixes before purchasing. Also look for MSG in pre-packaged dry mixes. Check the date before buying dips, especially dairy-based ones.

Preparation Ideas:

Cheddar Dip: Blend 1 cup shredded cheddar cheese with ½ tsp dry mustard and 2 Tbsp butter or cream until smooth.

Cheddar & Beer Dip: Combine 2 minced garlic cloves, ½ tsp dry mustard, 1 Tbsp Worcestershire Sauce, 2 drops Tabasco, ½ cup beer and 2 cups or 8 oz of grated sharp cheddar. Blend until smooth.

Cilantro Salsa: In a blender puree 1 bunch of cilantro (no large stems), 1 clove garlic, ½ jalapeño chile, 2-2½ Tbsp lime juice and 3 Tbsp corn or peanut oil until smooth. Add 4 chopped Roma tomatoes. Serve with corn chips.

Curry Yogurt: Try this dip with vegetables: 1 cup plain yogurt plus 1 Tbsp curry powder. Thicken yogurt with cornstarch.

Mellow out that hot salsa by adding **yogurt**. It will cool down the peppers, stretch the quantity and add a cheesy flavor.

Serve dips in bell peppers or melon halves.

Any of the seed seasonings (celery, poppy, dill or caraway) goes great in a cheese dip.

Thin **cream cheese** with sour cream, milk or yogurt. Flavor the dip with garlic, scallions, horseradish or chives. Flavor it with any of the above based on what you are dipping (vegetables or chips, for example).

Dips, Salsas and Spreads Preparation Ideas continued:

Clam Dip: Combine 8 oz of cream cheese, ½ cup crumbled blue cheese, 1 grated onion, 1 Tbsp chopped chives, 2 drops Tabasco and blend with a fork. Add 8-oz can of minced clams.

Easy Dressing Dip: Thicken a store-bought salad dressing with cornstarch and/or cream cheese and use as a dip.

Emergency Guest Dip: Melt a 2-lb box of Velveeta cheese in the microwave. Pour in a crockpot on low and add your favorite spicy salsa, diced tomatoes and/or chiles.

Gouda Blue Dip: Combine 8 oz of grated Gouda, ¾ cup blue cheese and ½ cup sour cream until smooth. Stir in 4 Tbsp soft margarine, 2 Tbsp lemon juice and 1 grated onion. Beat to blend.

Green Salsa: (1½ cups) Peel and bring to a boil 12 tomatillos. Chop them with 2 chiles, 1 onion, 1 clove garlic, and 1-2 Tbsp cilantro. Bring all to a boil in ½ cup water. Simmer 5-10 minutes until thick. Keeps a week, if refrigerated.

Grit Dip: Put a cup of cooked grits, a cup of sour cream, 1 tsp each of onion and garlic powder and blend for 5-6 minutes. Using this as a base for dips, add your favorite spice: cilantro, chives or jalapeño peppers. Chill until thickened.

Meaty Dips: Add cocktail sausages or small meatballs to your favorite cheese or salsa dip.

Red Salsa: (2 cups) Chop together 3 tomatoes, 1 small onion, 1-2 Tbsp cilantro, 1 Tbsp parsley, 2 chiles, 1 clove garlic and salt. Cook, puree slightly and cool. Use immediately.

Spicy Mint Dip: In a blender put 1 cup mint leaves, 1 tart chopped apple, ½ cup hazelnuts, 3 Tbsp fresh parsley, 1 Tbsp sugar, ¼ tsp cayenne, ½ tsp curry powder and 1 Tbsp lemon juice. Chill on ice or in the freezer and serve on crackers and cream cheese. Blend with whipped cream for a vegetable sauce. Also good on ham and reuben sandwiches. Try it on your next burger.

For something healthier than potato chips, try slicing up jicama, carrots or celery for dipping. Broccoli and cauliflower are also good.

Eating bread will get rid of the sting of hot salsas, as will milk or sugar.

Try using a particular sauce that you like (see Sauces and Gravies in this section) and thicken it with more spices and arrowroot or cornstarch.

Mustard Dip: Buy a flavored mustard or flavor prepared mustard with basil, chili powder or curry powder. Use as a dip for pretzels.

Rosemary Cream Cheese: Try ¼ tsp each rosemary and thyme with ½ tsp each celery seed and garlic powder, blended with 8 oz of softened cream cheese.

Tomato Dip: Take a can of diced tomatoes, add peppers, cilantro, onions, garlic or your favorite flavorings. Add yogurt or arrowroot to thicken.

Veggie Dip: Puree 2 cloves of garlic, 2 tomatoes, 1 bell pepper and cayenne in a blender. Dip away!

Eggplant (aubergine)

Benefits: Very low in calories, low in sodium

Seasonings to use with eggplant:

Allspice	Cinnamon	Parsley
Basil	Cumin	Pepper, White
Bay Leaf	Dill	Rosemary
Butter/Margarine	Garlic	Sage
Capers	Marjoram	Savory
Cayenne	Mint-peppermint	Thyme
Cheese	Nutmeg	Tomato
Chervil	Onion/Scallion	Turmeric
Chili Powder	Oregano	

How to Cook:
Most recipes call for salting and draining them. This removes vitamins and minerals. They will soak up oil, though, if not drained. Bake small ones 30 minutes at 425°. Microwave 7 minutes per pound.

Peel before serving.

Folklore refers to it as the *raging apple*, that had to be soaked in water to get rid of its insanity. There are white varieties that are egg-shaped, hence its name.

Buying Guide:
Avoid eggplants that are wrinkled, bruised, too large or soft. Loose bracts and stem mean it is spoiled. They should be heavy for their size. Use immediately.

Do not eat raw!

Preparation Ideas:

Appetizer: Grill ½" slices of eggplant brushed with olive oil on both sides. Spread with goat cheese, roll them up with a toothpick and warm them on the grill.

Casserole: Cube 1 eggplant and place in a baking dish. Add a chopped onion, 1 cup of cracker crumbs, 1¼ cups extra sharp cheddar and ½ tsp dried basil. Pour ½ cup milk over it all and bake covered for 40 minutes at 350°. Or **stuff it** by boiling it until tender, blend the pulp with ½ of the above ingredients, stuff and bake at 350° until brown.

Moussaka: (takes time) Steam 2 eggplants for 5 minutes after cutting them in ¼" rounds. Set aside to drain. Sauté 2 cups grated zucchini, 1 chopped onion and 1 clove of minced garlic. Add 1 large can of diced tomatoes, 2 Tbsp tomato paste, ¼ tsp each allspice and nutmeg. Simmer 10 minutes uncovered. In greased 8"x13" pan, place half the eggplant rounds, spread the vegetable mixture over this, then add the rest of the rounds. Add 1½ cups mozzarella and ½ cup Parmesan, shredded. Pour 1½ cups heated milk thickened with cornstarch over the top and bake 45 minutes at 350°.

Eggplant Curry: Sauté ½ tsp cumin seed, 1 tsp turmeric and ½ tsp cayenne in 3 Tbsp oil. Add 1 chopped onion and 1 chopped eggplant with skin. Stir until coated. Add 2 large chopped tomatoes and 1 cup water. Simmer covered for 20 minutes. Stir in 1 cup yogurt and 1 tsp salt and reheat.

Eggplant Pasta: Stir-fry a chopped onion, a *baked*, chopped eggplant, pimentos, oregano, pepper, some wine vinegar and a little brown sugar or molasses. Serve over pasta with grated feta or mozzarella cheese.

Eggs

Seasonings to use with eggs:

Basil	Fennel	Rosemary
Butter/Margarine	Garlic	Saffron
Capers	Horseradish	Savory-souffles
Cayenne	Lovage	Sorrel
Cheese	Marjoram	Tabasco
Chervil	Mint	Tarragon
Chili Powder	Mustard-deviled	Thyme
Chives-deviled	Nutmeg	Tomato
Cream & Milk	Onion/Scallion	Turmeric-deviled
Coriander	Oregano	Vinegar-deviled
Cumin-deviled	Paprika	Worcestershire Sauce-deviled
Curry Powder-deviled	Parsley-deviled	Wine
Dill	Poppy Seeds	

How to Cook:

Cook eggs at moderate temperatures to avoid toughness. To hard boil, simmer eggs 10 minutes or more (high altitudes). Peel by rinsing in cold water, cracking both ends and rolling in your palm.

When scrambling or making an omelet, add 1 Tbsp water or milk per egg. Sauté ingredients, such as onions first, then add eggs, cheese and finally fresh spices. Salted butter makes cooked eggs stick to the pan.

Buying Guide:

Fresh eggs have a rough, chalky shell. Old ones are smooth and shiny. Egg color has to do with the kind of hen, not the quality. Rotten eggs will float and 10-day old eggs will stand on end in salted water. Keep eggs about 3 weeks.

Preparation Ideas:

Green Bean & Egg Casserole: Cook 9 oz frozen green beans. Hard boil 5 eggs and then slice. Sauté ¼ cup minced onion in ¼ cup butter. Without heat stir in ¼ cup flour and then 2 cups hot milk until smooth and thick. Add pepper, thyme and parsley. In a greased dish layer beans, egg slices and sauce. Top with ½ cup grated Swiss cheese and ¼ cup bread or cracker crumbs. Bake 25 minutes at 350°.

Blue Cheese Eggs: Beat together 6 eggs (4 servings), 3 Tbsp heavy cream, 4 Tbsp dry white wine, a bit of crushed rosemary and ½ cup crumbled blue cheese. Melt 2 Tbsp butter, add egg mix and scramble on low heat stirring constantly. Garnish with chives or mint.

Cottage Cheese Scramble: (for 2) Beat 3 eggs, ⅓ cup cottage cheese and pepper. Scramble over low heat stirring constantly.

Egg Substitutions:

1 egg = 2 tsp arrowroot + 2 Tbsp apple juice + ¼ cup milk

1 large yolk = a large Tbsp
1 large white = 2 Tbsp

1 cup eggs = 5 large eggs or 8 egg whites or 13 egg yolks

*Eggs in recipes mean **large** eggs.*

A green ring on hard-boiled eggs means it was cooked too long.

Read labels on egg substitutes for its use. Some will not whip.

Egg Preparation Ideas continued:

Deviled Eggs: 1) Mix mustard with melted butter and pour over peeled and halved hard-boiled eggs. 2) Take the yolk out of the egg, add mustard and butter, blend and restuff the egg white. 3) Try ½ cup of yogurt for every dozen eggs. Mix the yogurt with the yolks, add chives, parsley, curry powder or mustard. Refill the whites. Add celery slices for crunch.

Egg & Bagel Dinner: Hard boil eggs, peel and slice. Place over toasted bagels. Make a thick Mornay sauce (see Sauces and Gravies in this section) and pour over the sliced eggs. Serve fruit on the side or mix fresh peas in the sauce.

Eggs Florentine: Sauté fresh spinach in butter. Add to eggs and scramble. Serve with Mornay sauce (see Sauces and Gravies).

Eggs for Kids: Cut a hole in a large piece of buttered bread. Place it in a frying pan with butter. Put an egg in the hole until it is set, flip and brown the other side. It's fun for kids.

Egg Sandwich: A small round bowl with straight sides is perfect for microwaving an egg that will then fit in between a toasted bagel. Spice up the egg or use flavored bagels. Add a slice of cheese, tomato, ham or bacon.

MaryJane's Eggbake: Place 4 slices of quartered, de-crusted bread in a greased 8" x 8" pan or 6 slices in 9" x 13" pan. Shred over bread ⅔-1 cup cheddar (based on pan size) and ⅔-1 cup Swiss or Monterey Jack. Fry and crumble ½ lb bacon over the cheese. Mix and pour over the top: 4 eggs (6 for bigger pan) and 2 cups milk (3 cups for bigger pan). Add 1 cup sliced mushrooms before baking at 350° covered for 45 minutes and uncovered for 15 minutes. Use a veggie or hot links instead of bacon. Add your favorite spices for variety (Italian blend, curry powder, garlic, mustard, onion or tomatoes). Not just for breakfast. Prepare the night before and bake it for brunch.

Omelets: Using an omelet pan, add 1 Tbsp water or milk for each egg. Allow eggs to run to the edge until it is all set. Add any ingredients or spices you like. Beat whites separately for fluffier omelets. Add a sauce (see Sauces and Gravies).

Add a pinch of cornstarch for fluffier omelets.

Whipping Egg Whites:
Whip egg whites at room temperature until smooth. If lumpy or spongy, you have gone too far (add another egg white). Egg whites expand to about 6 times their size when beaten. Use copper or stainless steel bowls to prevent falling. Extracts should go in at the end of whipping egg whites.

*If a **meringue** develops water drops on top let it cool first before refrigerating. For a harder meringue prop the oven door open halfway through cooking to vent steam. Add sugar slowly after beaten egg whites have formed peaks to avoid deflating.*

Scrambled Corn: Add a drained can of corn to 4 scrambled eggs and spice with tomato, oregano, basil or cayenne.

Use an Italian seasoning blend for **scrambled** eggs. Pesto sauce with basil is especially good. A spicy mustard also works well.

Make a **dessert omelet** by crushing ¼ cup nuts and adding 2 Tbsp cream for every 2 eggs. Sprinkle with powdered sugar and fruit.

Fondue

Seasonings to use with fondue:

Beer	Coffee	Marjoram
Butter/Margarine	Cream & Milk	Mustard
Caraway Seed	Cumin	Nutmeg
Cayenne	Curry Powder	Onion/Scallion
Cheese-esp. Swisses	Garlic	Pepper-white
Chives	Ginger	Tarragon
Chocolate	Liquid Smoke	Wine

How to Cook:

The key is picking the best cheeses (the essence of the flavor) and keeping them warm while you are dipping. A small crockpot works perfectly and you do not have to worry about an open flame.

Use a white wine, such as a Chardonnay, for traditional fondue. Red wines are a little strong. Also for success, prepare or cut the ingredients (dipping items) ahead of time. Don't forget the bread!

Buying Guide:

The best cheeses are the Swisses, including Gruyère, combined with any of the following: Emmental, Bel Paese, Cheddar, Edam, Fontina, Gouda, Jarlsberg, Mozzarella or Port Salut. With fondue you cannot avoid the fat, so indulge.

Preparation Ideas:

Beer Fondue: Mix 2 cups shredded Gruyère or Swiss cheese, 2 cups shredded Emmental, 1 Tbsp cornstarch, and ½ tsp dry mustard. Pour ⅔ cup warm beer in a pan over low heat and add dry ingredients slowly. Add 1 tsp Liquid Smoke. Dip with bread, fruits or vegetables.

Chocolate-Coffee Fondue: Melt 8 oz semisweet chocolate, 1 14-oz can sweetened condensed milk and ⅓ cup milk. Dissolve 2 Tbsp instant coffee into the milk before adding.

Chocolate-Peanut Butter Fondue: Warm 3 oz semi-sweet chocolate, ¼ cup sugar and ¼ cup milk until chocolate melts. Stir in ¼ cup chunky peanut butter. Makes 1 cup.

Traditional Fondue: Rub pan with a clove of garlic. Combine 1 Tbsp flour with ½ lb Gruyère and ½ lb Emmental grated. Heat 2 cups white wine in garlic pan and, before it boils, add cheese slowly, stirring until smooth. Add white pepper, nutmeg and 2 Tbsp Kirsch. Mix and keep heated. Dip in fruit slices, bread, bagel pieces and vegetables.

Originally made by thrift-minded peasants, who could use up old bread and cheese not suitable for guests.

A blackberry liquor, known as **kirsch** *or* **kirschwasser***, is usually associated with fondue. It is used to smooth the melted cheese, more than for flavor.*

Jack Fondue: Add in order: 3 Tbsp butter, 3 Tbsp flour, 1 tsp minced onion, ⅛ tsp garlic, ⅛ tsp cayenne, ⅔ cup or 5-oz can evaporated milk, ½ cup chicken broth and 1¼ cups shredded Monterey Jack cheese (5 oz). Serves 6.

Frostings & *Icings*

Seasonings to use with frostings and icings (Think extracts.):

Allspice
Butter/Margarine
Coffee
Cheese-cream cheese

Chocolate
Cream & Milk
Lemon Juice
Nutmeg

Orange
Sugar-powdered
Syrups & Extracts
Vanilla

How to Cook:
The key is to make them thick enough not to run, yet spreadable. Since most frostings call for a lot of powdered sugar, add almond, lemon, butter, mint or vanilla extracts for flavor. Be careful not to use extracts that will color your frostings something you do not want, such as brown with maple extract. Use milk to thin.

Frostings are richer and use butter more than icings. They hold up better as cake fillings, also.

Buying Guide:
There are many colored frostings now on sale with accompanying press patterns for decoration. Check the contents before buying and see if there is a date stamp. They will dry out if not used up after opening.

Preparation Ideas:

Caramel Frosting: Boil on low heat ½ cup condensed milk, ½ cup butter, ⅓ cup sugar and 2 Tbsp corn syrup. Stir constantly for 15 minutes or until deep gold in color. Good for an 8" cake.

Carrot Cake Frosting: Beat 8 oz soft cream cheese, ½ cup soft butter and 1 lb or 3½ cups of powdered sugar until smooth.

Chocolate Molasses Frosting: Beat 2 egg whites, 1 cup molasses and 2 squares melted unsweetened chocolate in a mixing bowl at medium speed for 15 minutes.

Coffee Flavored Frosting: Stir ½ cup packed brown sugar into ¼ cup melted butter. Boil and stir in 2 Tbsp instant coffee. Boil again, remove from heat and stir in ½ tsp vanilla. Let it cool. Blend in 4 oz softened cream cheese. Garnish with chopped nuts.

Corn Syrup Frosting: Beat 2 egg whites and 1 cup corn syrup in mixing bowl at medium speed 15 minutes. Add 1 tsp vanilla. Try other extracts if desired.

Cream Cheese Frosting: Cream ⅓ cup butter with 3 oz cream cheese. Add ½ tsp vanilla, 1½ cups powdered sugar. Instead of vanilla, use other extracts such as anise or almond, chocolate, lemon, mint or orange.

Orange Glaze: Mix 3 cups powdered sugar and 4-5 Tbsp orange juice until smooth.

Cookie Icing: (3 cups) Sift 3¾ cups powdered sugar. Add 3 egg whites, ½ tsp cream of tartar and 1 Tbsp water. Beat for 7 minutes. (Glycerin drops at your pharmacy can be added for increased glossiness.) Or use 3 Tbsp of meringue powder in place of raw egg whites and cream of tartar. Mix well into the powdered sugar and add 7 Tbsp of warm water. Beat for 5 minutes.

Simple Butter Frosting: Heat ½ cup butter until it is golden brown. Off the heat blend in 2 cups powdered sugar and 2 tsp vanilla.

Fruit

Benefits: Easy to digest with many vitamins and minerals depending upon variety

Seasonings to use with fruit:

Allspice-cooked apples or pears
Angelica-especially if tart
Angostura Bitters-salad
Anise-dried, especially figs
Basil-salad
Cardamom-salad
Chervil-salad
Cinnamon-cooked
Cloves-cooked

Coriander-cooked apples &
  peaches
Cream, Sour-use buttermilk on
  cherries and pears
Fennel-cooked apples & pears
Ginger-cooked apples & pears
Honey
Lemon Juice-salads
Marjoram-salads
Mint-salads

Nutmeg-bananas, apples
Nuts-salads
Rosemary
Sesame Seeds-salads
Star Anise
Syrups & Extracts
Tamarind-drinks
Turmeric-citrus
Vinegar-balsamic, salad

How to Cook:

Microwaving whole lemons, limes and oranges 30 seconds on high produces more juice. To soften raisins, cover them in a dish and microwave with 2 Tbsp water on high for 1 minute. Let stand 5 minutes.

Avoid washing berries until you use them. They will keep longer. Room temperature melons have more flavor.
Rhubarb, which is actually a vegetable, has poisonous leaves.

Buying Guide:

Bigger is not always better where fruit is concerned.

Avoid soft spots or bruising.

Preparation Ideas:

Add over-ripened bananas to the small muffin mixes at the grocery store to make **banana nut bread** or yummy **pancakes**.

In Baking: Raisins, dates, cranberries, prunes and figs are good in cookies and breads and can be bought in a dried form that will last a long time.

Baked Dessert: Sauté fruit, such as bananas, strawberries or peaches, in butter and then wrap them in foil with a little sugar and water. Bake at 350° for 15 minutes.

Easy Cobbler Crust: If preparing a fruit pie, here is a topping substitute for crust: Mix ½ cup flour, ½ cup sugar and 4 Tbsp melted butter. Blend until crumbly. Add ⅓ cup grated Parmesan, stir well, sprinkle over the fruit and bake.

Salad: Try any of the sweet spices like cinnamon, nutmeg, allspice, fennel or mint in your next fruit salad.

See Pairing of Cheese with Fruit under Cheese.

Buy **dried fruit** like apricots and before you need them, soak them in water overnight. Then mix them in a salad or have them over cereal for breakfast.

Main Dishes: Pineapple is used for its tangy, sweet taste at the end of cooking in Cajun or Creole dishes; Hawaiian dishes; in Asian sweet and sour dishes; with ham or other pork; on pizza; with seafood or in stir-frys.

Fruit Preparation Ideas continued:

Beverages: Some of the best beverages come from fruit and fruit juices, either by themselves, such as grapefruit, orange, apple, grape and prune or in combination. Fruit is used to flavor teas, such as with lemon or with the berry or apricot families. They are used to flavor punch, liquor, carbonated drinks, syrups and extracts.

Breakfast: Berries and yogurt are a great appetizer, while you are preparing breakfast. Put granola at the bottom of a tall, cone-shaped glass, add yogurt and berries on top for looks. Graham crackers on the side instead of granola also work.

Try blueberries, peaches, strawberries or bananas with your **pancakes and/or waffles**. Then sprinkle with walnuts or pecans! Use yogurt instead of syrup.

Dessert: Combine 1 pint strawberries, the juice of 1 lemon and ⅔ cup of fruity red wine. Add a little sugar and chill 1 hour.

Fruity Cheesecake: If you have a raspberry bush, buy the cheesecake mixes, add raspberries and blend them right in. Tastes great and it is easy. Buy a graham cracker crust and keep the crumbs in the package for other dessert ideas.

Gelatin: It is impossible to mention fruit and leave out gelatin. It is a great salad/filler for get-togethers and sometimes it is the only way to get kids to eat fruit. Although pineapple and bananas are popular, try other fruits for fun.

Lemons: Good to have on hand, lemons are not only used as a garnishment, but also to flavor teas, water and other drinks. They postpone apples and other cut fruit from browning and the juice is great over seafood. If they spoil, you can still use them down the disposal for a fresh smell. Anything with a bland taste can be perked up with a little lemon juice.

M & Mmmm Salad: Cut up 2 bananas, 1 apple and green grapes. Just before serving add whipped cream and M&M's. You are sure to get comments. (The candy will bleed, so leftovers are not attractive.)

Milkshake: Make your own with ice cream, strawberries, bananas and coconut for fun. Or blend fruit and buttermilk together.

Fruit Bowl: Use melon halves (cantaloupe or honeydew) as a bowl for dips, granola and/or yogurt. I suppose if you are really hungry, a watermelon . . .

Orange Syrup: Cook brown sugar in orange juice and zest over low heat and serve as a syrup on bananas, ice cream or even pancakes.

Fruit Salad: Combine 1 tart apple, 1 orange and 1 banana with ½ cup yogurt, 1 Tbsp brown sugar and ¼ tsp ginger or allspice.

Smoothie: Peel 2-3 peaches and a banana or 1 peach, some blueberries and a banana and cut into pieces. Put them in a blender with yogurt and ice. Thin with fruit juice if desired. Add 1 tsp vanilla or 2 tsp kirsch. Better than milkshakes!

Stir-Frys: Add apples for a different texture. Throw in some walnuts. Apples are also good with pork, onions and sausages.

Green Beans

Benefits: Very low in calories

Seasonings to use with green beans:

Anise	Garlic	Savory
Bay Leaf	Marjoram	Sesame Seeds
Butter/Margarine	Mint	Shallot
Caraway Seed	Mustard	Soy Sauce
Cayenne	Nuts-almonds, hazelnuts	Tomato
Cheese	Onion/Scallion	Turmeric
Chervil	Oregano	Thyme
Cloves	Parsley	Vinegar
Dill	Rosemary	Wine

How to Cook:

Snap fresh green beans and cut off the ends. Microwave ½ lb in ½ cup water for 6-10 minutes in a covered casserole dish.

Or stir-fry in a little oil until they are tender but still crisp.

Yellow wax beans can be spiced and cooked the same as green beans.

Buying Guide:

Snap a green bean to make sure it is fresh. If they bend, but do not snap, they are not fresh. Bumpy beans just mean mature seeds.

Preparation Ideas:

Almond Green Beans: Boil frozen French sliced green beans or microwave fresh beans for 6-10 minutes. Dry roast almonds in a pan stirring often until golden and pour over beans.

Green Bean & Egg Casserole: Cook 9 oz frozen green beans. Hard boil 5 eggs and then slice. Sauté ¼ cup minced onion in ¼ cup butter. Without heat stir in ¼ cup flour and then 2 cups hot milk until smooth and thick. Add pepper, thyme and parsley. In a greased dish layer beans, eggs and sauce. Top with ½ cup grated Swiss cheese and ¼ cup bread, cereal or cracker crumbs. Bake 25 minutes at 350°.

Hazelnut Green Beans: Boil 1 lb green beans 2 minutes and toast 1 cup of hazelnuts at 350° for 5 minutes. Sauté a sliced red onion. Add beans, ¼ cup dry white wine and 1½ tsp thyme. Sprinkle with 1½ cups grated cheddar. Cover the pan, turn off heat and let the cheese melt. Add toasted nuts.

Gritty Green Beans: Combine green beans with onions, canned hominy, pork sausage and scallions.

Add ½ tsp anise and 2 tsp fresh chervil to steamed green beans.

Tomato & Green Beans: Sauté 4 minced garlic cloves. Add 2 chopped tomatoes, 1 lb cut green beans and black pepper. Simmer with a lid for 10 minutes. Add 1 tsp oregano and 6 oz crumbled Feta cheese until melted.

Sauté 1 minced garlic, 1½ lb of green beans and 1 Tbsp sun-dried tomatoes.

Asian Green Beans: Add water chestnuts, mushrooms and shallots to green beans. Add soy sauce and sautéed almonds.

Grits (hominy, polenta)

Benefits: Enriched with vitamins, low in calories, no fat, good fiber source

Seasonings to use with grits:

Allspice	Chives	Pepper, White
Basil	Cinnamon	Sage
Bouillon Cubes	Garlic	Sugar-brown
Butter/Margarine	Mustard	Syrups & Extracts-maple
Cayenne	Nuts	Tabasco
Cheese-Parmesan, cheddar	Onion/Scallion	Tarragon
Chervil	Pepper, Bell-red	Thyme

How to Cook:
Use the proportion of 4 units of liquid (try milk, apple juice or broth for more flavor) to 1 of dry grits. Cooking longer at lower heat improves the outcome as does covering the pan after cooking and letting the grits steam on low heat a few minutes. For creamier grits, beat dry grits in a blender and add slowly to boiling water. To clean let the pan cool and grits will peel off.

Hominy absorbs flavors, so spice it up.

Buying Guide:
Instant grits are easy to make and are inexpensive.

Stone-ground grits are full of vitamin E and are good for facials.

Preparation Ideas:

Breakfast: Mix grits with a sunny side up or poached egg. Top it off with ham, sausage or bacon. Spice with garlic, pepper, tomato, Tabasco or your favorite flavorings.

Dinner: Fry bacon and cook up some shrimp, mushrooms and scallions in the bacon grease. Add garlic and crumpled bacon. Serve on cheesy grits.

Grits in a Casserole: Sauté a chopped onion in olive oil until golden. Add 2 cups chicken broth, pepper, ½ tsp rosemary and ½ tsp sage. Boil and slowly add ½ cup grits. Simmer 20 minutes covered. In the last 5 minutes add ⅓ cup of frozen peas. Remove from heat, stir in 3 Tbsp chopped flat-leaf parsley, ½ cup sautéed mushrooms and 1 Tbsp Parmesan cheese. Cover and let stand 10 minutes. Add spicy links for meat.

Baked Grits: Cook 1 cup grits for 30 minutes. Beat 3 egg yolks into grits. Beat 3 whites until stiff. Add to grits. Pour a layer of the grits in a greased pan. Alternate grits with 1 cup shredded, sharp cheddar cheese. Pour ½ cup milk over it and sprinkle with ½ cup dry bread crumbs. Bake 20 minutes at 350°.

Put sautéed vegetables on grits and top with shredded cheese.

Dip: Put 1 cup cooked grits, a cup of sour cream and 1 tsp each of onion and garlic powder in a blender and blend for 5-6 minutes. Using this as a base for dips, add your favorite spice: cilantro, chives or jalapeños. Chill until thickened.

Side Dish: Add a cup of cheddar cheese for every cup of dried grits. Flavor with butter, nutmeg or cayenne.

Starch Substitute: Use grits as a substitute for mashed potatoes, rice or pasta. Try it with gravy or salsa.

Ham

Seasonings to use with ham:

Angelica
Allspice
Basil
Bay Leaf
Cardamom
Cheese
Cilantro
Cinnamon
Cloves

Coriander
Curry Powder
Dill
Ginger
Honey-roasted
Horseradish
Juniper
Mace
Mint

Mustard
Pepper, Chile
Rosemary
Sage
Savory
Sugar-brown
Syrups & Extracts-maple
Tarragon
Thyme

How to Cook:

Ham comes precooked whether cured, smoked or canned. It can be cooked further at 10 minutes per lb or 130°. Fresh means uncooked and can take between 20-45 minutes per lb until it reaches 160-170°.

When boiling, leave ham in water after it is cooked until the water is cold. This adds juiciness and tenderness.

Add ginger to cut fattiness.

Buying Guide:

Select the most lean looking ham that is light pink in color. Cut in smaller chunks and freeze what you do not use. There is a turkey ham that is more lean than ham.

Preparation Ideas:

Slice ham on crackers with mint jam for an **appetizer**.

Use ham for **breakfast** instead of bacon. Put chunks of it in an omelet or mixed in with hashbrowns.

Make a tuna noodle **casserole** with ham instead of tuna and Swiss cheese instead of cheddar.

Glaze for Ham: Mix 1 cup of brown sugar, ½ cup fruit juice and 1 Tbsp dry mustard. If using pineapple juice, use more juice and decrease mustard to 1 tsp. Try basting your ham with 2 Tbsp of brandy or honey mixed with jam.

Kid's Meal: Use ham in a white sauce (see Sauces and Gravies in this section) served over toast or toasted bagels. Add peas. The kids will love it. (At least I did when I was a kid.)

What would split-pea **soup** be without ham?

Try ham with green beans over **pasta**. Add a sauce (see Sauces and Gravies in this section).

Pickling spices, such as dill, red chiles, allspice, bay and ginger go well with ham.

Ham is so easy to use since it is precooked. You can add it to almost anything and have protein in your meal—pastas, soups, salads or sauces.

Chowder: Look under Corn and try out the corn chowder with ham. It is very good.

If you are watching your fat intake, try turkey ham. It is hard to distinguish from the real thing.

Add ham to any meal involving cabbage or beans.

Kidney Beans

Seasonings to use with kidney beans:

Bay Leaf	Cumin	Oregano
Cardamom	Garlic	Pepper, Bell
Cayenne	Liquid Smoke	Pepper, Chile
Cheese-cream	Marjoram	Savory
Chili Powder	Mustard	Syrups & Extracts-molasses
Cilantro	Nuts-walnuts	Thyme
Cream, Sour	Onion/Scallion	Tomato

How to Cook:
Dry uncooked beans can be harmful to eat if undercooked.

Kidney beans can be purchased precooked in a can.

See Bean Varieties under Beans in this section for cooking times and other information on beans.

Buying Guide:
Red kidney beans are creamy colored on the inside and are more flavorful than the white kidney beans (cannellini).

Preparation Ideas:

Burritos: Rinse a can of kidney beans. Add them to ground beef and rice to make burritos. Any Mexican blend of spices like cumin, oregano, chili powder and peppers will work.

Chili: Empty a large can of pork and beans, tomato sauce and kidney beans in a pot. Add mustard, onion and garlic powder. Take 1-1½ pounds ground beef and brown it, adding chili powder, onion powder and garlic to taste. Drain the grease and re-spice. For an outdoor flavor add Liquid Smoke. Add meat to the pot. Warm or simmer in a crockpot for awhile. Add 1-2 Tbsp molasses, cayenne or chile peppers if you like.

Dip: Put a can of rinsed kidney beans in a blender. Add sour cream or softened cream cheese and either salsa, ketchup or tomatoes. Spice with cayenne, cumin, onion and/or garlic. Use this mix to stuff green or red peppers. Serve the dip this way or bake the peppers.

Kass' Taco Salad: Place tortilla chips as a base. Rinse a can of kidney (or black) beans. Add lettuce and 1 cup shredded cheddar or Monterey Jack. Add diced, cooked chicken or hamburger and chopped green onions. Use salsa as a dressing.

Salad: As a quick cold summer salad, add kidney beans to cooked pasta. Rinse mixed frozen vegetables in cold water after microwaving. Grate some cheddar cheese over it and add fat free Italian dressing.

Soup: Make a can of minestrone soup go further by adding a partial can of kidney beans. Add chile peppers, scallions or other spices. Add frozen vegetables after microwaving.

3-Bean Salad: Drain a can of limas, green and kidney beans. Add a chopped onion and red pepper. Pour 8 oz of Italian dressing over it and marinate for 1 hour. Drain and serve.

Lamb/Mutton

Benefits: Low in calories, high in protein, iron, niacin, B-12 and zinc

Seasonings to use with lamb/mutton:

Basil	Garlic	Orange
Bay Leaf-kabobs	Ginger	Oregano
Cardamom	Honey	Rosemary
Cheese	Lemon Juice	Sage
Cilantro	Marjoram	Savory
Cloves	Mint-peppermint	Tarragon
Coriander	Mustard	Thyme
Cumin	Nutmeg	Tomato
Curry Powder	Nuts	Worcestershire Sauce
Fennel	Onion/Scallion	Wine

How to Cook:
Trim fat and age the lamb 3-4 days unwrapped in the refrigerator to tenderize. Roast at 350° in a cup of liquid. Inside temperature should be 170° when done (about 25 minutes per pound). Broil chops 5-6 minutes per side.

In England, during King Arthur's time, the Knights would be treated with a feast of mutton (a year-old lamb) upon their arrival at a castle. The common person would also get meat, but it was just *the cold shoulder.*

Buying Guide:
The most tender cuts and mildest flavor are from the back and ribs (loin or rack of lamb). Legs or shanks are less tender. Age determines tenderness. Pick light-colored meat.

Preparation Ideas:

Chops: Broil lamb chops with salt, pepper, rosemary and garlic. When almost done spread with a mix of blue cheese and cream and broil until cheese is golden brown; or sprinkle with equal parts Roquefort cheese and flour, broil and then sprinkle with Worcestershire Sauce and water; or broil with a mix of honey and spicy mustard. Try plum preserves on one side during the last 2 minutes.

More Chops: Marinate them in lemon or orange juice, or after cooking, cover them with lemon juice and oregano or mint.

Irish Stew: Slow cook cubed lamb meat in a crockpot with your favorite spices. Stewed tomatoes make a good base. Add potatoes (or rice) and carrots. Turnips and onions are also good.

Kabob: Marinate lamb in Italian dressing and skewer with your favorite vegetables. Baste with the dressing 4-5 times during grilling for 15 minutes, depending upon size.

Savoy cabbage and eggplant go well with lamb.

Combine **lamb shanks**, carrots, celery and onion. Make a wine sauce (see Cooking with Wine and Food in Section 1), mix it together and microwave 30 minutes, turning often.

Unroll a rolled **leg of lamb**. Stuff with pesto (basil, garlic, pine nuts, Parmesan and olive oil) and re-roll to cook.

Use a mix of apricot or peach preserves, mint jelly, nutmeg and ginger to baste a **leg of lamb**.

Marinades

Seasonings to use with marinades:

Allspice-especially ham, pork	Fenugreek-vegetables	Oils & Fats-olive, peanut
Bay Leaf	Garlic	Onion/Scallion
Beer	Ginger-cuts fattiness	Oregano
Cayenne-red pepper flakes	Juniper	Soy Sauce
Chili Powder	Lemon Juice	Thyme
Cinnamon	Liquid Smoke	Vinegar
Cloves	Lovage	Wine
Coriander	Mint	Worcestershire Sauce

How to Cook:

A **marinade** is a flavored liquid that is absorbed by meats or vegetables. The act of soaking is **marinating**. It adds flavor and tenderizes via an acid base, such as lemon juice, vinegar, yogurt, beer or wine. Do not use an aluminum pan!

Marinate small chunks of meat or fish (after pricking with a fork) for 15-30 minutes at room temperature. Poultry or small meat pieces take 4 hours in the refrigerator or 1 hour at room temperature. Large, tough meat takes 2 days in the refrigerator.

Buying Guide:

Any marinade should have an acid, an oil and flavorings. Try Italian or other dressings as a marinade.

Use ½ cup marinade per pound of food to be soaked.

Preparation Ideas:

All Purpose Marinade: Soak 1½ lb meat in ¼ cup lemon juice, ¼ cup olive oil, ½ minced onion, 2 minced cloves of garlic and ⅛ tsp red pepper flakes.

Asian Marinade: Mix ½ cup peanut oil, ¼ cup sugar, ½ cup soy sauce, 1 tsp ginger, 1 clove minced garlic and 2 Tbsp sweet dry wine.

Hot & Spicy Chicken Marinade: Marinate chicken in 4 Tbsp olive oil, ¼ cup fresh chopped mint, 1 tsp thyme, 1½ tsp chili powder and 1 tsp black pepper for 3 hours and barbeque, using the leftover sauce for basting.

Pork Marinade: Soak 1 pound of pork for 1 hour in 2 Tbsp soy sauce, 1 tsp ginger, 2 cloves minced garlic and ¼ tsp cinnamon. Or try soaking pork in 1 cup apple juice, 2 Tbsp curry powder, ½ tsp cayenn and 1 tsp salt.

Seafood Marinade: Soak 1 lb seafood/fish for 30 minutes in ½ tsp coriander, ⅛ tsp allspice, juice of 1 lemon and a dash of olive oil. Soaking fish in milk first gets rid of the fishy taste.

*Dry marinades are **rubs**. They are stronger-flavored and form a crust of flavor on the outside to counter the unspiced food under it.*

Blend fruit juice with a different fruit jam and marinate before grilling.

Grilled Chicken: Mix and pour 6 Tbsp honey, 1 tsp ground rosemary and 1½ tsp Worcestershire sauce over 4 skinless chicken breasts for 30 minutes. Grill 8 minutes.

Meat Marinade: Soak meat overnight in: ¾ cup soy sauce, ⅛ cup Worcestershire Sauce, 1 cup red wine, ½ cup chopped scallion, 1 clove minced garlic, ¾ tsp oregano and 3 Tbsp lemon juice.

Mexican Foods (Southwestern)

Seasonings to use with Mexican foods:

Basil
Bay Leaf
Cayenne
Cheese
Chili Powder
Cilantro-sauces
Cinnamon

Cloves
Coriander-sauces
Cumin
Garlic
Marjoram
Nuts-peanuts, sauces
Onion/Scallion

Oregano
Paprika
Parsley
Pepper, Bell
Pepper, Chile
Saffron-rice
Tomato

How to Cook:
Pork lard is the traditional Mexican frying oil. Use bacon, safflower or peanut oil as an alternative. The traditional rice is long or extra long grain white rice. Mexican cheese is hard to get. Substitutions include Parmesan, Romano, Monterey Jack, mild Muenster or cheddar and Mozzarella for melting. Soften tortillas in microwave. Drape them over rungs of oven wrack at 350° for 6 min. to make crisp taco shells.

Buying Guide:
If Mexican food is authentic, it is fried and/or contains quite a bit of fat. Try to avoid frying in preparation. Read ingredient labels for fat content, especially with refried beans.

Preparation Ideas:

Quick Burritos: Sauté ground beef or diced chicken spiced up with cayenne, salsa, chili powder, onions, cumin or your favorites. Add a can of pork and beans and a can of corn or cream corn. Pinto or black beans can be substituted. Add tomato sauce if you want it juicier. Add arrowroot to thicken. Use instant rice or regular cooked rice instead of beans. Don't forget the tortillas. Melt pepper cheese over it. Put more salsa on top if desired. How's that for easy and tasty?

Basic Salsa: In a blender combine 1 quart (13) Italian plum tomatoes, 1 bunch scallions, 1 jalapeño, 1 lime, ⅓ bunch cilantro, pinch of cumin and salt. It lasts a week refrigerated.

Tamale Pie: Puree 1 lb tomatoes and 1-2 chiles. Brown 1 lb of ground beef in a frying pan. Remove all but enough grease to fry 1 small chopped onion and a clove of garlic. Add the puree to the frying pan and cook a couple minutes. Separately, add 1½ cups boiling water to ¾ cup cornmeal until smooth. Pour into casserole, fill with beef mix, cover with ¼ cup Mozzarella and bake 18 minutes at 375°.

Taco Seasoning: Add to 1 lb of ground beef or chicken:
½ tsp chili powder
¼ tsp black pepper
¼ tsp cumin
¼ tsp oregano
¼ tsp cayenne

Pepper Soup: Sauté 1 chopped onion, 1 minced garlic clove and 2 chopped red bell peppers in 2 Tbsp olive oil until bell peppers are soft (15 minutes). Add 3 red chile peppers after roasting, 4 cups broth, 1 tsp paprika and 1 dried ancho chile. Simmer uncovered for 25 minutes. Drain. Blend vegetables with ⅓ cup toasted almonds until smooth. Add to the soup.

Mexican Foods Defined

These foods were unknown in Europe before Columbus came to America: corn, tomatoes, chiles, bell peppers, beans, chocolate, vanilla, peanuts, avocados, turkey and pineapple. Other vegetables including green beans, broccoli, spinach, radishes, chard and tomatillos are still used extensively in Mexican cooking. Foods that we owe to our neighbors:

Carnitas-literally *little meats;* pork cooked until very tender, served with a sauce or in a tortilla.
Chorizo-hot pork sausage, sold in links or in bulk.
Empanadas-half-moon shaped turnovers usually made of wheat, filled with sweets or vegetables and meat and crimped on the round edge. They can be fried or baked.
Enchilada-a tortilla dipped in sauce or eggs, fried and filled with almost anything, topped with cheese.
Fajita-literally *little belt;* beef cooked in strips with onions. Sides of guacamole and sour cream are usually served with tortillas for wrapping.
Flauta-a flute-shaped tortilla, rolled with filling and fried.
Frijoles-beans. Beans used in Mexican cooking include: Great Northern, garbanzo, pinto, black, California pink (rojos) and kidney.
Frittata-an omelet that is cooked in a skillet or baked in an oven.
Gordita-a small flat cake softened by adding fat into masa. It is stuffed and then fried.
Huevo-an egg. Huevos rancheros are sunny side up eggs, placed on cooked tortillas and covered with sauce, cheese and beans.
Masa-a dough made of dried corn kernels, boiled in lime water. It is not the same as cornmeal.
Mole-Most of these sauces involve chiles ground in a paste and cooked in lard. Meats, often poultry, are added and cooked to absorb flavor. Sesame seeds and walnuts are used for thickening.
Nachos-tortillas which have been fried crisp to use as chips for dipping in sauces or as a base of chips covered with a sauce, beans, lettuce, guacamole and cheese.
Paella-made in a wok-like pan, it includes frying several meats with rice, flavorings and vegetables and is cooked by reducing liquids or slow simmering.
Polenta-a stew or porridge of grains or legumes; cornmeal cooked in hot water or porridge.
Posole-a stew of hominy (grits), pork, chiles and spices; any soup or stew with hominy.
Quesadilla-a wedge-shaped turnover made of masa, which has been filled with cheese, folded in half and cooked on both sides.
Sopaipilla (Buñuelo)-a pillow-shaped pastry usually served with honey on the side for dipping.
Sope-a small thick tortilla with a ridge to hold fillings. A canoe shaped one is a **chalupa**.
Taco-U-shaped or rolled, they are fried, hand held tortillas filled with various items.
Tamale-Masa usually filled with spicy pork filling, wrapped in corn husks and steamed. Served for holidays. Real ones take hours to prepare. They can be filled with beans, squash or meat or made sweet with sugar and cinnamon.
Tomatillo-a small green fruit or husk tomato covered with a paper-like brown skin, which is peeled. It is great in green sauces and does come canned.
Torta-flat omelet-like egg or potato cake, fried in fat and served covered in sauce.
Tortilla-a food staple or bread made of corn or white and wheat flour.
Tostada-a crisp, fried tortilla, used as a plate or base for a multitude of recipes.

Mushrooms

Benefits: Contains vitamin D

Seasonings to use with mushrooms:

Basil	Lemon Juice	Parsley
Butter/Margarine	Liquid Smoke	Rosemary
Caraway Seed	Marjoram	Sage
Chervil	Mint	Shallot
Chives	Mustard	Soy Sauce
Coriander	Oils & Fats-olive	Tarragon
Garlic	Onion/Scallion	Thyme
Ginger	Oregano	Vinegar
Leeks	Paprika	Wine

How to Cook:

Keep the heat medium, as high heat dissipates the flavor. Add salt to encourage the juices to flow. Most taste best when sautéed in butter or olive oil. They absorb the flavor of whatever they are sautéed with.

Mushrooms add substance and texture to foods, especially salads. They are not easily digestible.

Use an egg slicer to cut quickly.

1 oz dried mushrooms = 8 oz fresh

Buying Guide:

Tightly closed caps are good if used raw. If gills under the caps are showing, the flavor is better for cooking. Avoid mushrooms that are dry, wrinkled, wet or slimy. Store in paper, not plastic.

Preparation Ideas:

You can **bake** mushrooms 30 minutes at 350° in a tightly sealed dish with a lid. Sprinkle with parsley.

Creamed Mushrooms: Place 1 lb whole mushrooms in a saucepan with 1 Tbsp butter and enough milk to cover. Bring to a boil, reduce and cook gently 5 minutes. Add 1 Tbsp cornstarch (dissolved in water) to make sauce. Salt and serve. Add whatever vegetables or meat you have on hand and pour over toast or a bagel. Try it over pasta or rice.

Grill porcini mushrooms after dipping in an equal mix of olive oil and red wine vinegar, with salt, pepper, sage and parsley. You can substitute portobello, shiitake or cremini.

Marinate mushroom caps 30 minutes in a mix of ½ cup olive oil and 1 garlic clove. Use a bit of Liquid Smoke for an outdoor grill flavor. Grill 10 minutes, brushing with oil and garlic mix. Serve with a lemon wedge.

Try the flavorful **Mushroom Chowder**. Look under Soup.

Sauté mushrooms in bacon grease and poor hot over **salad,** especially spinach.

Sauté 2 minced garlic cloves or 1 shallot in 1 tsp of olive oil. Add ½ lb mushrooms and 2 Tbsp of parsley until mushrooms are soft. Add ⅛ cup white wine until almost evaporated. Sprinkle with lemon juice.

Stuff mushrooms with guacamole.

A Few Words about Mushrooms...

History/Folklore

Mushrooms are a fungi not a vegetable. They contain potassium, phosphorous and the rare and difficult-to-digest vitamin D. The cultivation of mushrooms probably started in Southeast Asia. Mushrooms are vulnerable to changes in temperature and humidity and thus, you will not find them in the same place from year to year. The Chinese use over 100 varieties for both medicine and cooking. They cultivated the wood ear mushroom (a blood thinner) as early as 300 BC.

The Romans thought mushrooms were too good for the common people. Aristocrats even cooked their own mushrooms in special cookware, called boleteria. You could tell how much you were held in esteem by the number and variety of mushroom courses you were offered by the host.

In Europe, cultivation came about 1650. By the 19th century the French were using caves for mass cultivation. In Bavaria the forests were almost eliminated because housewives believed morel mushrooms grew where there had been fires. In the US cultivation also came in the 19th century with the same varieties as the Europeans. In 1926 an American farmer discovered button mushrooms mixed in among his meadow mushrooms and so began the dominance of the button mushroom, out of which came the more mature versions—cremini and portobello. Like herbs and spices, we keep developing a taste for other varieties.

Buying, Storing, Cooking

When buying mushrooms, look for them to be slightly moist and plump. Caps should be tightly closed to hold moisture, when used raw. If not tightly closed (gills under the caps are showing), the flavor is more concentrated and they are better used for cooking. They should smell earthy. Avoid mushrooms that are dry, wrinkled, wet or slimy.

Washing mushrooms dilutes the flavor by soaking up the water. Thus, use a damp cloth (flannel is best) or a mushroom brush to wipe the surface. Trim the end of the stem.

Store them in a paper bag (except for enokis which hold up in plastic) in the refrigerator and use within one to two days. Mushrooms can be frozen for up to 2 months. Sauté them in butter first for about 5 minutes and let them cool. Then place them in plastic freezer bags and make sure to let out the air. Freezing fresh mushrooms without first sautéing them does not work well.

Dried mushrooms can last over 6 months. Use 1 oz of dry for every 8 ozs of fresh. You can purchase them dry, dry them in the sun yourself or put them in a 100° oven. Once mushrooms are dried, their flavor becomes more intense. Store them in a cool dry place. If mushrooms have been dried and frozen, rinse and then soak them in a covered pan with warm water for 30 minutes. Pat them dry afterward and use the leftover water for soups and sauces.

Mushroom Varieties

Buttons are white, rounded crisp mushrooms with a white stem. The most common mushroom in America, they are versatile, good in salads and sauces.

Chanterelles can be yellow to apricot and look like an inside-out umbrella or trumpet. They smell like apricots and taste nutty and spicy. They are good in eggs and in sauces.

Creminis (Romans) are dark-brown, fuller-flavored versions of the mature button mushroom. At its most mature, and most robust in flavor, the button is known as a portobello.

Enokis are white with long thin stalks and a small cap. It is best to buy them when they are crunchy and not limp. Add them for crunchiness, for a fruity flavor in salads or, when heated, for soups.

Matsutakes are white-capped and fleshy with light brown scales and thick bulbous stems. They smell and taste like pine. Use immediately.

Meadows have light reddish-brown caps and pink to light brown gills. They are a larger, firmer, and more open version of the common button mushroom with a more pungent, woodsy flavor.

Morels are creamy tan to dark gray with a hollow stem and a honey-combed, cone-shaped cap. They have a deep smoky and earthy flavor that intensifies with drying. They are used mostly in cream sauces and light meats, such as chicken. *Do not eat raw*, wash them well and use immediately. *Look for insects in the caps.*

Oysters are white, buff or gray and have oyster-shell-shaped caps, short stalks and wide white gills. They are fleshy and have a mild flavor. They dissolve easily and are best in soups, sauces and Asian stir-frys. Select small to medium-sized mushrooms and use immediately.

Porcinis have reddish-brown, puffy rounded caps with no gills and club-like stems. Remove soft pores and trim the stem. They have a meaty texture and their woodsy flavor intensifies with drying. Use immediately. Grill and spice after dipping in oil and vinegar.

Portobellos are a mature brown version of the button mushroom with a flat wide open cap and gills. Its flavor is similar to the button, but more robust. Use as a meat substitute in sandwiches and stir-frys. It can also be grilled.

Shiitakes have light brown, cupped caps with scales (*do not use the woody stems*) and have a strong, slightly garlicky flavor. They will keep for a week. The caps are thick and fleshy and are used as a meat substitute in Japan. They can withstand long cooking, but are good in stir-frys.

Straws are tan to gray and look like delicate, closed umbrellas. When dried, they have more flavor.

Truffles are black (vanilla flavored) or white (garlicky, cheesy). They are scaly, firm and have a strong odor. For $1,000 a pound they should not be any *truffle* at all.

Wood Ears are gray to black with a gel-like texture and no flavor. They actually do look like human ears and are used mainly in Asian cooking and medicine.

Interchange portobello, shiitake or cremini mushrooms for one another.

Pancakes/Waffles/French Toast

Waffles are from the German, meaning honeycomb.

Seasonings to use with pancakes, waffles and French toast:

Allspice	Coffee	Mace
Anise	Cream & Milk	Nutmeg
Butter/Margarine	Cream, Sour-Buttermilk	Nuts
Caraway Seed	Flowers-garnishment	Sesame Seeds
Cinnamon	Ginger	Sugar
Cloves	Honey	Syrups & Extracts
Cheese	Lemon Juice	Vanilla

How to Cook:

Do not over mix the batter. You don't need to grease your pan if you keep the temperature low enough to make water droplets dance. Turn pancakes over when the batter starts to bubble.

Keep pancakes and waffles warm by placing them on a cookie sheet in a 200° oven. Do not stack them when warming. Make lighter pancakes by separating the eggs called for in the recipe and beating the egg whites.

Buying Guide:

If you make your own, you avoid preservatives and happily cannot tell how many calories you are having. With frozen pancakes, waffles and French toast, the package tells you!

Preparation Ideas:

Using thin-sliced bread, make **French toast**. Melt a slice of cream cheese in-between. Sprinkle with cinnamon and powdered sugar. Top with fruit.

For a rich **French toast** flavor, add an extract (almond, coconut, walnut or strawberry) to the usual milk and egg *dipping* mix. Although many soak it, I prefer the bread not so gooey.

Cheesy, Fruity Pancakes: Blend ½ cup sour cream, ½ cup cottage cheese, 2 eggs, ¼ cup flour, ½ Tbsp sugar, ½ cup diced apples or whole blueberries. In a skillet with butter drop 4" pancakes. For syrup blend ½ cup cottage cheese, ½ tsp vanilla or maple extract and 1 Tbsp sugar. Makes 12.

Light Cheesy Pancakes: Blend until smooth, 6 eggs, 2 cups cottage cheese, ⅔ cup flour and 1 tsp salt. Cook as with regular pancakes. Add ¼ cup grated cheddar for cheesier flavor. **For dessert,** make these pancakes the same way except separate the whites, beat them until stiff and then fold them in at the end. Add cinnamon or flavored honey while blending.

Try yogurt with a little cornstarch and fresh fruit in place of syrup.

Use bananas, berries and walnuts with your syrup.

Use a mix of applesauce and brown sugar heated in a pan for syrup. Add allspice and/or caraway seed. Pour over waffles and sprinkle with powdered sugar.

Grate cheese and place it between pancakes and let it melt. Cheddar cheese and ground caraway seed are good with an apple-flavored syrup.

Warm and thin jam or jelly with yogurt or melted butter and use that as a syrup.

Pancakes, Waffles, French Toast Preparation Ideas continued:

Cornmeal and Rice Pancakes: Mix ½ cup each cornmeal and flour, 2 tsp baking powder, ½ tsp salt and 1 cup cooked rice. Separately, beat 2 egg yolks and add 1 cup milk. Add dry ingredients. Beat 2 egg whites until stiff and fold into mix.

Crêpes (8): Blend 2 eggs, ½ cup milk and ½ cup water. Add 1 cup flour and 2 Tbsp melted butter or margarine. Let stand 20 minutes. The batter should be like cream. Pour 2 Tbsp onto flat nonstick electric grill/skillet. Cook ½ minute until browned, then turn and remove to wax paper. Fill with a blend of fruit and yogurt (with vanilla or lemon flavoring).

German Pancake: Preheat oven to 450°. Beat 3 eggs until light, add ½ tsp salt and ½ cup flour and then ½ cup milk beating continuously. Spread bottom and sides of 10" pie plate generously with butter. Pour in batter. Bake 20 minutes. Reduce heat to 350° and bake until crisp and brown. Serve with powdered sugar and lemon juice. This rises higher at lower altitudes.

Gritty Pancakes: Mix 1 egg, ⅓ cup milk and 1 tsp powdered onion. Stir in 2 cups cooked grits with ½ tsp garlic powder, 2 cups water, ¼ cup flour, 1 tsp sugar and 1½ tsp baking powder. Cook as a pancake. Use applesauce or yogurt for syrup.

Pancake Sandwich: Make your favorite pancakes. Between them sandwich in your favorite fruit (bananas, apples, peaches, berries) with 1 Tbsp of yogurt. On top, sprinkle nuts and powdered sugar. Looks elegant, tastes great!

Leftover Waffles: Toast leftover waffles in a wide bagel toaster or use them in place of shortcake for strawberry shortcake. Kids love them cold (pancakes work also), spread with butter and sprinkled with cinnamon and sugar!

Cheese Waffles: Mix 2 cups flour, 2 Tbsp sugar, 2 tsp baking powder and 1 cup grated cheddar. Beat 2 egg yolks, 1½ cups milk and ¼ cup melted butter. Fold in 2 stiffened egg whites. You can substitute buttermilk for milk and add ¾ tsp baking soda instead.

Cornmeal Waffles: Combine 1 cup flour, 1 cup cornmeal, 3 tsp baking powder and 4½ tsp sugar. Separately, beat 2 egg yolks and add 1 cup milk and ¼ cup melted butter. Combine and fold in beaten egg whites. Makes 6.

French Toast: Buy a different bread, such as sourdough, fruitbread or a multi-grain and use it for French toast.

Ginger Waffles: Cream ¼ cup butter and ½ cup brown sugar. Beat in 2 egg yolks, ½ cup molasses and 1 cup milk. Separately, sift 2 cups flour, 1½ cups baking powder, 1 tsp each of ginger and cinnamon and ¼ tsp cloves. Add dry ingredients to butter mix. Fold in 2 beaten egg whites.

Gingerbread Waffles: Add 1 Tbsp lemon juice to a measuring cup, add milk to make a full cup and let sit for 5 minutes. Beat 3 eggs until light. Add ¼ cup sugar, ½ cup molasses and the milk. Separately, mix 1½ cups flour, 1 tsp baking powder, 1 tsp ginger and 1 tsp baking soda. Combine. Add ½ cup melted butter. Spice it up with cloves, nutmeg, allspice or cinnamon.

Pasta/Noodles

Seasonings to use with pasta/noodles:

Basil	Garlic	Parsley
Bay Leaf	Ginger	Pepper, Bell
Butter/Margarine	Hyssop	Poppy Seeds
Caraway Seed	Leeks	Rosemary
Cayenne	Lemon Juice	Sesame Seeds
Cheese	Marjoram	Shallot
Chives	Mustard	Thyme
Cilantro	Nutmeg	Saffron
Cream & Milk	Nuts-peanuts	Sage
Cream, Sour	Oils & Fats-olive	Tomato
Cumin	Onion/Scallion	Turmeric
Curry Powder	Oregano	Vinegar
Dill	Paprika	Wine

How to Cook:

Al dente-means "of the tooth" or cooked a bit underdone and a bit chewy. Choose pasta the same size as the meat or vegetables that will be added to it. Boil the water before adding the pasta to prevent sticking. Do not rinse pasta, since sticky starches help sauces and dressings get absorbed. Stir in a little butter to separate pasta not served at once. You can rinse leftover pasta in ice cold water to separate.

2 oz uncooked=1 cup cooked pasta

Buying Guide:

Look for 100% semolina or durum wheat on packages for best flavor. Japanese pastas such as Soba and udon are high in sodium. Pre-packaged pastas have a lot of salt and look for MSG in accompanying sauces.

Preparation Ideas:

Cheese Sauce: Mix ½ cup milk with ½ tsp cornstarch. Melt 4 oz margarine in a pan and add milk. Stir until thick. Add ⅛ cup (½ oz) each of diced Fontina, Gruyère and Provolone cheese. Stir until nearly melted. Pour over ½ lb linguine mixed with 2 Tbsp margarine.

Asian Noodles: Garlic cloves pickled in sweet or tart vinegar is great in Asian noodle dishes. Add ginger and sesame seeds.

Try a jar of artichokes hearts, including the oil they are soaked in, with your **pasta salad** for a nice little zing! For a warm pasta dish add sun-dried tomatoes and spicy diced sausages.

Extend a Salad: See Salad in this section for more ideas and add curly or ridged pasta (to hold dressings) to your salads.

Do not confuse pasta with antipasto, an appetizer.

See Sauces and Gravies in this section for further ideas. Try pasta for a week and just vary the sauce, meat and/or vegetables!

Add a Tbsp of curry powder, paprika, cumin or turmeric to pasta for color.

Add a little dill to your macaroni and cheese or add cayenne and mustard.

Pasta/Noodles Preparation Ideas continued:

Broccoli Bowtie Pasta: Blanch 1 lb broccoli in boiling water for a couple minutes and rinse. Separately, cook a minced shallot in a little olive oil. Add 2 chopped red bell peppers and 1 cup of stock. Simmer 10 minutes and add 1 large can diced tomatoes. Add 2 tsp basil, 1 tsp oregano and ½ tsp black pepper. Simmer another 5 minutes. Add the broccoli to the sauce. Serve over bowtie pasta. Sprinkle with grated Parmesan.

Baked Macaroni & Cheese: Start with a basic white sauce (see Sauces and Gravies in this section) with butter, flour and 1¼ cups milk. When it boils, stir in ½ cup grated cheddar (or ½ cup Gruyère) and then pour this over the al dente macaroni in a casserole dish. Add cayenne and mustard to taste and sprinkle ½ cup grated Parmesan on top. Bake until brown on top or about 30 minutes.

Dessert Pasta: Extend a fruit dessert by adding pasta to it. For example, add pasta to a mix of peaches and whipped cream. Add a few nuts.

Mushroom Pasta & Sauce: Sauté a sliced onion and 2 minced cloves of garlic in olive oil. Add 1 lb or 5 cups sliced mushrooms and ½ tsp rosemary. Add ½ cup dry white wine. Keeping heat on low, add a mix of 1 cup sour cream, 1 cup yogurt and ½ tsp cayenne. Serve over fettuccine. Add spicy sausage links or red pepper flakes instead of cayenne. Add summer squash or tomato for color.

Pasta Pancake: Cook 1 lb angel hair pasta al dente. Fry the pasta in 2 Tbsp olive oil until browned. Turn and brown the other side. Top with a sauce, which includes Asian spices.

Quick Noodle Soup: Boil thin egg noodles or ramen in chicken broth or bouillon cubes and water until tender. Add chopped scallions as well. Add mixed frozen vegetables cooked in a microwave. Add curry powder

Tuna Noodle Casserole: (Still an American classic, even with its fruitcake-like reputation.) Add a can of tuna and cooked frozen peas to noodles or pasta. Or chop up bits of bacon, ham or spicy hotdogs. Melt cheddar cheese with margarine and mustard for something a little different. Canned soups may have MSG, so use fresh mushrooms or diced celery.

Sauté a sliced apple with onion, add caraway seed and include this in **macaroni and cheese**.

Southwest Macaroni: Boil 2 lb macaroni until al dente. Mix 6 whole garlic cloves, ½ tsp black pepper, ½ tsp cinnamon, 2 tsp oregano, 4 Tbsp red wine vinegar and soak 1 lb of diced pork in it. Stir-fry pork, 1 chopped onion, 2 red bell peppers and 3 tomatoes until meat is browned. Put half of the macaroni in a baking dish, cover with half the pork mix and 1½ tsp raisins. Repeat. Top it with ½ lb shredded Monterey Jack cheese and bake at 350° until cheese is browned.

For a **different spaghetti** fry up ¼ lb of thick bacon. Save some oil and cook 1 chopped onion in it. Add the bacon to the onion, along with ¼ lb chopped ham, ¼ cup parsley and 1 cup diced Fontina cheese. Simmer until cheese melts. Add the meat mix and pepper to spaghetti noodles and toss. Grate Parmesan over the top.

𝒫asta 𝒱arieties

Pasta	Description
Agnolotti	Round or crescent-shaped ravioli filled with meat
Angel Hair	Thinnest pasta, long like spaghetti
Cannelloni	Flat squares of pasta rolled into large tubes around a stuffing
Cappelletti	*Little hats*; squares like ravioli stuffed with meat, cheese or vegetables
Conchiglie	Giant pasta shells that look like a conch sea shell
Farfalle	Pasta shaped like butterflies or ribbon bows
Fettuccine	Flat noodles ¼" wide, wider than linguini
Fiochetti	Bows
Fusilli	Cork screw shaped; traps sauces; good for cold pasta salads
Gnocchi	Pasta balls like dumplings made with potato, flour and egg (recipe under Potato)
Lasagna	Wide flat pasta for baked dishes
Linguine	Thicker than spaghetti, thinner than fettuccine, flat
Macaroni	Hollow pasta, many sizes, curved like an elbow
Mostaccioli	*Like a mustache*; diagonally cut, tube-shaped pasta, either ridged or smooth
Orecchiette	*Little ears*, round disc-shaped pasta easily filled with sauce
Orzo	Tiny pebble-like pasta as small as rice
Penne	Short smooth tubular pasta with diagonal ends; rigate variety has ridges
Ravioli	Pasta squares filled and pressed closed on all four edges
Rigatoni	Large-grooved, tubular pasta 3" in length
Rotini	Wheels or spirals
Shells	Shell-shaped pasta
Spaghetti	Dried thin long strands of round pasta
Tagliatelle	Long, thin noodles good in soup; same as fettuccine
Tortiglioni	Spirals curved to capture sauces, multi-colored
Tortellini	Small stuffed twists usually ring or hat-shaped, often stuffed with cheeses
Vermicelli	*Little worms*; very thin spaghetti good with light sauces
Ziti	Long thin tubes

Peas/Peapods/Snowpeas

Benefits: Low in sodium, good for stomach acids, pods are high in iron and calcium

Seasonings to use with peas, peapods and snowpeas:

Basil	Coriander	Onion/Scallion
Butter/Margarine	Garlic	Oregano
Caraway Seed	Ginger	Rosemary
Chervil	Marjoram	Sage
Chili Powder	Mint	Savory
Chives	Nutmeg	Tarragon
Cinnamon	Nuts	Thyme

How to Cook:

The tendency is to overcook peas. Frozen peas can be soaked in hot water for a few minutes and be ready, especially in cold salads. Microwave in half the time stated about 4 minutes per pound.

Although frozen peas seem fresh, unless you pick them from pods and keep them cold, their sugar turns to starch and toughens them.

Buying Guide:

Juicy wrinkle-free pods are freshest. Check by pricking pods with fingernail to see if juicy. Look for small fresh peas and avoid large dried ones.

Preparation Ideas:

Heat 2½ Tbsp of peanut oil in a pan, stir-fry ½ lb of snow peas, 1 tsp tarragon, ½ tsp spearmint and a dash of cayenne.

Try unsalted cashews with your peapods. Add mushrooms, onions, garlic and ginger.

Put fresh peas in your salads, including pasta salads, to add sweetness and color.

Slice 2½ cups mushrooms and warm in a pan for 3 minutes covered. Uncover and cook until liquid is absorbed. Add 2 cups peapods and ¼ cup water chestnuts. Mix and warm ½ minute. Cover and turn off heat. Serve by itself or with rice or pasta.

Make a basic white sauce (see Sauces and Gravies in this section) and pour over new potatoes and peas. Add onion and spice with mint, oregano or your choice.

Add fresh or frozen peas to your tuna noodle casserole.

Dried mint reduces the need for salt in split pea soup. Split peas are included under Beans.

Stir-fry almonds in butter until light brown and add peapods and mushrooms. You can thicken the juice with cornstarch.

Mint Peas: Sauté 2-3 chopped scallions in margarine. Add 1 tsp dried mint, 1 tsp lemon juice, 1 tsp sugar and ¼ tsp crushed rosemary. Add 2 cups frozen peas and simmer covered until tender.

Pork

Seasonings to use with pork:

Allspice
Angelica-stems
Basil
Bay Leaf
Caraway Seed
Cardamom
Cayenne
Cheese
Cilantro
Cinnamon
Cloves

Cumin
Curry Powder
Fennel
Five-Spice Powder
Garlic
Ginger-cuts fattiness
Honey-baste pork roast
Horseradish
Marjoram
Mustard
Onion/Scallion

Oregano
Pepper, Szechuan
Rosemary
Sage
Savory
Sesame Seeds
Shallot
Sorrel
Star Anise
Thyme
Vinegar

How to Cook:

Cook a roast with fat side up. Temperature should be taken while not touching a bone and should be between 150-160°. Juices will be clear when pork is done cooking.

All canned hams are precooked. Follow directions for uncooked hams.

Rewrap pork after purchasing to prevent freezer burn. Most forms of pork can be frozen up to 2 months.

Buying Guide:

Pork comes in roasts, chops, bacon, spareribs, ham and sausage (salami, bologna, pepperoni). Buy pork that has the least amount of fat, is whitish pink to pink in color and has a USDA stamp. Check dates.

Preparation Ideas:

Take ¼-½" thick lean pork (no bones), cut into 2" squares and brown on both sides. Add a can of stewed tomatoes and simmer. Add a clove of minced garlic, ground fennel and rosemary. Simmer covered until done.

Or, instead of the stewed tomatoes, when pork is almost done, cover the pork with a slice of gouda cheese. Cover the pan until the cheese has melted. Serve with mashed potatoes.

Dice up a tart apple or two (McIntosh, Winesap or Granny Smith), cook it with margarine and ¼-½" thick lean pork. Add allspice, cinnamon and/or five-spice powder. Onion or shallots with this is also very good.

Homemade Pork Sausage: Mix 1 lb of ground pork, ½ tsp each of cayenne, thyme, sage and black pepper and ¾ tsp sugar. Refrigerate overnight. Make patties for breakfast or add to meatloaf, spaghetti, lasagna or your own dinner creation.

An especially good spice combination for pork is sage, savory and basil.

For a pork gravy, try frying up some bacon and onions with sunflower seeds.

Using lean pork, pat dry and dip it in flavored honey. Dip into crushed crackers mixed with spices. Include pepper or cayenne to cut the sweet taste. Bake or microwave.

Stir-Fried Pork: Cut up lean pork and stir-fry it. Add Szechuan pepper, five-spice powder and frozen mixed vegetables microwaved for 3 minutes. Serve over rice.

Potato

Benefits: (with skins, no condiments) No fat, low in sodium, 1 baked potato = 100 calories

Seasonings to use with potatoes:

Basil-potato salad
Bay Leaf
Butter/Margarine
Caraway Seed
Cayenne
Cheese
Chili Powder
Chives-potato salad, baked
Cinnamon
Coriander
Cream, Sour
Cumin-potato salad

Curry Powder
Dill-potato salad
Fennel
Garlic-mashed, potato salad
Ginger
Horseradish-potato salad
Lemon Juice-potato salad
Mace-mashed
Mint-peppermint
Mustard-au gratin, potato salad
Nuts-mashed
Onion/Scallion- potato salad

Oregano-potato salad
Paprika-mashed
Parsley-potato salad
Pepper, Bell-mashed
Rosemary-mashed, potato salad
Sage
Savory-potato salad
Shallot
Sesame Seeds
Tarragon
Thyme-potato salad
Vinegar-mashed, potato salad

How to Cook:

For baking, mashing, French fries: Idahos and russets
For salads and casseroles: reds

Bake potatoes in about half the time by cutting a thin slice off both ends and boiling it in salted water 10 minutes before baking.

Microwave 2 pricked potatoes on high for 8 minutes, turning at 4 minutes. Place in a covered dish 10 minutes to finish cooking.

Peel potatoes after cooking to maintain nutrients and to absorb less water.

Buying Guide:

Aside from the usual potatoes, there are yellow and Peruvian purple varieties available.

Do not wash potatoes before storing.

Preparation Ideas:

Add plum tomatoes to your recipe of scalloped or au gratin potatoes. Add mozzarella, Parmesan, asiago or fontina cheese.

Instead of butter or gravy, spice up some stewed tomatoes with garlic, fennel and rosemary and pour over mashed potatoes. Yum! Thicken with cornstarch, if desired.

Instead of adding milk to make mashed potatoes, save some of the water it was cooked in and use it.

Spicy Baked Potatoes: Spray teflon roast pan with vegetable oil. Mix in the pan 2 Tbsp Dijon mustard, 1 tsp of paprika, ½ tsp cumin and ½ tsp chili powder. Sprinkle in some cayenne. Cut 8 small red potatoes in half and prick them with a fork. Add them to the mix and bake at 400° for 20 minutes until tender.

The potato originated in the Andes Mountains of Peru where it was worshiped as a god. It was rejected by Europeans for 200 years. The exception were the Irish, who grew nothing else. The potato blight and famine in Ireland in 1845 resulted in one of the largest American migrations.

Bake potatoes faster by cutting them in half, buttering the exposed side and placing them cut side down for 30 minutes at 400°. Time depends on size.

Potatoes Preparation Ideas continued:

Bangers & Mash: Cook your favorite sausage or kielbasa and serve over mashed potatoes. Flavor with rosemary and cayenne or scallions. Try it with stewed tomatoes.

Large Order of Biscuits: Mix 1 cup flour, 1 cup mashed potatoes, 3 tsp baking powder and ½ tsp salt. Cut in 2½ Tbsp margarine. Make a well in the center and pour in ½ cup milk. Mix after the flour is moistened. Knead on floured board for 20 seconds and roll ½" thick. Cut with cookie cutter, bake 400° for 4 minutes. Makes about 20 biscuits.

Cajun Crockpot Potatoes: In a crockpot cut 5 potatoes and 1 lemon into wedges. Add 6 whole cloves garlic, 2 red onions cut into wedges and 5 bay leaves. In a bowl mix 4 Tbsp lemon juice, ½ cup water, 1 pureed tomato, ⅔ tsp each black pepper and cumin, ½ tsp cayenne, 1¼ tsp each paprika and oregano and 4 Tbsp olive oil. Pour this into crockpot. Add hot spicy links or Canadian bacon if you want meat.

Chowder: Fry 2-3 slices of bacon. Add 1 chopped onion, a grated 1" piece of fresh ginger and 1 minced garlic clove. Once the onions are translucent, add 1 Tbsp flour and ½ cup milk, stirring until smooth. Add 3½ cups milk and 3 potatoes cut into ½" cubes. Simmer with a bay leaf for 10-15 minutes or until potatoes are tender. Add 2 cups light cream and bring to a boil. Add tiny shrimp, scallop pieces or clam meat and simmer 1-2 minutes.

Dumplings (gnocchi): Boil whole unpeeled Idaho potatoes and mash until very smooth. Add flour a little at a time until it is smooth and sticky. Roll the dough into ½" diameter ropes and cut into 1" pieces. Place a piece on your thumb and press with a fork. It will be hollow on one side and grooved on the other. Drop them into boiling water 15 seconds. Remove after they come to the surface. Gently stir in your favorite dressing or sauce (see Sauces and Gravies in this section). Treat as a warm pasta salad and add vegetables if you like.

Potato & Cabbage Patties: Boil milk with shredded cabbage and let it sit. Make mashed potatoes. Mix the two and cook as patties in margarine. Add cheese.

Next time you make mashed potatoes, make extra so you can try some of these interesting recipes.

Jicama can be sliced and cooked (8 minutes on high in microwave) and used as a potato substitute. Serve with yogurt or honey.

Hash Browns: Cook Idaho potatoes by boiling. Grate them and cook with bacon grease or olive oil. Mix in rosemary, crumbled bacon and/or shallots. Even though they are often cooked with onions, add any of your favorite spices. Cast iron pans work best. Bacon presses (weights) are good for even browning. Serve with eggs.

Mashed Potato Patties: Using leftover mashed potatoes, add a little flour, some rosemary or oregano and cook in butter, like a thick pancake. Flip when golden brown and do the other side. For a cheesy taste, add some cream cheese to the mashed potatoes before browning.

Potatoes Preparation Ideas continued:

Mix & Mashed: For fun and color mix in some pumpkin with your mashed potatoes. Applesauce, ground up nuts or porcini mushrooms will also add a different flavor.

Try whipping in olive oil instead of butter when making **mashed potatoes**. Cheese (Parmesan, fontina or Gruyère) and cream also add a variety of tastes.

Potato Pancakes: Boil and peel 3 medium potatoes and mash. Add 3 beaten eggs and ⅓ cup flour. Beat in ½ cup very hot milk and some nutmeg and pepper. Fold in 2 beaten egg whites and cook like pancakes.

Potato Salad: The key to a great potato salad is to mix in the dressing while the potatoes are still warm, so they will absorb the dressing and its flavor. Try a green or red pepper instead of pickles. Shallots can be used instead of onions.

Instead of mayonnaise in your **potato salad**, try using olive oil, white wine vinegar and mustard as a dressing. It will taste good and will be healthier for you.

Scalloped Potatoes: Boil 4 whole russets until tender, but firm. Peel and cut into ¼" slices. Cook a yellow sliced onion in margarine. Cover the bottom of a casserole dish with bread crumbs, layer with sliced potatoes, onions, ¼ lb ham and ¼ lb sliced mozzarella. Grate Parmesan on top, pour ½ cup milk over top and add slices of margarine. Bake 30-35 minutes at 400°. For variety use smoked sausage instead of ham and ½ lb Swiss instead of mozzarella.

Shepherd's Pie: Mash potatoes and put aside or use leftovers. Cook ground beef, drain fat, add corn and peas and spice up with rosemary, garlic, onion or your favorite spices. Drain the juices from this and thicken with a little flour or arrowroot into a gravy. Serve up the ground beef mix in oven-safe bowls and mold mashed potatoes completely over it. Pour the gravy over the mashed potatoes and grate Swiss cheese over the top. Microwave until melted, or for a crispy top, bake in the oven 10-15 minutes at 350°.

Slice a wedge or two of raw potato and stir it into a dish that has been spiced too heavily. The raw potato absorbs the flavors and mellows the taste, so you don't have to start over.

New Potatoes: In a large skillet cut 10-12 small new potatoes in half. Add 1 Tbsp of crushed coriander seeds and cook in 4 Tbsp olive oil until potatoes are golden. Add pepper. Simmer in a covered pan with ⅔ cup red wine for 15 minutes until tender. Stir occasionally to prevent sticking. Remove from heat and stir in 4 Tbsp chopped cilantro.

Potato Soup: Combine 1 cup peanuts, 4 chopped tomatoes, 3 medium Idaho potatoes and 5 cups stock or water. Sauté an onion. Add ¼ tsp red pepper flakes. Boil all together until potatoes are well done. Then place ½ of it in a blender and return it to the unblended half. Serve in bowls and top with green scallions or parsley for color.

Rice

Seasonings to use with rice:

Allspice
Basil
Bay Leaf
Bouillon Cubes-for cooking in
Caraway Seed
Cardamom
Chili Powder
Chives
Cinnamon
Coriander
Cumin

Curry Powder
Dill
Fennel
Fenugreek
Five-Spice Powder
Garlic
Horseradish
Leeks
Lovage
Mint
Nuts

Onion/Scallion
Pepper, Szechuan
Poppy Seeds
Saffron
Savory
Sesame Seeds
Soy Sauce
Tamarind
Tarragon
Thyme
Turmeric

How to Cook:
Browning rice in a hot dry skillet gives it a nutty flavor and reduces the cooking time 5-10 minutes. (Do not use instant rice in long cooking.) Add ¼ tsp salt for every cup of rice and every 2 cups of water. Bring to boil. Simmer covered 20 minutes if using these quick cooking rices: **converted, Texmati, Wehani, wild pecan, white, short or long grain**. Let stand 5 minutes and fluff with a fork. A few drops of lemon juice will separate grains. Use coconut milk instead of water for creaminess.

Buying Guide:
Brown rice is more nutritious than white, which is basically starch. Long grain is dry and fluffy, while short grain is sticky and more tender. By adding spices, which contain vitamins, you can justify using instant rice!

Preparation Ideas:

Easy Burritos: Add cooked or instant rice to cooked ground beef and corn. Add Mexican spices such as cumin, chili powder and cayenne or salsa. Place in a tortilla. Melt cheese on top.

Fried Rice: Microwave frozen mixed vegetables. Fry cooked rice with soy sauce, curry powder, five spice powder and Szechuan pepper. Scramble an egg in it and add the vegetables.

Meat & Rice Salad: Mix cooked rice with pecans, crumbled bacon, chicken, mushrooms, onion and a sun-dried tomato. Serve as a cold salad with a mustard-flavored dressing.

Rice Salad: Cook 1 cup instant rice and refrigerate. Slice fresh cilantro, flat-leaf parsley, 1½ cups mushrooms and 1 apple. Add to rice. Use a vinegar and oil or Italian dressing. Serve on lettuce leaves to dress it up.

Cereal: Heat leftover rice with raisins, milk and allspice.

Use leftover rice in place of crackers for **dipping** meats.

Crust: Mix 2 egg whites, 2 cups cooked rice and 2 Tbsp Parmesan. Grease a pie plate, pat into a crust and bake at 375° for 10-15 minutes.

Rice Muffins: Mix ¾ cup leftover rice, ¼ cup sugar, 1 egg, 4 tsp oil and 1 cup milk. Separately, mix 5 tsp baking powder, ½ tsp salt and 2¼ cups flour. Combine. Bake 425° for 30 minutes.

Salad (lettuce, spinach, greens)

Benefits: Low in calories, provides roughage; high in calcium, iron, vitamins A and C; greens high in nutrients

Seasonings to use with salad:

Angelica	Garlic	Paprika
Anise	Horseradish-red radish also	Parsley
Basil	Hyssop	Pepper, Bell
Burnet	Lemon Juice	Pepper, Chile
Capers	Leeks	Poppy Seeds
Caraway Seed	Lovage	Rosemary
Cardamom	Mace	Savory-cooked vegetables
Celery Seed	Marjoram	Sesame Seeds
Cheese	Mint	Shallot
Chervil	Mustard	Sorrel
Chives	Nutmeg	Tarragon
Cilantro	Nuts	Thyme
Cumin	Oils & Fats-bacon, olive or salad oil	Tomato
Dill	Onion/Scallion	Turmeric
Fennel-seed sprouts	Oregano	Vinegar

How to Cook:

Add lemon juice to a bowl of cold water and soak lettuce for an hour to remove sogginess. Use pasta or rice to go with your salad. Use large lettuce leaves as a dish liner or garnishment.

Pat salad ingredients dry or use a salad spinner. Moisture does not let dressings adhere or absorb.

Do not store or reheat spinach. Nitrates build up and can harm children.

Buying Guide:

Pick greens that are crisp, dark green (more nutrients) and chilled. Avoid wilted, yellow leaves and woody, rough stems. Head lettuce should be heavy for its size. Cut items are not as fresh as whole ones.

Preparation Ideas:

Cilantro-Pasta Salad: Combine 1 bunch of cilantro, 1 orange bell pepper, 3 scallions, cooked pasta and sunflower seeds. Tasty and colorful.

Spicy Cabbage Salad: Chop up a fresh package of chervil and Italian parsley and an Anaheim pepper. Shred ½ cabbage head and add peanuts. Use a fat-free Italian dressing or, better yet, add a jar of artichoke hearts, including the oil. Blanch the cabbage in boiling water to soften it a little, if desired.

Old Reliable Salad: Add vegetables like tomatoes, celery and carrots to your salad. Of course, if you are going to settle for that, you have missed the point of the book!

Leave the cover off when cooking spinach to maintain color. No need to salt, since it is already high in sodium.

Use zucchini in place of cucumbers and combine with peanuts for a tasty salad.

Chives are light and spicy and good in potato salads.

My bias against food that bounces prevents me from including gelatin salads.

Salad Preparation Ideas continued:

For those of us in a hurry and who cannot eat a whole head of lettuce before it rots, buy the bags of mixed lettuce and greens in the grocery store. It is easy and healthy and you can add whatever raw fruits or vegetables you like. Cabbage also works well and lasts longer than lettuce.

Dessert Salad: Cut up a banana, grapes and an apple. Refrigerate. Just before serving blend with whipped cream or yogurt and add M & M's™ (peanut or chocolate). The colors will bleed, so leftovers are not attractive.

Green Bean Pasta Salad: Microwave fresh green beans and add almonds. Yellow snap beans add contrasting color. Add pasta with oil and vinegar dressing. Scallions are also good.

Cheesy Fruit Salad: Coat 4 diced and peeled apples with lemon juice. Slice and quarter 2 oranges. Blend ¼ cup mayonnaise and ⅓ cup yogurt. To the yogurt blend add the apples, oranges and 8 oz of diced Gouda cheese. Serve on lettuce or spinach.

Melon Breakfast Salad: Combine grapes or a variety of berries (blueberry, raspberry, blackberry or strawberry) with melon balls in the half shell of a melon. Serve with yogurt and nuts or granola. Whipped cream also works. Sprinkle with mint and/or lemon juice.

Pea Salad: Combine 1⅓ cups of peas, ½ head shredded lettuce and a small minced onion. Mix with Thousand Island dressing, then add 2 hard-boiled eggs and 2 diced tomatoes.

Veggie Pasta Salad: One of my favorite no fuss salads is curly pasta with lightly cooked mixed frozen vegetables (or a bag of stir-fry vegetables) and a fat free Italian dressing. Grate your favorite cheese over the top. Add kidney beans for protein or spicy links for meat and a slight bite. Add nuts, sunflower seeds, cabbage and/or celery for crunchiness.

Fruit Salad: Combine pears, walnuts, celery and apples with a thinned cream cheese dressing.

Salads are so versatile you may add any vegetable: zucchini, peas, green beans, radishes; any fruit: raisins, bananas, peaches; any nut: pecans, cashews, peanuts, walnuts; or any starch: rice, potato, pasta; and even meat and beans. For a great looking presentation add any of the edible flowers (see Flowers to Eat in section 1).

For crunchiness add celery, sunflower seeds, nuts or with fruit salads, add shredded coconut.

Try artichoke hearts, jicama (absorbs flavor of the dressing) and/or baby corn in your salads. Water chestnuts also add texture.

Letting frozen peas stand in warm water is usually all they need to make them salad-ready.

Try a salad of cantaloupe, tomato and avocado with salt and pepper.

What Seasoning for What Salad?

CAESAR SALAD:

(2 heads romaine, 2 eggs, 2 cups croutons, 7 anchovy fillets)

Cheese (4 oz Parmesan)
Garlic (rub on bowl)
Lemon Juice (5 Tbsp)
Mustard (¼ tsp)
Oil-olive (6 Tbsp)
Pepper, Black (¼ tsp)

CHICKEN SALAD:

Cayenne
Chives
Dill
Horseradish
Nuts
Oregano
Tarragon

EGG SALAD:

Dill
Horseradish
Marjoram
Mustard
Onion/Scallion
Tarragon

FRUIT SALAD:

Angelica
Cardamom
Celery Seed
Lemon Juice
Mace
Nuts-coconuts, walnuts
Rosemary

GREEN SALAD:

Burnet
Basil
Cheese
Chervil
Chives
Leeks
Marjoram
Mint
Nuts
Onion/Scallion
Tarragon
Thyme

POTATO SALAD:

Basil
Cumin
Dill
Garlic
Horseradish
Lemon Juice
Mustard
Onion/Scallion
Oregano
Parsley
Rosemary
Savory
Thyme
Vinegar

SEAFOOD SALAD:

Cayenne
Lemon Juice
Mint-especially tuna
Oregano

SPINACH SALAD:

Anise
Caraway Seed
Chervil
Chives
Dill
Lemon Juice
Mace
Marjoram
Nutmeg
Nuts
Oils & Fats-bacon, olive
Onion/Scallion
Oregano
Radish
Rosemary
Sorrel
Tarragon
Thyme

TUNA SALAD:

Celery Seed
Chives
Dill
Mint
Nuts

WALDORF SALAD:

(2 apples, 2 celery, 2 Tbsp mayonnaise)

Cream, Sour (½ cup)
Nutmeg (⅛ tsp)
Nuts (¼ cup walnuts)
Raisins (½ cup)

Salad Varieties

Although there are numerous lettuce varieties, in the US they are grouped in one of four kinds:

- ☙The **butterheads** have small, round loose heads with sweet-tasting leaves of pale green. Examples include Bibb and Boston.
- ☙**Crispheads or icebergs** have larger, more compact heads and few nutrients. They are wilt-resistant and taste bland.
- ☙**Leaf lettuces** are not as compact, usually come from a single stalk, are darker green, have more vitamins, are more flavorful and spoil faster than head lettuce.
- ☙**Romaine (Cos)** is oblong-shaped with dark green outside leaves (lighter toward the middle). Romaine is used in Caesar salads, is crunchy and slightly bitter in flavor.

Greens are edible plant leaves. They come from chicory, collards, dandelions, mustards and turnips and are rich in nutrients. Simmer 10 minutes, steam or eat raw. See also Cabbage.

Arugula-is a salad green with a peppery, slightly bitter flavor and a crisp texture.

Bibb-is a butterhead lettuce with a soft texture and a sweet, nutty flavor.

Bok choy-looks like celery with wider white stalks and dark green leaves; cook or eat raw.

Boston-is a butterhead lettuce with a soft texture, a loose, light head and a sweet flavor.

Chard-(Swiss chard) Cook stalks as you would asparagus and the leaves like spinach. **Tatsoi** are a substitute and are dark green heads with flat leaves and white ribs. Use in salads or stir fries.

Chicory (curly endive)-is tangy to bitter with a crisp texture. Leaves are eaten raw in salads or cooked as greens. Ground roots of some kinds are a coffee substitute or mixed in with coffee.

Collard greens-are a green leaf cabbage, loose on a stem. These greens are confused with kale, taste like a mix of cabbage and kale and are prepared the same as cabbage.

Dandelion greens-are leaves with a bitter, but tangy, flavor. Cook them like spinach or eat raw in salads. They are full of nutrients and are best eaten before they flower.

Endive-is related to chicory and has a slightly bitter flavor, a crisp texture and a creamy color. It is good for fighting infections, should be kept out of the light and be used immediately.

Escarole-is a kind of endive, also related to chicory. The leaves are broad and pale green with a less bitter flavor than endive.

Kale-is a cabbage with frilly edible leaves and lots of nutrients. Use quickly as you would spinach.

Kohlrabi-is a cabbage (bulb), related to the turnip, with attached leaves. Use the leaves in stir-frys or soups. The bulb tastes like a milder turnip.

Mustard greens-are also in the cabbage family. They taste like a peppery mustard and are dark green. Steam or simmer them.

Radicchio-is slightly bitter with a crisp texture mostly used in salads, for baking and sautéing. It is a red-leafed chicory, related to the endive.

Spinach-are loose, dark green, coarse leaves with a slightly bitter taste. Use raw in salads or cook as a vegetable (a la Florentine).

Turnip greens-are full of nutrients. Younger are sweeter, so pick small ones. Stir-fry, boil or steam them.

Watercress-is a relative of mustard. It is crisp, dark green and slightly bitter and peppery in flavor. Use it raw in salads, put it in soups or use it for a garnish.

Salad, Dressings for

Seasonings to use with dressings for salads:

Basil
Burnet
Celery Seed
Chervil
Chives
Coriander
Cream, Sour
Cumin
Curry Powder
Dill
Garlic

Honey
Horseradish
Lemon Juice
Marjoram
Mint
Mustard
Oils & Fats-olive, salad
Onion/Scallion
Oregano
Paprika
Parsley

Pepper, Black or White
Savory
Sesame Seeds
Sugar
Tabasco
Tarragon
Thyme
Turmeric
Vinegar
Worcestershire Sauce

How to Cook:

There are so many store-bought dressings available that you should never have to spend much time in preparation. But if you get caught short, try one of these.

Thicken a salad dressing with cornstarch and/or cream cheese and use it as a dip or spread it on a sandwich.

Buying Guide:

Premade dressings are varied, tasty and easy. Just make sure to read the labels if you are concerned about fat, sodium or MSG.

Preparation Ideas:

Add ¼ tsp thyme to French Dressing for use on green salads.

Mix plain yogurt with equal amounts of olive oil and lemon or lime juice. Add ground white pepper. For variety add other seasonings, such as garlic, basil or horseradish.

Mustard is a healthy substitute for mayonnaise. Combine yogurt and Dijon mustard with your favorite spices to create a tasty dressing over salads.

Avocado Dressing:
Cover or use before discoloring.
Makes 1⅔ cups.
¾ cup Sour Cream
⅓ cup Milk
1 Tbsp Lemon Juice
Tabasco (a few drops)
1 mashed Avocado

Hot Bacon Dressing:
(good on spinach salads)
Oil from 3 crisp Bacon slices
¼ cup Vinegar
1 tsp Sugar

French Dressing:
1½ Tbsp Lemon Juice
6 Tbsp Salad Oil
⅛ tsp Paprika
⅛ tsp white Pepper
1½ Tbsp Vinegar

Honey Mustard:
2 Tbsp Honey
3 Tbsp prepared Mustard

Oil and Vinegar:
¾ cup Olive Oil
¼ cup Vinegar
1 tsp Sugar
Black Pepper

Russian Dressing:
1 cup mayonnaise
3 Tbsp Horseradish
⅓ cup Ketchup
1 Tbsp prepared Mustard
2 Tbsp Worcestershire Sauce

Sour Cream:
1 cup Sour Cream
2 Tbsp Sugar
2 tsp Dijon Mustard
1 Tbsp Vinegar
White Pepper

Sandwiches

Seasonings to use with sandwiches:

Butter/Margarine	Horseradish	Pepper, Bell
Cayenne	Hyssop	Pepper, Chile
Cheese	Liquid Smoke	Soy Sauce
Chili Powder	Marjoram	Tabasco
Chives	Mustard-prepared	Thyme
Dill	Onion/Scallion	Tomato
Fennel	Oregano	Turmeric
Garlic	Pepper (from peppercorns)	Worcestershire Sauce

How to Cook:
Most sandwiches are prepared cold. Hot dogs are precooked. Reheat in boiling water; broil 3 minutes (slice and butter the outside first); grill; or microwave in a hot dog bun in a paper towel for 30 seconds.

Because most sandwiches involve meat and/or mayonnaise, few are low in fat content. Try substituting mustard for mayonnaise and go for turkey breast instead of ham, salami or bologna.

Buying Guide:
Although children love hot dogs, they contain nitrates, which are not so lovable. Many sandwich meats have nitrates. Lean meats are obviously healthier, but you need to get used to reading the packages.

Preparation Ideas:

Try a salad dressing instead of mayonnaise or thicken up yogurt with cornstarch and spices. Make a cream cheese dressing by thinning it with milk. Serve sandwiches on different breads or bagels. Add chives, garlic or turmeric to your mayonnaise to spice it up. The longer it stands the more flavor is absorbed.

Toasted Cheese is still an all-time favorite. Use a different cheese next time or add a slice of tomato to it. Try using different breads. My husband dips them in tomato soup!

An onion, mustard and asparagus sandwich adds variety for vegetarians, but kids still prefer **peanut butter and jelly**.

Leftover **meatloaf sandwiches** with lots of ketchup used to be a real treat when I was a kid.

Thicken up spaghetti sauce and serve as a **sloppy joe** sandwich, especially on a bagel. Make a **meatball** sandwich.

A **portobello** mushroom makes a meaty sandwich. Add Liquid Smoke for a grilled taste.

Deli, corned beef, hoagies . . .

Bacon is often added to sandwiches, as is a slice of tomato. **BLT**'s are still good.

Tuna, chicken or egg salad sandwiches are messy, but great. Add pickle relish, celery, tarragon and onion.

For an appetizer or snack make **cucumber and cream cheese** sandwiches. Add chili powder or ground fennel.

Reuben: Rye bread, Swiss cheese, Thousand Island Dressing, sauerkraut and corned beef is a favorite. Butter the rye and grill until the cheese melts.

Sauces & Gravies

Seasonings to use with sauces and gravies:

Allspice-brown gravy
Angostura Bitters
Arrowroot-thickener
Basil-gravy
Bay Leaf
Bouillon Cubes
Burnet
Butter/Margarine
Caraway Seed
Cayenne-red pepper flakes
Celery Seed-gravy
Cheese
Chili Powder
Chocolate
Cilantro

Coriander
Cream, Sour
Cream & Milk
Cumin
Dill
Fennel
Five-Spice Powder
Garlic
Ginger
Honey
Horseradish
Lemon Juice
Marjoram
Mint
Mustard

Oils & Fats-olive
Onion/Scallion
Oregano
Paprika
Pepper, Chile
Rosemary
Shallot-buttery sauces
Sorrel-cream sauces
Soy Sauce
Star Anise
Tarragon
Thyme
Tomato
Turmeric
Vinegar

How to Cook:
The key to a good sauce is in the thickening. Mix the thickener with cool water or warm fat before adding to a heated dish. Use equal parts flour and butter or fat to prevent lumps. More flour may be needed if baking with moist foods. Also puree cooked foods (asparagus, potatoes) to thicken sauces. Plan on ⅓-½ cup sauce per serving.

A little baking soda will get rid of excess grease.

Buying Guide:
You don't have time to make a sauce? Buy a packaged one and add your own spices. Beware of MSG, if you are allergic, and watch for excess sodium or salt.

Preparation Ideas:

Basic White Sauce is composed of 3 Tbsp butter/margarine, 3 Tbsp flour and 2 cups milk. Melt the butter on low first, then add the flour and cook low for 2 minutes. Gradually add *hot* milk and stir to keep smooth. If adding cheese, do it with the burner off and stir until melted. Use ½-¾ cup or 2-3 oz of cheese for mild flavor.

Basic Gravy: In a saucepan mix 3 Tbsp of warm fat from cooked meat to 3 Tbsp flour. Heat and stir 3 minutes. Slowly add 2 cups *hot* water, milk or broth until smooth and thick. Season depending upon the meal. This will make 2 cups or 4-6 servings. (To add more color, place the flour in a skillet on low heat and stir to avoid burning until brown throughout.)

The difference between a sauce and a gravy is that **gravy** *involves meat juices.* **Sauces** *are any thickened liquid used to enhance the flavor of food.*

Deglaze *means to add a little liquid to loosen the cooked-on residue in pans, which contains great flavor for making gravies.*

Sauce and Gravies Preparation Ideas continued:

Aioli: For 1½ cups, add 4 cloves minced garlic to 1¼ cups mayonnaise. From France this sauce is good on fish, cooked vegetables, dips, breads and on sandwiches as a condiment.

Alfredo Sauce: A white sauce made by mixing 1½ cups milk and 2 Tbsp cornstarch over low heat until thick. Add 1 cup sour cream, 3 oz Parmesan cheese and pepper. Add whatever other spices to taste. Try an Italian blend.

BBQ Glaze: Mix 6 Tbsp honey, 1⅓ Tbsp paprika, 2 tsp dry mustard and 1 tsp cayenne. Brush on after 5-6 minutes of cooking chicken on the grill.

Bechamel: This is a fancy name for basic white sauce.

Cheese Sauce: Mix 3 Tbsp butter and 3 oz mild gorgonzola.

Fruit Sauce: Mix the zest of 1 lemon, 2 cups of buttermilk, ½ cup sugar and a dash of salt. Chill until ice cold. Place over your favorite fruit, especially berries and peaches.

Glaze: Mix 3 Tbsp honey and 2 Tbsp soy sauce.

Harissa Sauce: Mix 2 oz dried red chiles, 2 cloves garlic, 2 tsp coriander seeds, 1½ tsp cumin, 1 tsp caraway seeds, 1 tsp dried mint, 2 Tbsp olive oil and salt. It is good for marinating grilled chicken, seafood or as a condiment.

Hoisin is a soybean sauce with five-spice powder and dried chiles used in stir-frys and in Szechuan cooking.

Horseradish Sauce: Combine 2 Tbsp margarine with 2 Tbsp flour. Mix and add 1 cup of hot milk slowly. Add 2 Tbsp horseradish at the end.

Hummus is a puree of chickpeas and ground sesame seeds.

Lemon Sauce: Mix 1 Tbsp cornstarch with 1 cup sugar. Melt ¼ cup margarine and add dry mix to it. Slowly add ¼ cup water and ½ tsp grated lemon zest. Boil for 3 minutes. Add 1½ Tbsp lemon juice. Serve warm over cake or ice cream.

Lemon Custard Sauce: Use this on pancakes, waffles or French toast. Beat 3 eggs and 1 cup sugar. Add ¼ cup lemon juice, 1 tsp lemon zest and 2 Tbsp melted margarine. Cook in a double boiler for 15 minutes on medium or until the mix coats a spoon.

Marinara/Red Sauce: Chop 3 onions and 2 cloves of garlic. Dice 2 carrots and sauté all in ¼ cup olive oil until onions are transparent. Add a large can of diced tomatoes. Blend it all in a blender. Simmer 15 minutes. Add 3 Tbsp margarine, 1 tsp basil and 1½ tsp oregano. Simmer.

Pasta or Meatball Sauce: Mix 1 can jellied cranberry sauce, 3 Tbsp steak sauce, 2 tsp brown sugar and 1 tsp prepared mustard. Beat and heat.

Mole Sauce: Puree 1 28-oz can of tomatoes, ½ small chopped onion, 1 tsp chile powder, 2 cloves of garlic, 1 tsp flour and ½ square unsweetened chocolate or 1 Tbsp cocoa. Pour into a frying pan. Simmer on until thick. This is good on chicken or any poultry.

Sauce and Gravies Preparation Ideas continued:

Mornay Sauce: To a basic white sauce add ¼ cup of grated Gruyère cheese and ¼ cup of Parmesan. Make it richer by adding 1 slightly beaten egg yolk and ¼ cup heavy cream. Try a different, strong-tasting Swiss cheese.

Pasta Mushroom Sauce: Boil 2 cups heavy cream with a little nutmeg and salt. Simmer uncovered 15 minutes. Separately, sauté 1 whole shallot and 2 garlic cloves and then add ½ tsp salt, 1 lb cremini and ½ lb shiitake mushrooms, thickly sliced. Cook covered 4 minutes and then uncovered 2 minutes. Stir ⅓ cup of grated Parmesan and some black pepper into cream and, finally, add this to the mushrooms.

Peanut Dipping Sauce: Mince 2 garlic cloves and ½ tsp dried red pepper flakes. Mix in ½ cup vinegar, ¼ cup sugar dissolved in ¼ cup hot water and ¾ cup chopped peanuts.

Peanut Sauce: (Chicken or Pork) Heat ¼ cup oil in a pan. Sauté ½ cup dry-roasted peanuts, 6 crumbled saltines and 1 chopped clove of garlic until golden brown. Drain, leaving oil in pan. Chop 4 tomatoes, 1 onion and 1 garlic clove in a blender and heat in oil. Process the peanut mix in the blender and then add it to the tomato mix. Boil until thick.

Pesto Sauce: Put 1 cup fresh basil, 3 Tbsp walnuts, 3 Tbsp Parmesan and 3 cloves garlic in a blender and add enough olive oil for a smooth paste. You may also use pine nuts. Use cilantro instead of basil for an Asian pesto and spice it up with red pepper flakes and tamari.

Potato Sauce: Mix 1 tsp olive oil with 2 Tbsp each of tomato paste and paprika, 3 Tbsp wine vinegar and a dash of cayenne.

Easy Red Sauce: Cut up the tomatoes in a can of stewed tomatoes. Keep the juice and add a minced clove of garlic, ground rosemary and fennel. Add ½ cup cool water mixed with cornstarch or arrowroot to thicken.

Red Sauce: Blend 2 Tbsp olive oil, 2 Tbsp butter, 5 plum tomatoes, 8 basil leaves and ¼ cup Parmesan cheese.

Seafood Sauce: Mix 1 cup yogurt with 3 Tbsp minced dill weed and 1½ tsp Dijon mustard.

Squash/Sweet Potato Sauce: Add sugar and cinnamon to plain yogurt. Add nuts.

Sweet & Sour Sauce: Mix 1 Tbsp soy sauce, 1 10-oz jar of currant jelly, 3 Tbsp of vinegar, ½ tsp garlic powder and ½ tsp ginger. Heat to boiling.

Tartar Sauce: Mix 1 cup mayonnaise, ½ cup chopped onion, ½ cup chopped dill weed and pepper. Add some pickle relish if you like.

Tomato/Cheese Sauce: Heat 1 cup grated cheddar or other strong cheese, ½ can tomato soup and 1 Tbsp tomato paste in a pan. When cheese is melted, add ½ cup milk.

Vanilla Sauce: This makes 2 cups and is good with fruit or dessert. Mix ½ cup instant vanilla pudding, 1 cup milk, 1 Tbsp vanilla and 1 cup Half & Half.

Your Favorite Sauce: Mix 2 cups whipping cream with 2⅔ tsp dried basil and some ground pepper. Bring to a boil. Simmer 10 minutes and strain. You can use tarragon or your favorite spice in place of basil.

A Few Words about Thickening . . .

The most common choices for thickening a sauce are flour, cornstarch and arrowroot. **Flour** is best thickened with room temperature fat to create a paste. The paste makes an opaque sauce. If water is used instead of fat, whisk quickly to dissolve lumps. To remove the raw flour taste, cook 2-3 minutes before adding to the sauce. A **roux** is an equal mix of flour and fat cooked to remove the flour taste and used to darken a sauce. The sauce is then added to the roux.

Mix 2 Tbsp flour with 2 Tbsp warm fat for every 1 cup of liquid (sauce).

Arrowroot or cornstarch makes a thickening paste when added to cool water. Both need gentle handling, since too much stirring can thin the sauce. A little salt or sugar separates the paste. If the temperature difference between the sauce and the paste is too extreme, warm the paste first by adding a little of the sauce to it and then add the warmed paste to the sauce. The heavier the concentration of the paste the thicker the sauce will be. The sauce will be clear.

Mix 1 Tbsp cornstarch or arrowroot with 2 Tbsp of *cool* water for every cup of liquid (sauce).

What Seasoning for What Sauce?

BBQ SAUCE:
Chili Powder
Honey
Horseradish
Liquid Smoke
Mustard
Pepper, Black
Syrups & Extracts-molasses
Tomato

CHEESE SAUCE:
Caraway Seed
Celery Seed
Cheese
Chervil
Chives
Mustard
Parsley
Pepper, White
Poppy Seed
Sage
Tarragon
Thyme

MUSTARD SAUCE:
Dill
Mustard
Pepper, White
Tarragon

RED/TOMATO SAUCE:
Allspice
Anise
Basil
Cilantro
Cinnamon
Cumin
Marjoram
Oils & Fats-Olive
Oregano
Pepper, Black
Pepper, Chile
Rosemary
Sage
Savory
Thyme
Vinegar

SEAFOOD SAUCE:
Dill
Marjoram
Mustard
Pepper, White
Tarragon

WHITE CREAM SAUCE:
Basil
Capers
Cayenne
Celery Seed
Cheese
Chervil
Chives
Curry Powder
Horseradish
Marjoram
Nutmeg
Pepper, White
Sorrel
Tarragon

Sausages & Links

Seasonings to use with sausages and links:

Allspice	Cumin	Oregano
Anise	Dill	Paprika
Basil	Fennel	Pepper, Black
Caraway Seed	Garlic	Pepper, Chile
Cardamom	Horseradish	Sage
Cayenne	Mace	Savory
Cheese	Marjoram	Syrups & Extracts-molasses
Chili Powder	Mustard	Tomato
Coriander	Onion/Scallion	

How to Cook:
Many sausages contain pork, so cook them thoroughly. Links (shaped like hot dogs) are cooked in water and simmered 5 minutes in a covered pan. Read the label to see if they have been pre-cooked.

Bulk sausage is made into patties, which take 12-15 minutes to cook on low heat. Juices should be clear. Roll sausages and links in flour to reduce shrinkage.

Buying Guide:
Look for pink color and a fresh smell. Use sausages right away: smoked sausages in 1-2 weeks and dried ones within 3 weeks. Freeze 2 months after first re-wrapping.

Preparation Ideas:

Hot, spicy links are handy to have around when you do not want to spend a lot of time defrosting or preparing meat. Take 2 spicy links, cook in water in the microwave for 1-2 minutes and slice into small pieces. Add them to **stir-frys, salads, casseroles, a red sauce with pasta** (see Sauces and Gravies in this section) and **soups**. It adds a nice bite and includes meat in a meal for those who want protein.

Sausages are still good with **breakfast**. No bacon? No problem—just add spicy links to your omelets, scrambled eggs or hashbrowns. Try a veggie sausage for a leaner choice.

Make **burritos** with cut up hot links, rice, beans, corn and salsa. It may not be authentic, but then we want something tasty and easy to prepare, don't we?

I've added spicy links to **lasagna** along with or instead of ground beef.

Add small chunks of spicy sausage to **spaghetti**.

Sausage and links are a good combination with **pork and beans**, whether spicy or not. Add mustard and molasses.

If you are making a **stew** or **chili**, add a spicy link or two.

Make your own version of **jambalaya** with hot links, ground beef, ham, rice, onion and tomatoes. Spice with garlic, cayenne, paprika and oregano.

Include chopped links in your **Shepherd's pie** (see Beef/Veal in this section) or in MaryJane's Eggbake (see Eggs).

Seafood/Fish

Seasonings to use with seafood/fish:

Allspice-boiled fish
Angelica
Anise
Basil
Butter/Margarine
Caraway Seed
Cardamom
Cayenne
Celery Seed
Cheese
Chervil
Chives
Curry Powder

Dill
Fennel
Garlic
Honey
Horseradish
Lemon Juice
Mace
Marjoram
Mint
Mustard
Nutmeg
Nuts
Onion/Scallion

Oregano
Paprika
Parsley
Rosemary
Sage
Savory
Shallot
Sorrel
Tarragon-tartar sauce
Thyme
Turmeric
Vanilla
Wine

How to Cook:

Thaw fish in milk for a fresh-caught flavor. *Never refreeze.* Cook fish until it reaches 140° or 10 minutes for every inch of thickness. Allow ½ lb per person, more if buying whole fish, less if fillets. Create a sauce to add flavor and/or to hide overcooking. Lemon juice after cooking prevents sogginess. If the knife is hot after inserting it into the thickest part for 5 seconds, then it is done. Otherwise, it is done when it is no longer translucent and is firm to the touch.

Buying Guide:

Fresh fish do not smell fishy and have scales that are firmly affixed. Gills are bright red or pink and eyes are clear. When buying frozen avoid ice on packages; it has been refrozen. Center cuts are best and are U-shaped.

Preparation Ideas:

Appetizer: Mix 8 oz of cream cheese, 1 Tbsp Worcestershire, ½ clove minced garlic and 1 8-oz can of minced clams. Serve on crackers. Or mix 8 oz of cream cheese, 2 tsp curry powder and 4 Tbsp red wine. Spread on crackers with a small shrimp on top.

Appetizer: Place a variety of fish, such as salmon, sardines, tuna or shrimp on a plate with artichoke hearts, tomato slices, celery, scallions or hard-boiled eggs. Add sides of tartar, cocktail or other sauce and crackers or small pieces of toast.

Clam Soup (2): Scrub 24 soft clams. Steam them until shells open. Remove round bellies and throw away the rest. Keep a little of the liquid and to it add 2 cups light cream, 2 Tbsp butter and a dash of nutmeg or mint. Simmer 2 minutes, add bellies and 1 tsp wine. Simmer just one more minute.

Deep fry frozen fish fillets, scallops or shrimp at 365° for 4-6 minutes. Use a thermometer. Dip the fish in milk and then flour, crumbs or cornmeal and fry until golden.

Sauté fillets after seasoning them with herbs and flour. Place in a pan with very hot butter and brown both sides.

Steam fish by wrapping it in cheesecloth. Boil 2" of water, and place seafood on a rack above it. Spice the water, as desired. Cover tightly and steam 1 minute per ounce.

What Seasoning for What Seafood?

CLAMS:
Butter/Margarine
Caraway Seed
Lemon Juice
Marjoram
Mint-spearmint
Paprika
Vinegar

COD:
Anise
Shallot

CRAB:
Anise
Basil
Marjoram
Nuts-almonds, peanuts
Paprika
Savory
Thyme

LOBSTER:
Dill
Paprika
Tarragon
Vanilla

OYSTERS:
Anise
Caraway Seed
Celery Seed
Chervil
Curry Powder
Horseradish
Marjoram
Mint-spearmint
Nutmeg
Oregano
Paprika

SALMON:
(Use red sockeye if canned.)
Basil
Bay Leaf
Dill
Honey
Mace
Marjoram
Mint-spearmint
Mustard
Savory

SCALLOPS:
(Bay scallops are more tender than sea scallops.)
Curry Powder
Thyme

SHRIMP:
Anise
Basil
Curry Powder
Dill
Horseradish
Mint-peppermint
Nuts-peanuts
Oregano
Savory

SOLE:
Dill
Sage
Savory
Thyme

TROUT:
Mint

TUNA:
(White solid tuna is better than the dark flaky canned tuna.)
Basil
Marjoram
Mint
Tarragon

....

Perhaps the reason seafood is so successful in soups and chowders is because it is familiar with a liquid habitat.

SEAFOOD SUBSTITUTIONS
(Interchange these fish to avoid going to the store.)

Calls for	Substitute with
*Carp	Haddock
*Cod	Haddock, Sea Bass
*Flounder	Perch, Sole
*Haddock	Carp, Cod
*Halibut	Lobster, Sea Bass
Herring	Mackerel
Mackerel	Herring
Perch	Flounder, Sole
Salmon	Swordfish
*Sea Bass	Cod, Halibut
*Sole	Flounder, Perch
*Swordfish	Salmon, Tuna
Tuna	Swordfish

*Baste with butter if baking.

Seafood Varieties

Quick to prepare and fairly lean (2 to 10% fat)—what more do you want from a meat? It comes fresh, canned and frozen. If you overcook it, you can prepare a sauce (see Sauces and Gravies in this section) to go on top and no one will notice it being dry. Cook fish on the same day that you thaw it. Do not clean (scale or bone) fish until you are ready to cook it. Serve immediately to prevent sogginess. Use leftovers to make a seafood dip with cream cheese or sour cream. Use the water from boiling shellfish for soups. Because fish has a tendency to taste bland, be generous with your spicing or top it with a sauce.

Clams-Use soft shell clams for white chowder, hard shell for Manhattan chowder. Buy shells that are firmly closed. If they close when you touch them, they are still alive and about as fresh as you can get! Allow 6-8 clams for ½ cup. Throw away broken or opened clams. Rinse and soak in salt water for 30 minutes and steam until they are partially open.

Crabs-Dungeness crabs are good in salads. Crabs will die in fresh water, so soak in salt water 30 minutes, bring to a boil and simmer 15 minutes. The shells will be reddish when cooked. Rinse, crack open and throw away spongy material. The hardness of the shells has to do with their molting stage, since they cast off old shells and make new ones.

Crayfish-Similar to a small lobster, you should use 12 unpeeled or ½ lb peeled crayfish per serving. Pull the middle tail fin to discard items not eaten and then boil them for 5-7 minutes. Fry it for appetizers.

Lobsters-Most people are familiar with the Pacific coast red lobster. Maine lobsters are bluish green. To see if a lobster is cooked correctly straighten the tail. It should curl back in place. Putting live lobsters in fresh water or ice will kill them. Boil them alive in salted water in a covered pan 15 minutes (for 2 lb) or until opaque.

Mussels-Cultured mussels are bigger and easier to cook than wild ones. Live mussels will snap shut when tapped. Allow 12 per serving. Cook immediately after cleaning and cutting away the fringe. Steam mussels 5 minutes until the shells open. Make them plumper by adding flour, which also helps eliminate sand trapped in their shells.

Scallops-Sea scallops are much larger than bay scallops and not as tender. Look for moist texture and avoid strong smells in shelled scallops. Stir-fry them in butter or olive oil for 5-7 minutes until golden and firm.

Shrimp-Shrimp are either fresh or frozen. Fresh are gray green in color and firm, while frozen should be ivory not white. Black spots mean they are old and tough. Shrimp looses a size when cooked. Allow 10 small shrimp per serving. Boil small shrimp 2 minutes, sauté for 5 minutes or stir-fry until pink. Be careful, it is easy to overcook them.

Soup

Seasonings to use with soup:

Angostura Bitters
Anise
Basil
Bay Leaf
Bouillon Cubes
Burnet
Caraway Seed
Cayenne
Cheese
Chervil
Chili Powder
Chives
Cilantro

Cloves
Cream & Milk
Cream, Sour
Curry Powder
Fennel
Ginger
Hyssop
Leeks
Lemon Grass
Mace
Marjoram
Mint-peppermint
Mustard

Onion/Scallion
Oregano
Paprika
Rosemary
Sage
Savory
Soy Sauce
Tabasco
Tamarind-hot & sour
Tarragon
Thyme
Wine
Worcestershire Sauce

How to Cook:
Save the juices from microwaving or cooking vegetables. It makes a great soup starter or stock. Use arrowroot as a thickener or puree cooked vegetables (carrots or potatoes) to thicken soups.

Bisque is a thick cream soup.
Bouillabaisse is a chowder made of various fish, veggies and seasonings.
Chowder is a thick soup with chunks of fish or other food.
Consummé is a thin soup served hot or cold made of broth with a strong flavor of meat or fish.

Buying Guide:
Read the label on soup cans and packets. Many soups have MSG and a great deal of salt/sodium. Keep in mind chunkier soups are more filling and you avoid paying for what is mostly flavored water.

What Seasoning for What Soup?

BEANS/PEA SOUP:
Basil
Cloves-split pea
Fennel
Mace
Marjoram
Mint
Oregano
Rosemary
Sage
Savory
Thyme

CHICKEN SOUP:
Bay Leaf
Mace
Marjoram
Sage
Thyme

CREAM SOUP:
Cayenne
Chervil
Chives
Rosemary
Sage
Tarragon

POTATO SOUP:
Chives
Cloves
Curry Powder
Rosemary

TOMATO SOUP:
Basil
Chili Powder
Cloves
Fennel
Rosemary
Sage

VEGETABLE SOUP:
Anise
Basil
Bay Leaf
Caraway Seed
Marjoram
Savory

New Twist to an Old Favorite: *Add a whole sweet potato with skin at the start of your chicken soup.*

Soup Preparation Ideas continued:

Bisque: Chop and stir-fry 2 lb chicken and 1 carrot. Heat and simmer for 5 minutes ¼ cup oil, 1 tsp thyme, 2 bay leaves, 2 tomatoes, ½ onion and ½ cup white wine. Add 3 cups stock, ¾ cup uncooked rice and 1 tsp pepper. Combine all and simmer 25 minutes. Blend all but the chicken in a blender. Add ½ cup heavy cream and a dash of Tabasco. Add the meat back in and serve in a bread bowl.

Broccoli Cheese Soup: Sauté a diced yellow onion in ½ cup of melted margarine until soft. Add ½ cup flour and cook low, stirring 4 minutes. Slowly add 6 cups of warm milk. When thick, add 2-3 cups of chopped broccoli, 1 tsp cayenne, 1 Tbsp Dijon mustard and ½ cup beer. Simmer until broccoli is soft. Add 1 cup light cream and 1 tsp Worcestershire Sauce. Add 1 lb or 4 cups grated cheddar and stir until melted.

Clam Chowder: Cook ¼ lb bacon in a pan. Remove the bacon and to the grease add 1 chopped onion and 1 cup cubed potatoes. Simmer 15 minutes. Add 2 cups chopped clams and 2 cups milk.

Try water chestnuts in cream soups.

Mushroom Chowder: Boil 2 small diced potatoes until done. In a large saucepan, sauté 2 Tbsp butter, 1 lb chopped mushrooms and a chopped onion. Add the potatoes, 2 beaten egg yolks, 3 cups yogurt, ¼ tsp each of thyme, mace and cloves. Finally add black pepper and ¼ cup kirsch. Heat to just below boiling. Add heated chopped links or cooked chopped leftover chicken for meat. Intense, in a good way!

Mushroom/Veggie Soup: Slice ¾ lb meadow, chanterelles or oyster mushrooms. In a large sauce pan sauté in olive oil ½ cup diced onions, 1 clove garlic, ½ cup diced red potatoes and ¼ lb green beans for 2 minutes. Add more oil and the mushrooms. Cover and cook 2 minutes on low. Add 2½ cups chicken broth, 1 can stewed tomatoes, ¼ tsp basil, ¼ tsp thyme, ⅛ tsp sage and a bay leaf. Boil, then reduce heat and simmer for 25 minutes. Sprinkle with Swiss cheese.

Miso is a Japanese stock made by fermenting and aging soybeans and rice. It is used for chicken, soups and vegetables.

There is no turtle in **Mock Turtle Soup**. *It is actually made with a calf's head.*

Easy Kid's Noodle Soup: Kids love noodles. Boil frozen mixed veggies and ramen noodles together. Add spices, water and salt or soy sauce and thicken with arrowroot. Or make canned soup go a little further by adding ramen noodles and/or mixed vegetables to it. Again add water and spice it up!

Potato Soup: Boil 5 diced potatoes in 4 cups of chicken broth and 5 chopped scallions until done. Blend broth and potatoes in blender with 8 oz cream cheese.

Zucchini Soup: Simmer sliced zucchini, tomatoes and an onion with a bouillon cube and water until soft. Add spices of your choice, puree for soup. For variety add canned milk or puree just half and add back the rest for a chunky soup. Sprinkle with cheese.

Squash (winter)

Benefits: Low in sodium, good potassium and vitamin A

Seasonings to use with squash:

Allspice	Garlic	Parsley
Basil	Ginger	Pepper, Bell
Butter/Margarine	Honey	Raisins
Caraway Seed	Lemon Juice	Rosemary
Cardamom	Marjoram	Saffron
Cayenne-red pepper flakes	Nutmeg	Savory
Cinnamon-acorn squash	Onion/Scallion	Sugar-brown sugar
Cloves	Oregano	Thyme

How to Cook:

Most **winter squash** is cut in half, the pulp and seeds are removed and then it is baked for 45 minutes to an hour at 350°. Varieties include: acorn, butternut and spaghetti. (Zucchini is a **summer squash** and is listed separately.)

Winter squash pieces can steam for 20 minutes or simmer on low in a covered pan for 30 minutes until tender.

Squash are related to cucumbers and melons and their flowers are edible.

Buying Guide:

The winter squashes have a hard outer shell and take longer to grow and cook than summer squash. Avoid dark spots or bruises on outer shells.

Preparation Ideas:

Stuff a squash with butter and brown sugar and bake.

Pumpkin Soup: Melt ¼ cup butter and sauté 3½ lb chopped pumpkin (or other winter squash) and 1 sliced onion until clear. Add 8½ cups water or broth. Boil and reduce to simmer for 30 minutes until pumpkin is soft. Strain the pumpkin and onion and puree it. Add ¼ cup butter and reheat. You can add tomatoes, orzo pasta or potatoes in the soup and use milk instead of broth. Add ginger, a cinnamon stick or cloves. Thicken with arrowroot.

Squash & Bean Stew: Sauté a chopped onion in 4 Tbsp bacon fat. Add 2 lb cubed squash and cook 5 minutes. Add 2 sliced red bell peppers and cook for 5 more minutes. Rinse and add 1 can kidney beans, one can black-eyed peas, 4 Roma tomatoes, 2-3 Anaheim chile peppers (or ⅓ tsp red pepper flakes) and 3 chopped garlic cloves. Boil and then simmer covered 30 minutes until soft. Sweet potatoes will also work.

Scrape out pumpkin and squash seeds with the top of a canning lid.

Serve winter squash with a mushroom, tomato or cheese sauce (see Sauces and Gravies).

Salad: After cutting 1 lb hubbard or butternut squash into ½" cubes, steam them for 10 minutes. Add a sliced apple, 2½ Tbsp lemon juice, ½ cup raisins (golden) and ⅔ cup chopped walnuts. For dressing, use a mix of 4 Tbsp yogurt, ¼ tsp Dijon mustard and ½ tsp honey and some black pepper over all. Chill and serve.

Stew

Seasonings to use with stew:

Anise
Basil
Bay Leaf
Bouillon Cubes
Caraway Seed
Cardamom
Cayenne
Celery Seed
Cinnamon
Chili Powder-beef
Cilantro
Cinnamon-beef
Cloves-pork or beef
Fennel

Fenugreek
Garlic
Ginger
Hyssop
Lemon Grass
Lovage
Marjoram
Mustard
Onion/Scallion
Orange-beef
Oregano
Paprika
Parsley
Pepper, Bell

Pepper, Chile
Rosemary
Saffron-chicken
Sage
Savory
Shallot
Soy Sauce
Syrups & Extracts-molasses
Tabasco
Tamarind
Thyme
Tomato
Vinegar

How to Cook:
Add most flavorings to stews in the last 45 minutes of cooking time. Add fresh herbs 15 minutes before the end of slow cooking.

The difference between a soup and a stew is that a stew is simmered, while soup is boiled. Stews also tend to be a little thicker. **Ragout** is a highly seasoned stew of meat and vegetables.

Buying Guide:
Check for MSG and lots of sodium in prepared or canned stews. Any meat will tenderize if cooked over a long period, thus you can use cheaper meats when using a crockpot for stews.

Preparation Ideas:

Crockpot Stew: Brown 1-1½ lb stew meat or ground beef. Drain grease. Spice with your favorites (onions, garlic or rosemary). Add cut potatoes and carrots (2 lb each) to fill a crockpot. Add 1 large can tomato sauce. Cook on low all day. Add 3 bay leaves, seeds from 1-2 cardamom pods and/or cayenne or chile peppers. Before serving stir in 2-3 Tbsp of molasses. It will mellow the peppery taste.

Shiitake Goulash: Sauté 2 chopped onions and 3 cloves of garlic until golden. Add 1 tsp salt and ¾ lb of quartered shiitake mushroom caps. Cover and simmer 10 minutes. Dice and add 1 lb new potatoes, 1 tsp caraway seeds, 1 tsp paprika, 1 red bell pepper in strips and 2 tomatoes in wedges. Add water, cover, bring to a boil, then simmer until potatoes are done.

Add a pinch of cinnamon in your next stew.

Vegetable Stew: Cut 2 onions, 7 carrots, and 3 potatoes into 1" chunks. Simmer in a saucepan with ¼ cup butter and 2 garlic cloves for 10 minutes. Add 5 cups water and ½ tsp ground pepper and simmer 15 minutes. Add a cabbage cut into 8 wedges. Simmer 10 minutes. Sprinkle ⅓ cup of blue cheese in a bowl and pour stew over it.

Stir-Frys

Seasonings to use with stir -frys:

Anise	Five-Spice Powder	Onion/Scallion
Cayenne	Garlic	Pepper, Chile
Cilantro	Ginger	Pepper, Szechuan
Cloves	Honey	Sesame Seed
Coriander	Horseradish-daikon	Soy Sauce
Curry Powder	Lemon Grass	Star Anise
Fennel	Lemon Juice	Vinegar
Fenugreek	Nuts	Wine

How to Cook:

The essence of **stir-frying** is to sauté meat and vegetables quickly, at a high heat and with very little oil. You can marinade meat 15 minutes before cooking in ¼ cup soy sauce, a minced garlic clove and 2 slices of minced ginger root.

Stir-fry meat first and set aside. Then cook an equal amount of vegetables in the order it takes to cook them. That is, carrots before cauliflower, celery and onions with cabbages, mushrooms and peas last. Add meat back and serve.

Buying Guide:

You may buy frozen stir-fry vegetables. Stir-frys are often enjoyed in restaurants. Ask about MSG and sodium and be careful of any pre-packaged sauces that may contain MSG.

Preparation Ideas:

Fried Rice is a variation on stir-frys. Use instant rice and sauté garlic and onion. Add curry powder and small frozen vegetables like corn and peas. Cut up a hot spicy sausage link and/or add zucchini for sweetness. Make a hole and scramble an egg in the middle and mix throughout. Salt with soy or tamari sauce. Add any of the above flavorings.

Stir-frying is a great way to experiment with spices. Use any meat to start, even leftover ham or chicken. That and some vegetables is all you need. The most time is spent in cutting up the meat and vegetables, if using fresh ones. Look for the healthier, quicker cooking rices, such as Texmati or Wehani instead of instant. Dry roast rice first to quicken cooking time.

Italian Stir-Fry: Stir-fry meat with Italian spices and tomatoes and serve over pasta.

Add a chopped apple to your stir-fry for a different texture and flavor. Nuts and seeds are also good and add crunchiness.

Honey-Dipped Stir-Fry: Pat chicken or pork dry, dip in flour with Szechuan pepper and then in a flavored honey. Finally dip in cracker crumbs and stir-fry. Use the sweet spices like five-spice powder and allspice to flavor other vegetable ingredients.

Partially cook frozen vegetables in the microwave before adding to a stir-fry. Use the juice from the vegetables, some soy sauce and arrowroot (or cornstarch) to make a sauce. Or try a peanut sauce (see Sauces and Gravies in this section).

Sweet Potato/Yam

Benefits: Very high in vitamin A and niacin

Seasonings to use with sweet potato/yam:

Allspice	Garlic	Onion/Scallion
Butter/Margarine	Ginger	Poppy Seeds
Cardamom	Honey	Raisins
Cinnamon	Mace	Rosemary
Cloves	Nutmeg	Sugar-brown
Five-Spice Powder	Nuts-coconut, walnuts	Syrup & Extracts-maple

How to Cook:

Microwave sweet potatoes after pricking with fork and placing on a paper towel. Two potatoes will take 9 minutes. Place in a covered dish and let stand for 3 more minutes. Oven cooking takes 1½ hours.

Sweet potatoes, originally from the West Indies, are a fleshy root. **Yams,** from Southeast Asia and Africa, are not related. They are fleshy stems and are not grown much in the US.

Buying Guide:

Pick ones that have pointy ends and avoid ones with spots.

Preparation Ideas:

Appetizers: For an interesting topping for crackers, blend leftover sweet potatoes with garlic, ginger and onion.

Baked Sweet Potatoes: Bake sweet potatoes with syrup, brown sugar and marshmallows. **Kass' Tropical Glaze:** Slice baked sweet potatoes. In a pan put 1 cup orange juice, ½ cup each of papaya nectar, pineapple juice and sugar. Simmer, then pour glaze over potatoes and warm in oven 15 minutes.

Chips: A Korean friend showed me how to slice raw sweet potatoes very thin and throw them in vegetable oil to make sweet potato chips! Even kids will eat these.

Honey & Yogurt Sweet Potatoes: After baking, peel sweet potatoes. Add 2 Tbsp butter, 1½ Tbsp honey and 1 Tbsp yogurt for each potato. Add pepper, ginger and cloves and beat like mashed potatoes. Add walnuts for crunch.

Mashed Sweet Potatoes: Try a little rum in your sweet potatoes. Better yet mix butter, brown sugar, rum and yogurt with mashed sweet potatoes and sprinkle with nuts and raisins.

Sweet potatoes are in the same family as morning glories. They originated in Central America and were grown in Polynesia and New Zealand by the late 15th century. They came to Virginia in 1648 and were more popular along the southeastern coast.

Muffins/Biscuits: Blend ¾ cup leftover mashed sweet potatoes with ⅔ cup milk and 4 Tbsp melted butter. Mix 1¼ cups flour, 4 tsp baking powder, 1 Tbsp sugar and ¼ tsp cinnamon. Combine. Fill greased muffin pan and bake for 15 minutes at 450°.

Tomato

Benefits: Low in calories, high in vitamins and cleansing acids

Seasonings to use with tomatoes:

Anise	Coriander	Onion/Scallion
Basil	Cumin	Oregano
Bay Leaf	Dill	Parsley
Capers	Fennel	Rosemary
Cheese	Garlic	Saffron
Chervil	Lemon Juice	Sage
Chives	Marjoram	Savory
Cilantro	Mint-peppermint	Tarragon
Cinnamon	Nutmeg	Thyme
Cloves	Oils & Fats-olive	Vinegar

How to Cook:

To peel, soak tomato in boiling water for 10 seconds, then soak in cold water. Cut out the core from the top, but peel from the bottom.

Do not eat any green parts.

Refrigerating tomatoes takes away flavor and stops the ripening process.

Plum or Roma tomatoes are good for long cooking in sauces and stews.

Buying Guide:

Tomatoes will ripen quicker in a closed brown paper bag. Buying in season is good, depending upon cost and appearance. Sometimes it is better to buy canned.

Preparation Ideas:

Appetizer/Salad: Slice a tomato and put fresh mint leaves on top with a dollop of yogurt. Stuff a tomato with guacamole.

Side Vegetable: Sauté 2 chopped cloves of garlic in olive oil. Add 2 cups cherry tomatoes and continue sautéing 2 minutes. Add 2 Tbsp minced fresh chives. Remove from heat and serve.

Stuffed Tomatoes: Slice off the tops of 4 (the number of people you are serving) tomatoes and scoop out pulp in a bowl. Moisten ½ cup bread crumbs with garlic dressing. Mix in pulp, ¾ cup yogurt, ¼ cup grated cheddar and some pepper. Fill tomatoes and place in oiled baking dish. Top with grated cheese. Bake at 375° 15-20 minutes. Also try mint, rosemary, oregano or onion. Adding rice will soak up more of the moisture. These are very tasty, but any leftover tomatoes will be soggy and unattractive.

Sprinkle a little sage on freshly sliced tomatoes! A dash of cinnamon brings out their sweetness.

Canned **stewed tomatoes** are wonderful over lean pork tenderloin. Add fresh garlic and crushed dried rosemary and fennel. Or you may thicken stewed tomatoes for a pasta sauce with mixed vegetables and spicy hot links or sausages.

I love to melt thin slices of cheddar cheese in my tomato **soup**.

Turkey & Stuffing

Benefits: 20% protein, white meat contains less fat than chicken.

Seasonings to use with turkey and stuffing:

Allspice	Fennel	Oregano
Basil	Garlic	Paprika
Bay Leaf	Ginger	Parsley
Beer-marinade,tenderizer	Honey	Pepper, White
Cardamom	Juniper-stuffing	Raisins-stuffing
Cayenne	Leeks	Rosemary
Celery Seed	Lemon Grass	Sage-stuffing
Chervil	Mace	Savory
Chives	Marjoram	Sesame Seeds
Cilantro	Mint	Shallot
Cinnamon	Mustard	Tarragon
Cloves-stuffing	Nutmeg	Thyme
Cumin	Nuts-almonds, cashews, pistachios	Turmeric
Curry Powder	Onion/Scallion-stuffing	Wine
Dill-pot pies	Orange-stuffing	

How to Cook:
Remove giblets. Rub outside with butter. Wrap airtight in foil at 450° for 3½ hours for a 20 lb turkey. Unwrap last 30 minutes. Baste to brown. Add an hour if unwrapped and lower the oven to 325°. Thermometer should be at 175° when done. Microwaving keeps turkey moist. If stuffing, use 1 cup stuffing per lb of turkey and add 3 minutes per lb for cooking. Carve after letting it sit covered for 15 minutes. Use 2 Tbsp fat for every cup of nonfat juice to make gravy.

5 lb poultry = 3 cups diced cooked

Buying Guide:
Turkey is lean with less fat in the white meat vs the dark meat. Look for moist, tender skin. Hens have more meat on them than toms. A flexible breast bone means the turkey is tender.

Preparation Ideas (see Chicken also):

Ground turkey can be used as a healthier ground beef substitute for hamburgers, spaghetti or meatloaf. Use butter, since turkey does not have much fat and it will stick to pans. Use more spices, since little fat means less flavor.

A goose has a lot more bone and fat, so buy larger.

Stuffing: (*Stuffing is cooked inside the bird; dressing is cooked outside.*) Make your own by melting some butter, throwing in the spices you want and then add the croutons. Add the cooked, cut up giblets from the bird, if desired. Or use packaged croutons, but add more of the spices you like. Apples, nuts, celery and red onions are especially good.

Cover the carcass in water. Simmer with 1 onion, 2 stalks of celery, and 2 carrots. Save the liquid for soup or gravy. Use the leftover meat in soup.

❧ Thawing Turkey ❧
(never at room temperature)

Weight	Time in Refrig.	Time in Cold Water
8 lb	1 day	5 hours
12 lb	2 days	6 hours
16 lb	3 days	7 hours
20 lb	4 days	8 hours

Vegetables

Seasonings to use with vegetables: Vegetable color that will go with the seasoning is indicated.

Allspice-yellow, red
Anise-carrots
Basil-green
Burnet
Butter/Margarine
Caraway Seed-red
Cheese
Chervil
Chives-green
Cilantro
Cinnamon-orange, yellow
Cloves-orange, yellow
Curry Powder

Cumin-red
Dill-white
Fennel
Ginger
Horseradish-red
Hyssop
Lemon Juice
Marjoram
Mint-peas
Nutmeg-yellow, orange
Nuts
Oils & Fats-olive
Onion/Scallion

Oregano-red
Paprika-red
Parsley-red
Poppy Seeds-cooked
Rosemary-stuffed
Sage-red, orange
Savory-red, yellow, orange
Sesame Seeds-red, yellow, orange
Tabasco
Tarragon
Thyme
Turmeric

How to Cook:

The key to vegetables is: the less you cook, the more nutrients remain. Generally cover vegetables that grow below the ground (except potatoes) when cooking and uncover those above ground.

Covering vegetables with a loose fitting lid or vented plastic wrap in a microwave retains moisture and accelerates cooking time. Stir half way through to equalize heat. *Salt after cooking.*

Buying Guide:

See individually listed vegetables.

Generally, the older the vegetable, the less flavor it has.

Canned vegetables are precooked.

Preparation Ideas: (See specific vegetable listings.)

Cream one stick of butter (½ cup). Add ⅛ tsp white pepper, 1 tsp parsley and stir in slowly 1½ Tbsp lemon juice. Pour over vegetables.

Sauté vegetables in sesame oil and add roasted sesame seeds.

Simmer your veggies in a mix of lemon, pepper and garlic.

Foil wrap vegetables, add spices and roast in an oven or on the grill.

Kebab them. (See Marinades.)

Store vegetable juices after cooking them and use them for a soup or stew base. Use quickly, since they will not keep long. Use them when mashing potatoes or for making sauces.

Vegetable Gumbo: In a crockpot put 1 chopped onion, 3 cloves minced garlic, 1 diced red bell pepper, ⅓ head of kale, 2 large chopped tomatoes, 3 celery stalks with leaves, 5 sliced okra, ½ tsp red pepper flakes, 4 cups broth or water, 1 tsp cumin and 1 tsp thyme. Add 1 can of corn and ½ tsp Tabasco 20 minutes before serving over rice in a bowl. Add spicy links or pork if you want meat. You can use other cabbages for kale.

Storing Fresh Vegetables

The crisper in your refrigerator should be used to keep foods **warmer and more humid** than the rest of the refrigerator. Humidity prevents vegetables from wilting, so store them in the crisper.

Do not sprinkle or wash produce before storage, since that just encourages rot.

If you want items to be stored **cold and humid**, put them in a plastic bag or an airtight container in the back of the refrigerator. This also prevents absorption of odors from other refrigerated items.

Generally, the greener the vegetable the more vitamins and food value it has. Most dark yellow vegetables and carrots have vitamin A. All vegetables contain vitamins A, C and B2, minerals including potassium, magnesium, calcium, iron and phosphorous and good old roughage.

Keep vegetables cool and in the dark, while storing, to help them maintain nutrients. Most should not be trimmed in order to maintain vitamins and minerals. For the same reason, do not wash vegetables after slicing or cutting. To maintain color sprinkle with lemon juice.

Buying vegetables in season reduces the chance of more harmful chemicals being used for growth during the off season. Organically grown vegetables reduce the chance of chemical additives even more,

although they can some times look inferior in size or glossiness.

For more information on a particular vegetable, go to that particular listing in this section of the book.

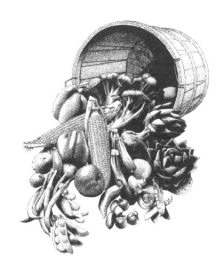

A more detailed description of how to store vegetables and how to microwave them follows. Take note of how long various vegetables last and plan your meals accordingly.

Keep the temperature in your refrigerator between 34° and 40° F. Freezers should be kept at 0° F if you are storing items for more than two weeks.

Storing and Microwaving Fresh Vegetables

FRESH VEGETABLE	HOW TO STORE	DAYS OF STORAGE	MICROWAVING Minutes to Cook
Artichoke	crisper	1-2	6-8 each
Asparagus	crisper in damp cloth; standing in water	2-3	6 per lb
Broccoli	crisper	2	8 per lb-spears
Brussels Sprouts	crisper	2-3	10 per lb
Cabbage	crisper, cover cut areas with clear wrap	14	8 per lb shredded
Cabbage-red	cover red cabbage with foil	14	8 per lb shredded
Carrot	crisper	21	8 per ½ lb sliced
Cauliflower	crisper	3-5	13 per lb flowerets
Celery	crisper, in a plastic open bag	7-14	13 per 4 cups ½" slices
Chard-leaves	plastic bag in crisper	2-3	6 per lb
Chard-stems	rolled in wet paper	8	8
Corn -on the cob	crisper still in husk	3-4	6 per 2 cobs
Cucumber	crisper	6-7	not cooked
Eggplant	crisper	5-6	7 per lb
Fennel	crisper	14	8 per 2 quartered bulbs
Green Beans	plastic bag	3	8 per ½ lb in ½ cup water
Kale	cool and moist in crisper	2	6 per lb
Leeks	crisper	10	9 per 2 whole
Peas	crisper	1-2	4 per lb
Potato	cool dark; not refrigerated	21	8 per 2 + cover 10
Spinach	nitrates will develop if stored at all	Do not store	6 per lb
Sweet Potato	cool dark; not refrigerated	14	9 per 2 potatoes
Tomato	crisper, closed paper bag to ripen	5-6 if refrgd.	Blanch 10 seconds, peel
Zucchini	crisper	3-4	6 per lb

Yogurt

Benefits: Quickly digested, replenishes beneficial bacteria killed by antibiotics, can reduce yeast infections
Externally: Bleaching effect on freckles, good for skin

Seasonings to use with yogurt:

Basil	Curry Powder	Nutmeg
Burnet	Fennel	Parsley
Caraway Seed	Garlic	Pepper, Chile
Cardamom	Honey	Raisins
Cilantro	Lemon Juice	Syrups & Extracts
Cinnamon	Onion/Scallion	Tomato
Coffee	Mint-peppermint	Vanilla

How to Cook:
Add ½ tsp baking soda for each cup of yogurt, when baking with it. Use yogurt at room temperature at the end of cooking to prevent curdling. Low temperatures and short exposure to heat are best.

Homemade yogurt is easy to make, less expensive and lower in calories. It is healthier than the packaged flavored yogurts, since you can make it with skim milk and avoid sugar and additives.

Buying Guide:
Buy plain yogurt and add flavors or fruit to it yourself. Although non-fat it can have lots of sugar. Read the labels.

Preparation Ideas:

For Breakfast: Add yogurt to oatmeal, sprinkle with cinnamon and fruit. The yogurt will cool oatmeal and is thicker and richer than milk. Yogurt is also great with granola and fruit.

Cheese: You can easily make cream cheese from yogurt by placing it in several layers of cheesecloth and tying it over your faucet. Stir it and let it drain overnight unrefrigerated. It has fewer calories (250 per cup) than does a cup of cream cheese (800) and lasts about a week refrigerated. Add spices for spreads or use on fruit. Salt if desired and drain longer if you want it thicker. Use the flavorings listed under Flavored Butters in the front spice section of the book.

Cheese Sauce: Make a cheese sauce with cheese and yogurt and your favorite spices. Pour over pasta and add whatever veggies you have on hand.

Although yogurt has been around for 4,000 years, it has been available commercially only since 1925. Isaac Carasso, a Spanish businessman, marketed his yogurt cultures in Barcelona and opened his first plant, naming it after his son Daniel, thus the Danone Company. The Dannon name came during WWII when Daniel moved to New York and started a branch in the US before moving back to France. Flavors were added in 1946 to make yogurt more appealing to the sweets-loving US market.

Yogurt Preparation Ideas continued:

Cream Substitute: Substitute yogurt for heavy creams in soups and sauces or in place of whipped cream on desserts. Remember that you cannot use it under high heat.

Crêpe Sauce or Syrup Substitute: Make thin pancakes. Mix plain yogurt with fresh fruit and dollop inside and roll it up. Or place a spoonful of yogurt on top of pancakes with fruit.

Cucumbers & Yogurt: Mince fresh mint with plain yogurt and sliced cucumbers. Add garlic and white pepper.

Dessert Sauce: Pour this over vanilla ice cream or shortcake. Mix 1 pint fruit, ½ cup yogurt, ½ tsp vanilla, 2 Tbsp brown sugar and ¼ tsp extract (almond, mint or chocolate).

Dips: Use yogurt instead of cream or cream cheese to make dips. Flavor it with onion, garlic or curry powder. Add tomatoes for a salsa or stir plain yogurt into a spicy salsa for a cheesy chip dip. Stuff tomatoes or bell peppers with yogurt and spice for dipping. Add cornstarch or drain it to thicken.

Dressing: Make a dressing for fruit salad with ½ cup plain yogurt, 2 tsp honey, ⅛ tsp of cardamom and 1 tsp of coconut.

Meat Marinade: Use yogurt to marinate meat. Then make a gravy with it.

Mayonnaise Substitute: Use yogurt in place of mayonnaise in coleslaws and salads for less fat. Thicken with cornstarch.

Muffins: Sift 1¼ cups flour, ⅛ cup sugar, 1 tsp baking powder and ½ tsp baking soda (½ cup blueberries optional). Separately, combine 1 beaten egg, ½ cup yogurt and 2 Tbsp melted butter. Add this to dry ingredients and stir until moistened. Should be lumpy. Fill greased tins ⅔ full and bake at 400° for 25 minutes until golden brown.

Yog-sicles: Take a cup of yogurt and mix with any fruit (berries are good) or fruit concentrate. Place in a mold with sticks and freeze. Add sugar if the fruit is tart. Blend the fruit first if you like.

To keep yogurt from separating, fold in 2 tsp cornstarch dissolved in 3 tsp water for every cup of yogurt.

Use a dollop of yogurt to "cool down" a spicy dish.

Pudding Snack: Flavor plain yogurt with fruit-flavored extracts or honey, when you do not have any fruit on hand. Sprinkle with cookie sprinkles to interest kids.

Sauce: Mix yogurt with a bouillon cube broth and spice it to taste. Pour this mix over leftover meats, vegetables or pasta.

Smoothies: Make your own smoothies with plain yogurt, crushed ice, blueberries, strawberries, peaches, bananas or your favorite fruit. Add a little vanilla or other flavored extract (anise or mint). Or add a fruit-flavored liquor like kirsch.

Sour Cream Substitute: Use yogurt instead of sour cream on baked potatoes. Yogurt plus 2 Tbsp of flour can be used instead of sour cream to make a sauce. Remember to avoid high heat when using yogurt.

Zucchini (courgettes, summer squash)

Benefits: Low in calories and sodium, easy to digest

Seasonings to use with zucchini:

Allspice	Curry Powder	Nuts-peanuts, walnuts
Basil	Five-Spice Powder	Onion/Scallion
Bouillon Cube	Garlic	Oregano
Butter/Margarine	Ginger	Pepper, Bell
Caraway Seed	Lemon Juice	Sesame Seeds
Cayenne-red pepper flakes	Liquid Smoke	Shallot
Cheese	Marjoram	Tarragon
Cream, Sour	Mint	Thyme
Cumin	Mustard	Tomato

How to Cook:
Boil whole ones about 5 minutes. Microwave 6 minutes per lb. Add them last when stir-frying, in soups or stews and in the last 15 min if cooking in a crockpot. Do not peel. They will absorb grease when fried.

3 medium, sliced= 3 cups
4 cups shredded = 1 lb
2 zucchinis, grated = 1 cup

Pureed zucchini makes a good base for a vegetable soup.

Buying Guide:
Pick medium-sized zucchinis that are 7" long. When the skin can be easily cut with a fingernail, you know it is fresh.

Preparation Ideas:

Appetizer: Spread zucchini slices with cream cheese. Sprinkle with garlic or onion powder or sesame seeds. Use it with or without a cracker. Top with a slice of Roma tomato or hard-boiled egg. Or try tuna salad, ham or pepperoni.

Zucchini Bread (2 loaves): Mix 3 beaten eggs, 1 cup apple-sauce, ¾ cup sugar, 2 cups grated, packed zucchini and 2 tsp vanilla. Separately, mix 2¼ cups flour, 1 cup rolled oats, 1 tsp each baking powder and baking soda and 3 tsp cinnamon. Add ¾ cup raisins or 1 cup nuts. Bake at 350° for 1 hour. Remove after 10 minutes.

Zucchini Casserole: Slice 2 zucchinis and add cooked pinto beans, corn and cubed cheese. Bake or microwave until cheese has melted. Add cayenne, curry powder or cumin.

Try a **casserole** of peas, zucchini and mushrooms. Layer with a white mustard or cheese sauce (See Sauces and Gravies). Bake at 275° for 30 minutes covered and add seeds (sesame or sunflower) or nuts and bake uncovered 15 minutes more.

When zucchini is on sale, buy a bunch, slice it in ¼" slices, blanch for 3 minutes, then dip in ice water 3 minutes to stop the cooking. Drain and freeze in plastic bags. Leave ½" for expansion.

Zucchini goes well with these cheeses: Swiss, Parmesan, Romano, Mozzarella, Cheddar and Gruyère. . . And with the following vegetables: broccoli, carrots, celery, corn, eggplant, green peppers, mushrooms, peas and tomatoes.

For a white sauce with zucchini, use mustard, Swiss cheese and onions.

Zucchini Preparation Ideas continued:

Walnuts & Zucchini: Sauté 2 lb (6) zucchini in butter until tender. Melt more butter. Mix in 2 tsp curry powder and add 1 cup of walnuts and cook until toasted. Add the zucchini.

Zucchini-Corn Chowder: Cook 4 strips bacon, crumble and set aside. Sauté 3 cups sliced zucchini, 1 cup minced onion and 1 minced garlic clove in bacon grease. Add 1 can corn, 1 cup water, ¼ tsp basil and ¼ tsp tarragon and bring to boil. Simmer low for 10 minutes. Separately, mix 2 cups milk and 2 beaten eggs and add to the pot. Simmer until thickened, but do not boil. Sprinkle on bacon bits. Serve it in a bread bowl.

Zucchini Scramble: Before adding to eggs, sauté diced zucchini in curry powder and shallots. Add tomatoes.

Zucchini Hash Browns: Instead of potatoes, shred zucchini, and add a little caraway seed or any listed spice, pepper and cheese. Let brown on both sides with a little butter.

Zucchini Jam: A Creole dish made by browning salted zucchini in fat and simmering it until the liquid evaporates and the mix turns amber.

Zucchini & Peanut Salad: Add sliced zucchini raw to salads. Add peanuts for a little protein and a great taste. Tomatoes also work well. Use a variety of lettuces.

Cook up sliced zucchini, tomatoes and onion with a bouillon cube and water until soft. Add spices of your choice, puree for **soup**. For variety and to stretch it further add canned milk. Sprinkle with cheese for fun.

Mix zucchini with sausage and/or ground beef in casseroles.

Zucchini Parmesan: Heat ⅓ cup olive oil and add 2 sliced garlic cloves until browned. Discard garlic. Slice thinly 7 small zucchini and add them to oil. Add ½ cup or 2 oz of grated Parmesan. Put in a greased baking dish, sprinkle with ¼ cup additional Parmesan and bake at 350° for 15 minutes. Pepper to taste.

Zucchini & Apple Stir-Fry: Slice and core 2 apples and slice 4 zucchini. Add the sweet spices of allspice, five-spice powder or mint. For a contrast add onion. Serve over pasta or rice. Add chicken or pork at the beginning, if desired.

Zucchini & Cabbage Stir-Fry: Slice 4 zucchini and shred ½ head of cabbage. Add onion, garlic, a little sugar, red pepper flakes and/or peanuts or seeds. Add meat at the beginning if desired. Serve over rice.

Stuffed Zucchini: Hollow out zucchini and fill with any meat or spices. Add Liquid Smoke for a grilled flavor. Bake 25 minutes at 350°. As an appetizer stuff with spiced, thinned cream cheese and serve cold.

Zucchini-Stuffed Tomato: Cut off the top of a tomato and scoop it out. Stuff it with diced sautéed zucchini, instant rice and your favorite spices (Italian blend is good). Add sour cream and stuff the tomato. Sprinkle with cheddar. Add water to prevent burning the bottoms of the tomatoes. Cook 20 minutes at 350°.

Flavor Substitutions
See Equivalency Charts for Baking Substitutions

Use these substitutions if you are missing a particular flavor and will settle for a flavor that is a bit stronger or weaker instead of running to the store.

EXCHANGE:	WITH ANY ONE OF THESE ITEMS:
Allspice	Cinnamon, Cloves, Nutmeg or a mix of the three
Almonds	Peanuts, Sesame Seeds
Angelica	Anise, Honey, Juniper, Lovage, Sugar
Anise	Chervil, Cilantro, Fennel, Star Anise
Basil	Summer Savory, Tarragon
Bouillon Cubes	Soup or Stock, Boil water with carrots, celery and soy sauce
Capers	Salt
Caraway Seed	Anise ground with toasted Sesame Seeds, Dill Seed
Cardamom	Cumin, Curry Powder, Ginger
Cayenne	Red Pepper Flakes, Chili Powder (hot), Horseradish, Black Pepper, Tabasco
Celery Seed	Fenugreek
Chervil	Anise, Cilantro, Fennel, Flat Leaf Parsley, Star Anise
Chili Powder	Cayenne, Chile Peppers, Red Pepper Flakes, Szechuan Pepper, Tabasco
Chives	Leeks, Scallions (upper green part), Shallot
Cilantro	Anise, Chervil, Fennel, Star Anise
Cinnamon	Allspice
Cloves	Allspice
Coriander	Lemon Grass
Cream-whipping	A can of ice cold evaporated milk
Cumin	Cardamom, Curry Powder
Curry Powder	Cumin + Mustard (dry) + Allspice + Black Pepper
Dill Seed	Caraway Seed
Dill Weed	Parsley
Fennel	Anise, Chervil, Cilantro, Star Anise
Fenugreek	Celery Seed
Garlic	Leeks, Red Onion, Shallot
Ginger	Cardamom, Turmeric, ⅓ Mace + ⅔ Lemon Peel
Honey	Angelica, Sugar, Syrup
Horseradish	Chile Peppers, Dijon or dry Mustard, Szechuan Pepper, Tabasco
Leeks	Chives, Garlic, Red Onion, Shallot
Lemon Grass	Coriander
Lemon Juice	Vinegar, Wine
Liquid Smoke	Soy Sauce, Steak Sauce, Worcestershire Sauce
Lovage	Angelica, Celery Seed
Mace	Nutmeg
Maple (extract)	Vanilla, Brown Sugar, Molasses

Flavor Substitutions continued

EXCHANGE	WITH ANY ONE OF THESE ITEMS:
Marjoram	Oregano
Mint	Basil, Thyme
Mustard	Cayenne, Horseradish, Szechuan Pepper
Nutmeg	Allspice, Mace
Olive Oil	Canola or Peanut Oil (all low in cholesterol)
Onion	Garlic, Leek, Scallion, Shallot
Orange	Grand Marnier, orange-flavored Honey
Oregano	Marjoram
Parsley	Anise, Chervil, Dill Weed
Peanuts	Almonds, Sesame Seeds
Pepper, Black	Cayenne, Chile Peppers, Red Pepper Flakes, Szechuan Pepper, Tabasco
Peppers, Chile	Cayenne, Black Pepper, Red Pepper Flakes, Szechuan Pepper, Tabasco
Pistachios	Almond + Vanilla Extract
Rosemary	Mint + a little ground Ginger or Sage
Saffron	Marigolds (flower), Turmeric
Salt	Capers, Soy Sauce
Savory	Thyme
Scallion	Garlic, Leek, Onion, Shallot
Sesame Seeds	Almonds, Peanuts
Shallot	Chives, Garlic, Leek, Onion, Scallion (green tops are mild)
Sour Cream	Cottage or Cream Cheese (blended), Yogurt
Soy Sauce	Capers, Salt, Bouillon Cube dissolved in a little water
Star Anise	Anise, Chervil, Cilantro, Fennel
Sugar	Angelica, Fruit, Honey, Syrup & Extracts
Syrup-maple	Brown Sugar, crushed Pecans; Extracts for other syrups
Szechuan Pepper	Cayenne, Horseradish, Mustard (hot), Black Pepper, Tabasco
Tabasco	Cayenne, Chile Peppers, Horseradish, Black Pepper, Red Pepper Flakes
Thyme	Savory
Turmeric	Cardamom, Ginger, Saffron
Vanilla	Maple Extract, Walnut Extract
Vinegar	Lemon Juice, Wine
Wine	Lemon Juice, Vinegar
Worcestershire	Bouillon Cubes, Liquid Smoke, Steak Sauce
Yogurt	Cream or Cottage Cheese (blended), Sour Cream

Cooking and Preparing Definitions

Bake-Use in desserts, with meat and vegetable cooking. Make sure your dish is full and covered to keep in moisture. If you are cooking mostly vegetables, do not add water, as they produce their own juices. A few drops of oil will keep food from scorching. Place the oven's rack in the middle.

Boil-Use for vegetables, grains, pastas and some desserts. Boiling cooks food in hot water in a covered pan. It is faster than steaming, but takes away nutrients.Timing starts after the food is added and the water boils again. **Parboiling** partially boils items such as carrots that take a while. This allows you to add it to items that do not take as long, so everything gets done at the same time. **Blanching** is boiling food for 1-2 seconds in water and then rinsing in cold water. It sets color, aids in peeling (such as tomatoes) and is done before freezing. Use water for sauces and soups.

Braise-Use for long slow cooking on top or in the oven in a tightly covered pan with a little liquid. Meats or vegetables are first **browned** in oil (cooked on the outside until brown in color, thereby sealing in the juices and flavor) and then cooked on low heat.

Broil-Although meats can handle the intense heat of 550°, most vegetables cannot, except when kabobing. Broiling is also used to add a crust or color to casseroles and desserts after cooking. The broiler is the top heating element in an electric oven and the bottom drawer on a gas stove.

Casserole-is a mixture of foods, cooked in a covered dish in the oven or on top of the stove. It can be reheated or frozen. Little liquid is needed, since steam drips back in from the cover.

Chopping-is cutting food in uneven pieces about ½" x ¼". **Cubing** is cutting into ½" x ½" pieces or larger. **Dicing** is cutting into small even squares about ¼" x ¼." **Julienne** is cutting vegetables into thin match-like strips. **Mincing** is cutting food into uneven small pieces, slightly larger than ground or **crushed. Grating** is making fine pieces or particles by rubbing over a course grater. **Shredding** is using the fine side of a grater to make very narrow strips.

Crockpot-is a heated dish that slowly cooks (half or all day) soups or stews. It is used to maintain vitamins and nutrients and allows the food and seasonings to mingle together.

Double Boiler-A pan, placed in another pan with a single lid. The lower pot is half-filled with hot simmering (not boiling) water. It is used when consistent, gentle cooking is desired.

Fry-Cooking food in oil that can handle high temperatures. Season prior to placing in hot oil.

Folding-Folding is gently stirring a fluffy substance, such as egg whites, into a mixture without deflating it. Cut through the middle of the mix and stir a spoon along the bottom and up the side of the bowl gently until evenly blended.

Cooking and Preparing Definitions continued

Grill/Barbeque-Although heat is not easily controlled, grilling beats cooking indoors on a hot summer day. Wrap vegetables, such as corn, potatoes, tomatoes and onions in aluminum foil. Baste all meats in your favorite barbeque sauce or marinade. Be careful not to overcook the meat.

Microwave-Although often used on leftovers, microwaving is a great way to cook fresh vegetables. It saves time and nutrients. Meatier pieces are best placed on the outside edges. Fresh herb flavors may not be released, so do a taste test and add more if necessary. *Keep a spray bottle of water nearby and spritz on leftovers when reheating, thus steaming the item.*

Pickle-To pickle is to preserve or flavor meat, fish or vegetables in a brine, or a mix of vinegar and other seasonings.

Poach-Poaching is simmering an item in water, not quite covering it, and keeping it just below the boiling point. It is usually associated with eggs or salmon.

Pressure Cook-Pressure cooking is a way of quick cooking at a high temperature in a tightly sealed pot by building up steam. Food maintains nutrients. It is used for dense foods such as beans, grains and tough meat. It tends to overcook less dense vegetables.

Roast-A dry cooking method, roasting is done in the oven in an uncovered pan. It browns on the outside and if the meat is tender to begin with, it will be moist on the inside.

Puree-Food is mashed to a thick, smooth texture. It is often used to thicken soups or sauces.

Sauté/Stir-Fry-Cook and/or brown thin slices of food in a pan with a little oil or butter, stirring constantly. Stir-frying is done at a higher temperature. If pieces are thick, lower the temperature so the center is cooked before the surface burns. Use less oil by heating the pan first.

Simmer/Stew-Simmering is considered a slow boil and a great way to blend flavors in a sauce or slow cook meat so that it is not tough. Stewing is the same, but with a lid.

Steam-Steam items to maintain nutrients. Place food in a basket or on a rack above, but not touching, boiling water. The steam gently cooks the food, usually vegetables.

Sweat-Sweating is another way of slow cooking. Use a little fat and heat food in a tightly covered pan just below boiling for two minutes. Then add a little water and continue heating. Seasonings are added at any point. Another procedure is to first wrap the food in foil and let it cook in its own juices.

Equivalency Chart: Measurements

Measurement Equivalents (Metric measurements are rounded.)

Less than ⅛ tsp = **pinch**
¼ tsp = a **dash** = 3 drops
½ tsp = a **sprig** = 2½ ml
1 tsp = ⅛ oz = 5 ml = 5 grams
3 tsp = 1 Tbsp
⅓ Tbsp = 1 tsp
½ Tbsp = 1½ tsp
1 rounded Tbsp = a **scoop or dollop**
1 Tbsp = ½ fluid oz = 15 grams
2 Tbsp = ⅛ cup = 1 fluid oz
3 Tbsp = a **jigger** = 1½ fluid oz
1 oz = 2 Tbsp = ⅛ cup = 30 ml = 28 grams
2 oz = 4 Tbsp = ¼ cup = 59 ml = 58 grams
3½ oz = 100 grams
4 oz = 8 Tbsp = ½ cup = 118 ml = 115 grams
8 oz = 16 Tbsp = 1 cup = 235 ml = 225 grams
16 oz = 1 lb = 450 grams
⅛ cup = 2 Tbsp
⅜ cup = ¼ cup + 2 Tbsp (⅛ cup)
⅝ cup = ½ cup + 2 Tbsp (⅛ cup)
⅞ cup = ¾ cup + 2 Tbsp (⅛ cup)
1 cup = ½ pint = 8 fluid oz = 237 ml
2 cups = 1 pint = 16 fluid oz = 473 ml
4 cups = 2 pint = 1 qt = 32 fluid oz = 1 liter
16 cups = 4 qt = 1 gallon = 128 fluid oz
1 liter = about 1 qt
1 lb = .45 kilogram
1 kilogram = 2 lb 3 oz

Rectangular & Loaf Pan Equivalents

Lower oven temperature 25° when using glass.

8" x 8" x 2" = 8 cups = 8-16 servings*
9" x 9" x 1½" = 8 cups = 8-16 servings
9" x 9" x 2" = 10 cups = 9-16 servings
9" x 3½" tube = 12 cups = 18-20 servings
9" x 5" x 3" loaf = 8 cups = 10-12 servings

*To figure out capacity of a pan, count the number
of cups of water it will hold up to the rim of the pan.

Abbreviations

BBQ=barbeque
lb = pound(s)
min =minute(s)
ml = milliliter(s)
oz = ounce(s)
qt = quart(s)

refrgd = refrigerated
SW = Southwest(ern)
tsp = teaspoon(s)
Tbsp = Tablespoon(s)
US = United States

Power Outage
Frozen items keep 24-36 hours without electricity; the refrigerator will stay cool 4-6 hours.

Measurements of cups or spoons should always be level in US cookbooks. Outside the US, assume heaping spoonfuls.

Temperatures
(all temperatures in the book are Fahrenheit)

Room temperature = 70°
Lukewarm = 90°
Simmer = 115°
Low Oven = 250-300°
Moderate Oven = 325-375°
Hot Oven = 400-475°
Broil = 550°

Microwave
Cookbooks assume a 700 watt oven, so you may have to adjust the timing up or down.

Water Boils
at 212° at sea level
at 203° at 5,000 ft.
at 194° at 10,000 ft.

Can Sizes

No.	Oz	Cups
300	14-16	1¾
303	16-17	2
1	11½	1⅓
2	20	2½
2½	29	3½
3	46	5¾

Converting Fahrenheit to Celsius
Subtract 32, multiply by 5 and then divide by 9.

(212-32) x 5 ÷ 9 = 100

Equivalency Chart: Baking

Chocolate Equivalents
1 oz unsweetened chocolate = 3 Tbsp unsweetened cocoa + 1 Tbsp butter
1 oz chocolate = 1 square
12 oz chocolate chips or carobs = 2 cups

Dairy Equivalents
Butter 1 cup = ½ lb butter = 2 sticks = ⅞ cup shortening + ½ tsp salt
Cheese ¼ lb = 1 cup grated cheese = 4 oz (Use 2-4 oz per serving.)
¾ cup cream = 1 cup yogurt + ½ tsp baking soda (for baking only)
1 cup heavy cream = ¾ cup whole milk + ⅓ cup butter
1 cup light cream = ⅞ cup milk + 3 Tbsp butter
1 cup half & half = 1½ Tbsp butter + whole milk to equal 1 cup
                  = 1 cup evaporated milk
1 cup sour milk = 1 Tbsp lemon juice + 1 cup sweet milk
1 cup buttermilk = 1 cup yogurt =
                1 cup milk + ¾ Tbsp cream of tartar =
                1 cup milk + 1 Tbsp vinegar (let stand 5 minutes)

> ½ cup salted butter contains ¼ tsp salt

Egg Equivalents
1 cup = 5 large eggs or 8 egg whites or 13 egg yolks
1 egg = 2 tsp arrowroot + 2 Tbsp apple juice + ¼ cup milk

Flour Equivalents
4 cups white sifted flour = 1 lb = 500 grams = 3 cups whole wheat sifted
1 cup white flour = ¾ cup wheat + ⅔ of butter called for in a cookie recipe
1 cup self-rising flour = 1 cup flour + 1¼ tsp baking soda
2 Tbsp flour = 1 Tbsp cornstarch = 1 Tbsp arrowroot (for thickening sauces and gravies)

Sugar/Honey/Molasses Equivalents
2 cups sugar = 2¼ cups packed brown sugar = 1 lb
1 cup sugar = 1¾ cups unsifted powdered sugar (2¼ cups sifted)
1 cup honey = 1¼ cups sugar + ¼ cup water
1 cup sugar = ⅔ cup honey (or maple syrup) + ¼ cup flour
1 cup brown sugar = 1 cup white sugar + 4 Tbsp molasses
1 cup powdered sugar = ½ cup honey + 1 Tbsp granulated sugar
1 cup corn syrup = 1 cup sugar + ¼ cup water (boil together until syrupy)
1 cup molasses = ¾ cup sugar + ¼ cup water (increase spices in recipe)
1⅓ cup honey = 1 lb
3½ cups powdered sugar = 1 lb

> When substituting sugar with honey or syrup, reduce heat by 25° and cook a little longer to prevent burning.

Other Baking Equivalents
1 tsp baking powder = ¼ tsp baking soda + ½ tsp cream of tartar
1 tsp baking powder = 4 tsp quick tapioca
2 oz compressed yeast = ¾ oz of dry yeast
1 tsp lemon juice = ½ tsp vinegar

> **High Altitude Baking** (5,000 ft.)
> Reduce butter by 10%
> Reduce sugar by 25%.
> Reduce baking powder by 25%.
> Add 2 Tbsp liquid for 1 cup of liquid.
> Add 2 tsp flour for 1 cup of flour.
> Increase oven temperature by 25°.
> Decrease baking time a little.

Equivalency Chart: Sizes & Substitutions

Crumb/Cracker Equivalents
1 cup Bread crumbs = ¾ cup cracker crumbs
22 Vanilla wafers = 1 cup crumbs
15 Graham crackers = 1 cup crumbs
28 Saltines = 1 cup crumbs

Fruit Equivalents
Apples   1 lb = 2 large = 3 cups sliced
Bananas 1 lb = 3-4 whole = 2 cups sliced
             = 1¾ cups mashed
Coconut 1 lb = 5 cups shredded or flaked
Dates   1 lb = 2⅔ cups chopped and pitted
Figs   1 lb = 2⅔ cups chopped
Juice   ¼ cup fresh juice = 1 Tbsp concentrated
Lemon   2½ Tbsp juice = 1½-2 tsp zest
Orange   ⅓ cup juice = 1½-2 Tbsp zest
Peaches 1 lb = 4 medium = 3 cups sliced, peeled
Prunes   1 lb = 2¼ cups pitted
Raisins   1 lb = 3 cups
Strawberries 1 qt = 4 cups sliced

Grain & Starch Equivalents
Bread   1 lb = 12 slices
               ½ cup soft bread crumbs = ⅓ cup dry
Cornmeal ⅓ lb = 1 cup uncooked = 4 cups cooked
Grits   ⅓ lb = 1 cup uncooked = 3½ cups cooked
Oats   1 cup uncooked = 1¾ cups cooked
Pasta   2 oz uncooked = 1 cup cooked
Potatoes 1 lb = 3 medium = 2¼ cups cooked
               = 1¾ cups mashed
Rice, white   1 cup uncooked = 3-3½ cups cooked
Rice, brown, wild 1 cup uncooked = 4 cups cooked

Nut Equivalents (out of the shell)
1 cup of nuts weighs 4 oz
1 lb almonds = 3 cups whole
                = 4 cups slivered
1 lb coconut = 5 cups shredded
1 lb peanuts = 4 cups
1 lb pecans = 3½ cups
1 lb pistachios = 3½ cups
1 lb walnuts = 3¾ cups

Spice & Herb Equivalents
3-4 tsp of fresh herb = 1 tsp dried herb

Garlic   1 clove = ¼ tsp garlic powder
              = ¾ tsp minced
Mustard 1 tsp dry = 1 Tbsp prepared
Onion   1 small = 1 Tbsp minced
              = 1 Tbsp onion powder
              = ¾ cup chopped
Scallions 9 with green tops = 1 cup sliced

Vegetable Equivalents
Asparagus 1 lb = 18 spears
Bell Pepper 1 large = 1 cup diced
Broccoli   1 lb = 2 cups chopped
Cabbage   1 lb = 3½ cups shredded raw
                = 2 cups cooked
Carrots   1 lb = 2½ cups shredded raw
Cauliflower 1 lb = 1½ cups chopped
Celery   3 stalks = 1 cup diced
Corn   2 ears = 1 cup kernels
Eggplant   1 lb = 3-4 cups diced
Mushrooms 1 lb fresh = 2 oz dried
                = 5 cups sliced
                = 2 cups sliced, cooked
Tomato sauce 2 cups
                = ¾ cup paste + 1 cup water
Tomatoes   1 lb = 3 medium = 8 oz can
                = 1½ cups chopped

*I*ndex-Featured Flavors are in **Bold**; Featured Foods are in **BOLD CAPITALS**.

*I*ndex continued

*I*ndex continued

Index continued

Copy this Order Form

Phone: 303-765-1220

On-line orders: www.bellwetherbooks.com

By Mail: Bellwether Books • P O Box 9757 • Denver, CO 80209 USA

Please print the **shipping** address where you want the book(s) sent:

Name:_____

Care of or Company (if applicable):

_____

Address: _____

City: _____ State: _____ Zip:_____

Phone/Email: (_____)_____
(for questions on orders)

Send _____ copy(s) at $22.98 each $ _____

Shipping/Handling: ❑ $5 US for one book; ❑ $2 for each additional _____

Subtotal _____

Sales Tax: Colorado residents add 4.1% _____

Grand Total $ _____

Payment: ❑ Check #_____ Order Date: _____

If ordering as a gift for someone, call and ask about a *free* gift card.

Copy this Order Form

Phone: 303-765-1220

On-line orders: www.bellwetherbooks.com

By Mail: Bellwether Books • P O Box 9757 • Denver, CO 80209 USA

Please print the **shipping** address where you want the book(s) sent:

Name:_____

Care of or Company (if applicable):

_____

Address: _____

City: _____ State: _____ Zip:_____

Phone/Email: (_____) _____
                     (for questions on orders)

Send _____ copy(s) at $22.98 each $ _____

Shipping/Handling: ❏ $5 US for one book; ❏ $2 for each additional   _____

Subtotal   _____

Sales Tax: Colorado residents add 4.1%   _____

Grand Total $ _____

Payment: ❏ Check #_____   Order Date: _____

If ordering as a gift for someone, call and ask about a *free* gift card.